EIGHT HUNDRED LEAGUES ON THE AMAZON

JULES VERNE

1st WORLD
LIBRARY
Literary Society

Eight Hundred Leagues on the Amazon

Jules Verne

© 1st World Library – Literary Society, 2005
PO Box 2211
Fairfield, IA 52556
www.1stworldlibrary.org
First Edition

LCCN: 2006905730

Softcover ISBN: 1-4218-2159-1
Hardcover ISBN: 1-4218-2059-5
eBook ISBN: 1-4218-2259-8

Purchase *"Eight Hundred Leagues on the Amazon"*
as a traditional bound book at:
www.1stWorldLibrary.org/purchase.asp?ISBN=1-4218-2159-1

1st World Library Literary Society is a nonprofit
organization dedicated to promoting literacy by:

- Creating a free internet library accessible from any computer worldwide.
- Hosting writing competitions and offering book publishing scholarships.

**Readers interested in supporting literacy
through sponsorship, donations or
membership please contact:
literacy@1stworldlibrary.org
Check us out at: www.1stworldlibrary.ORG
and start downloading free ebooks today.**

CONTENTS

PART 1. THE GIANT RAFT

I. A CAPTAIN OF THE WOODS 9

II. ROBBER AND ROBBED 18

III. THE GARRAL FAMILY 32

IV. HESITATION 44

V. THE AMAZON 54

VI. A FOREST ON THE GROUND 64

VII. FOLLOWING A LIANA 73

VIII. THE JANGADA 92

IX. THE EVENING OF THE FIFTH OF JUNE 102

X. FROM IQUITOS TO PEVAS... 112

XI. FROM PEVAS TO THE FRONTIER 123

XII. FRAGOSO AT WORK 137

XIII. TORRES.. 149

XIV. STILL DESCENDING 158

XV. THE CONTINUED DESCENT 167

XVI. EGA.. 178

XVII. AN ATTACK 191

XVIII. THE ARRIVAL DINNER... 204

XIX. ANCIENT HISTORY 214

XX. BETWEEN THE TWO MEN 222

PART II. THE CRYPTOGRAM

I. MANAOS 236

II. THE FIRST MOMENTS 241

III. RETROSPECTIVE 250

IV. MORAL PROOFS 258

V. MATERIAL PROOFS 268

VI. THE LAST BLOW 275

VII. RESOLUTIONS 289

VIII. THE FIRST SEARCH 296

IX. THE SECOND ATTEMPT 304

X. A CANNON SHOT 310

XI. THE CONTENTS OF THE CASE 320

XII. THE DOCUMENT 328

XIII. IS IT A MATTER OF FIGURES? 340

XIV. CHANCE! 352

XV. THE LAST EFFORTS 363

XVI. PREPARATIONS 371

XVII. THE LAST NIGHT 381

XVIII. FRAGOSO 391

XIX. THE CRIME OF TIJUCO 401

XX. THE LOWER AMAZON 410

PART I - THE GIANT RAFT

CHAPTER I

A CAPTAIN OF THE WOODS

"Phyjslyddqfdzxgasgzzqqehxgkfndrxuj uglocytdxvksbxhhuypohdvyrymhuhpuydk joxphetozlsletnpmvffovpdpajxhyynojy ggaymeqynfuqlnmvlyfgsuzmqIztlbqqyug sqeubvnrcredgruzblrmxyuhqhpzdrrgcro hepqxuflvvrplphonthvddqfhqsntzhhhnf epmqkyuuexktogzgkyuumfvIjdqdpzjqsyk rplxhxqrymvklohhhotozvdksppsuvjhd."

THE MAN who held in his hand the document of which this strange assemblage of letters formed the concluding paragraph remained for some moments lost in thought.

It contained about a hundred of these lines, with the letters at even distances, and undivided into words. It seemed to have been written many years before, and time had already laid his tawny finger on the sheet of good stout paper which was covered with the hieroglyphics. On what principle had these letters been arranged? He who held the paper was alone able to tell. With such cipher language it is as with the locks of some of our iron safes - in either case the protection is the same. The combinations which they lead to can be counted by millions, and no calculator's life would suffice to express them. Some particular "word" has to be known before the lock of the safe will act, and some "cipher" is necessary before that cryptogram can be read.

He who had just reperused the document was but a simple "captain of the woods." Under the name of *"Capitaes do Mato"* are known in Brazil those individuals who are engaged in the recapture of fugitive slaves. The institution dates from 1722. At that period anti-slavery ideas had entered the minds of a few philanthropists, and more than a century had to elapse before the mass of the people grasped and applied them. That freedom was a right, that the very first of the natural rights of man was to be free and to belong only to himself, would seem to be self-evident, and yet thousands of years had to pass before the glorious thought was generally accepted, and the nations of the earth had the courage to proclaim it.

In 1852, the year in which our story opens, there were still slaves in Brazil, and as a natural consequence, captains of the woods to pursue them. For certain reasons of political economy the hour of general emancipation had been delayed, but the black had at this date the right to ransom himself, the children which were born to him were born free. The day was not far distant when the magnificent country, into which could be put three-quarters of the continent of Europe, would no longer count a single slave among its ten millions of inhabitants.

The occupation of the captains of the woods was doomed, and at the period we speak of the advantages obtainable from the capture of fugitives were rapidly diminishing. While, however, the calling continued sufficiently profitable, the captains of the woods formed a peculiar class of adventurers, principally composed of freedmen and deserters - of not very enviable reputation. The slave hunters in fact belonged to the dregs of society, and we shall not be far wrong in assuming that the man with the cryptogram was a fitting comrade for his fellow *"capitaes do mato."* Torres - for that was his name - unlike the majority of his companions, was neither half-breed, Indian, nor negro. He was a white of Brazilian origin, and had received a better education than befitted his present condition. One of those unclassed men who are found so frequently in the distant countries of the New World, at a time when the Brazilian law still excluded mulattoes and others of mixed blood from certain employments, it was evident that if such exclusion had affected him, it had done so on account of his worthless character, and not because of his birth.

Torres at the present moment was not, however, in Brazil. He had just passed the frontier, and was wandering in the forests of Peru, from which issue the waters of the Upper Amazon.

He was a man of about thirty years of age, on whom the fatigues of a precarious existence seemed, thanks to an exceptional temperament and an iron constitution, to have had no effect. Of middle height, broad shoulders, regular features, and decided gait, his face was tanned with the scorching air of the tropics. He had a thick black beard, and eyes lost under contracting eyebrows, giving that swift but hard glance so characteristic of insolent natures. Clothed as back-woodsmen are generally clothed, not over elaborately, his garments bore witness to long and roughish wear. On his head, stuck jauntily on one side, was a leather hat with a large brim. Trousers he had of coarse wool, which were tucked into the tops of the thick, heavy boots which formed the most substantial part of his attire, and over all, and hiding all, was a faded yellowish poncho.

But if Torres was a captain of the woods it was evident that he was not now employed in that capacity, his means of attack and defense being obviously insufficient for any one engaged in the pursuit of the blacks. No firearms - neither gun nor revolver. In his belt only one of those weapons, more sword than hunting-knife, called a *"manchetta,"* and in addition he had an *"enchada,"* which is a sort of hoe, specially employed in the pursuit of the tatous and agoutis which abound in the forests of the Upper Amazon, where there is generally little to fear from wild beasts.

On the 4th of May, 1852, it happened, then, that our adventurer was deeply absorbed in the reading of the document on which his eyes were fixed, and, accustomed as he was to live in the forests of South America, he was perfectly indifferent to their splendors. Nothing could distract his attention; neither the constant cry of the howling monkeys, which St. Hillaire has graphically compared to the ax of the woodman as he strikes the branches of the trees, nor the sharp jingle of the rings of the rattlesnake (not an aggressive reptile, it is true, but one of the most venomous); neither the bawling voice of the horned toad, the most hideous of its kind, nor even the solemn and sonorous croak of the bellowing frog, which, though it cannot equal the bull in size, can surpass him in noise.

Torres heard nothing of all these sounds, which form, as it were, the complex voice of the forests of the New World. Reclining at the foot of a magnificent tree, he did not even admire the lofty boughs of that *"pao ferro,"* or iron wood, with its somber bark, hard as the metal which it replaces in the weapon and utensil of the Indian savage. No. Lost in thought, the captain of the woods turned the curious paper again and again between his fingers. With the cipher, of which he had the secret, he assigned to each letter its true value. He read, he verified the sense of those lines, unintelligible to all but him, and then he smiled - and a most unpleasant smile it was.

Then he murmured some phrases in an undertone which none in the solitude of the Peruvian forests could hear, and which no one, had he been anywhere else, would have heard.

"Yes," said he, at length, "here are a hundred lines very neatly written, which, for some one that I know, have an importance that is undoubted. That somebody is rich. It is a question of life or death for him, and looked at in every way it will cost him something." And, scrutinizing the paper with greedy eyes, "At a conto [1] only for each word of this last sentence it will amount to a considerable sum, and it is this sentence which fixes the price. It sums up the entire document. It gives their true names to true personages; but before trying to understand it I ought to begin by counting the number of words it contains, and even when this is done its true meaning may be missed."

In saying this Torres began to count mentally.

"There are fifty-eight words, and that makes fifty-eight

contos. With nothing but that one could live in Brazil, in America, wherever one wished, and even live without doing anything! And what would it be, then, if all the words of this document were paid for at the same price? It would be necessary to count by hundreds of contos. Ah! there is quite a fortune here for me to realize if I am not the greatest of duffers!"

It seemed as though the hands of Torres felt the enormous sum, and were already closing over the rolls of gold. Suddenly his thoughts took another turn.

"At length," he cried, "I see land; and I do not regret the voyage which has led me from the coast of the Atlantic to the Upper Amazon. But this man may quit America and go beyond the seas, and then how can I touch him? But no! he is there, and if I climb to the top of this tree I can see the roof under which he lives with his family!" Then seizing the paper and shaking it with terrible meaning: "Before to-morrow I will be in his presence; before to-morrow he will know that his honor and his life are contained in these lines. And when he wishes to see the cipher which permits him to read them, he - well, he will pay for it. He will pay, if I wish it, with all his fortune, as he ought to pay with all his blood! Ah! My worthy comrade, who gave me this cipher, who told me where I could find his old colleague, and the name under which he has been hiding himself for so many years, hardly suspects that he has made my fortune!"

For the last time Torres glanced over the yellow paper, and then, after carefully folding it, put it away into a little copper box which he used for a purse. This box was about as big as a cigar case, and if what was in it was all Torres possessed he would nowhere have been considered a wealthy man. He had a few of all the coins of the neighboring States - ten double-condors in gold of the United States of Colombia, worth about a hundred francs; Brazilian reis, worth about as much; golden sols of Peru, worth, say, double; some Chilian escudos, worth fifty francs or more, and some smaller coins; but the lot would not amount to more than five hundred francs, and Torres would have been somewhat embarrassed had he been asked how or where he had got them. One thing was certain, that for some months, after having suddenly abandoned the trade of the slave hunter, which he carried on in the province of Para, Torres had ascended the basin of the Amazon, crossed the Brazilian frontier, and come into Peruvian territory. To such a man the necessaries of life were but few; expenses he had none - nothing for his lodging, nothing for his clothes. The forest provided his food, which in the backwoods cost him naught. A few reis were enough for his tobacco, which he bought at the mission stations or in the villages, and for a trifle more he filled his flask with liquor. With little he could go far.

When he had pushed the paper into the metal box, of which the lid shut tightly with a snap, Torres, instead of putting it into the pocket of his under-vest, thought to be extra careful, and placed it near him in a hollow of a root of the tree beneath which he was sitting. This proceeding, as it turned out, might have cost him dear.

It was very warm; the air was oppressive. If the church of the nearest village had possessed a clock, the clock would have struck two, and, coming with the wind, Torres would have heard it, for it was not more than a couple of miles off. But he cared not as to time. Accustomed to regulate his proceedings by the height of the sun, calculated with more or less accuracy, he could scarcely be supposed to conduct himself with military precision. He breakfasted or dined when he pleased or when he could; he slept when and where sleep overtook him. If his table was not always spread, his bed was always ready at the foot of some tree in the open forest. And in other respects Torres was not difficult to please. He had traveled during most of the morning, and having already eaten a little, he began to feel the want of a snooze. Two or three hours' rest would, he thought, put him in a state to continue his road, and so he laid himself down on the grass as comfortably as he could, and waited for sleep beneath the ironwood-tree.

Torres was not one of those people who drop off to sleep without certain preliminaries. HE was in the habit of drinking a drop or two of strong liquor, and of then smoking a pipe; the spirits, he said, overexcited the brain, and the tobacco smoke agreeably mingled with the general haziness of his reverie.

Torres commenced, then, by applying to his lips a flask which he carried at his side; it contained the liquor generally known under the name of *"chica"* in Peru, and more particularly under that of *"caysuma"* in the Upper Amazon, to which fermented distillation of the root of the sweet manioc the captain had added a good dose of *"tafia"* or native rum.

When Torres had drunk a little of this mixture he shook the flask, and discovered, not without regret, that it was nearly empty.

"Must get some more," he said very quietly. Then taking out a short wooden pipe, he filled it with the

Jules Verne

coarse and bitter tobacco of Brazil, of which the leaves belong to that old *"petun"* introduced into France by Nicot, to whom we owe the popularization of the most productive and widespread of the solanaceae.

This native tobacco had little in common with the fine qualities of our present manufacturers; but Torres was not more difficult to please in this matter than in others, and so, having filled his pipe, he struck a match and applied the flame to a piece of that stick substance which is the secretion of certain of the hymenoptera, and is known as "ants' amadou." With the amadou he lighted up, and after about a dozen whiffs his eyes closed, his pipe escaped from his fingers, and he fell asleep.

[1] One thousand reis are equal to three francs, and a conto of reis is worth three thousand francs.

CHAPTER II

ROBBER AND ROBBED

TORRES SLEPT for about half an hour, and then there was a noise among the trees - a sound of light footsteps, as though some visitor was walking with naked feet, and taking all the precaution he could lest he should be heard. To have put himself on guard against any suspicious approach would have been the first care of our adventurer had his eyes been open at the time. But he had not then awoke, and what advanced was able to arrive in his presence, at ten paces from the tree, without being perceived.

It was not a man at all, it was a "guariba."

Of all the prehensile-tailed monkeys which haunt the forests of the Upper Amazon - graceful sahuis, horned sapajous, gray-coated monos, sagouins which seem to wear a mask on their grimacing faces - the guariba is without doubt the most eccentric. Of sociable disposition, and not very savage, differing therein very greatly from the mucura, who is as ferocious as he is foul, he delights in company, and generally travels in troops. It was he whose presence had been signaled from afar by the monotonous concert of voices, so like the psalm-singing of some church choir. But if nature has not made him vicious, it is none the less necessary to attack him with caution, and under any circumstances a sleeping traveler ought not to leave himself exposed, lest a guariba should surprise him when he is not in a position to defend himself.

This monkey, which is also known in Brazil as the "barbado," was of large size. The suppleness and stoutness of his limbs proclaimed him a powerful creature, as fit to fight on the ground as to leap from branch to branch at the tops of the giants of the forest.

He advanced then cautiously, and with short steps. He glanced to the right and to the left, and rapidly swung his tail. To these representatives of the monkey tribe nature has not been content to give four hands - she has shown herself more generous, and added a fifth, for the extremity of their caudal appendage possesses a perfect power of prehension.

The guariba noiselessly approached, brandishing a study cudgel, which, wielded by his muscular arm, would have proved a formidable weapon. For some minutes he had seen the man at the foot of the tree, but the sleeper did not move, and this doubtless induced him to come and look at him a little nearer. He came forward then, not without hesitation, and stopped at last about three paces off.

On his bearded face was pictured a grin, which showed his sharp-edged teeth, white as ivory, and the cudgel began to move about in a way that was not very reassuring for the captain of the woods.

Unmistakably the sight of Torres did not inspire the guariba with friendly thoughts. Had he then particular reasons for wishing evil to this defenseless specimen of the human race which chance had delivered over to him? Perhaps! We know how certain animals retain the memory of the bad treatment they have received, and it is possible that against backwoodsmen in general he bore some special grudge.

In fact Indians especially make more fuss about the monkey than any other kind of game, and, no matter to what species it belongs, follow its chase with the ardor of Nimrods, not only for the pleasure of hunting it, but for the pleasure of eating it.

Whatever it was, the guariba did not seen disinclined to change characters this time, and if he did not quite forget that nature had made him but a simple herbivore, and longed to devour the captain of the woods, he seemed at least to have made up his mind to get rid of one of his natural enemies.

After looking at him for some minutes the guariba began to move round the tree. He stepped slowly, holding his breath, and getting nearer and nearer. His attitude was threatening, his countenance ferocious. Nothing could have seemed easier to him than to have crushed this motionless man at a single blow, and assuredly at that moment the life of Torres hung by a thread.

In truth, the guariba stopped a second time close up to the tree, placed himself at the side, so as to command the head of the sleeper, and lifted his stick to give the blow.

But if Torres had been imprudent in putting near him in the crevice of the root the little case which contained his document and his fortune, it was this imprudence which saved his life.

A sunbeam shooting between the branches just glinted on the case, the polished metal of which lighted up like a looking-glass. The monkey, with the frivolity peculiar to his species, instantly had his attention distracted. His ideas, if such an animal could have ideas, took another direction. He stopped, caught hold of the case, jumped back a pace or two, and, raising it to the level of his eyes, looked at it not without surprise as he moved it about and used it like a mirror. He was if anything still more astonished when he heard the rattle of the gold pieces it contained. The music enchanted him. It was like a rattle in the hands of a child. He carried it to his mouth, and his teeth grated against the metal, but made no impression   on it.

Doubtless the guariba thought he had found some fruit of a new kind, a sort of huge almost brilliant all over, and with a kernel playing freely in its shell. But if he soon discovered his mistake he did not consider it a reason for throwing the case away; on the contrary, he grasped it more tightly in his left hand, and dropped the cudgel, which broke off a dry twig in its fall.

At this noise Torres woke, and with the quickness of those who are always on the watch, with whom there is no transition from the sleeping to the waking state, was immediately on his legs.

In an instant Torres had recognized with whom he had to deal.

"A guariba!" he cried.

And his hand seizing his manchetta, he put himself

into a posture of defense.

The monkey, alarmed, jumped back at once, and not so brave before a waking man as a sleeping one, performed a rapid caper, and glided under the trees.

"It was time!" said Torres; "the rogue would have settled me without any ceremony!"

Of a sudden, between the hands of the monkey, who had stopped at about twenty paces, and was watching him with violent grimaces, as if he would like to snap his fingers at him, he caught sight of his precious case.

"The beggar!" he said. "If he has not killed me, he has done what is almost as bad. He has robbed me!"

The thought that the case held his money was not however, what then concerned him. But that which made him jump was the recollection that it contained the precious document, the loss of which was irreparable, as it carried with it that of all his hopes.

"Botheration!" said he.

And at the moment, cost what it might to recapture his case, Torres threw himself in pursuit of the guariba.

He knew that to reach such an active animal was not easy. On the ground he could get away too fast, in the branches he could get away too far. A well-aimed gunshot could alone stop him as he ran or climbed, but Torres possessed no firearm. His sword-knife and hoe were useless unless he could get near enough to hit him.

It soon became evident that the monkey could not be reached unless by surprise. Hence Torres found it necessary to employ cunning in dealing with the mischievous animal. To stop, to hide himself behind some tree trunk, to disappear under a bush, might induce the guariba to pull up and retrace his steps, and there was nothing else for Torres to try. This was what he did, and the pursuit commenced under these conditions; but when the captain of the woods disappeared, the monkey patiently waited until he came into sight again, and at this game Torres fatigued himself without result.

"Confound the guariba!" he shouted at length. "There will be no end to this, and he will lead me back to the Brazilian frontier. If only he would let go of my case! But no! The jingling of the money amuses him. Oh, you thief! If I could only get hold of you!"

And Torres recommenced the pursuit, and the monkey scuttled off with renewed vigor.

An hour passed in this way without any result. Torres showed a persistency which was quite natural. How without this document could he get his money?

And then anger seized him. He swore, he stamped, he threatened the guariba. That annoying animal only responded by a chuckling which was enough to put him beside himself.

And then Torres gave himself up to the chase. He ran at top speed, entangling himself in the high undergrowth, among those thick brambles and interlacing creepers, across which the guariba passed like a steeplechaser. Big roots hidden beneath the grass lay often in the way. He stumbled over them and again started in pursuit. At length, to his astonishment, he found himself shouting:

"Come here! come here! you robber!" as if he could make him understand him.

His strength gave out, breath failed him, and he was obliged to stop. "Confound it!" said he, "when I am after runaway slaves across the jungle they never give me such trouble as this! But I will have you, you wretched monkey! I will go, yes, I will go as far as my legs will carry me, and we shall see!"

The guariba had remained motionless when he saw that the adventurer had ceased to pursue him. He rested also, for he had nearly reached that degree of exhaustion which had forbidden all movement on the part of Torres.

He remained like this during ten minutes, nibbling away at two or three roots, which he picked off the ground, and from time to time he rattled the case at his ear.

Torres, driven to distraction, picked up the stones within his reach, and threw them at him, but did no harm at such a distance.

But he hesitated to make a fresh start. On one hand, to keep on in chase of the monkey with so little chance of reaching him was madness. On the other, to accept as definite this accidental interruption to all his plans, to be not only conquered, but cheated and hoaxed by a dumb animal, was maddening. And in the meantime Torres had begun to think that when the night came the robber would disappear without trouble, and he, the robbed one, would find a difficulty in retracing his way through the dense forest. In fact, the pursuit had taken him many miles from the bank of the river, and he would even now find it difficult to return to it.

Torres hesitated; he tried to resume his thoughts with coolness, and finally, after giving vent to a last imprecation, he was about to abandon all idea of regaining possession of his case, when once more, in spite of himself, there flashed across him the thought of his document, the remembrance of all that scaffolding on which his future hopes depended, on which he had counted so much; and he resolved to make another effort.

Then he got up.

The guariba got up too.

He made several steps in advance.

The monkey made as many in the rear, but this time, instead of plunging more deeply into the forest, he stopped at the foot of an enormous ficus - the tree of which the different kinds are so numerous all over the Upper Amazon basin.

To seize the trunk with his four hands, to climb with the agility of a clown who is acting the monkey, to hook on with his prehensile tail to the first branches, which stretched away horizontally at forty feet from the ground, and to hoist himself to the top of the tree, to the point where the higher branches just bent beneath its weight, was only sport to the active guariba, and the work of but a few seconds.

Up there, installed at his ease, he resumed his interrupted repast, and gathered the fruits which were within his reach. Torres, like him, was much in want of something to eat and drink, but it was impossible! His pouch was flat, his flask was empty.

However, instead of retracing his steps he directed them toward the tree, although the position taken up by the monkey was still more unfavorable for him. He could not dream for one instant of climbing the ficus, which the thief would have quickly abandoned for another.

And all the time the miserable case rattled at his ear.

Then in his fury, in his folly, Torres apostrophized the guariba. It would be impossible for us to tell the series of invectives in which he indulged. Not only did he call him a half-breed, which is the greatest of insults in the mouth of a Brazilian of white descent, but *"curiboca"* - that is to say, half-breed negro and Indian, and of all the insults that one man can hurl at another in this equatorial latitude *"curiboca"* is the cruelest.

But the monkey, who was only a humble quadruman, was simply amused at what would have revolted a representative of humanity.

Then Torres began to throw stones at him again, and bits of roots and everything he could get hold of that would do for a missile. Had he the hope to seriously hurt the monkey? No! he no longer knew what he was about. To tell the truth, anger at his powerlessness had deprived him of his wits. Perhaps he hoped that in one of the movements which the guariba would make in passing from branch to branch the case might escape

him, perhaps he thought that if he continued to worry
the monkey he might throw it at his head. But no! the
monkey did not part with the case, and, holding it with
one hand, he had still three left with which to move.

Torres, in despair, was just about to abandon the chase
for good, and to return toward the Amazon, when he
heard the sound of voices. Yes! the sound of human
voices.

Those were speaking at about twenty paces to the right
of him.

The first care of Torres was to hide himself in a dense
thicket. Like a prudent man, he did not wish to show
himself without at least knowing with whom he might
have to deal. Panting, puzzled, his ears on the stretch,
he waited, when suddenly the sharp report of a gun
rang through the woods.

A cry followed, and the monkey, mortally wounded,
fell heavily on the ground, still holding Torres' case.

"By Jove!" he muttered, "that bullet came at the right
time!"

And then, without fearing to be seen, he came out of
the thicket, and two young gentlemen appeared from
under the trees.

They were Brazilians clothed as hunters, with leather
boots, light palm-leaf hats, waistcoats, or rather tunics,
buckled in at the waist, and more convenient than the
national poncho. By their features and their complex-
ion they were at once recognizable as of Portuguese
descent.

Each of them was armed with one of those long guns of Spanish make which slightly remind us of the arms of the Arabs, guns of long range and considerable precision, which the dwellers in the forest of the upper Amazon handle with success.

What had just happened was a proof of this. At an angular distance of more than eighty paces the quadruman had been shot full in the head.

The two young men carried in addition, in their belts, a sort of dagger-knife, which is known in Brazil as a *"foca,"* and which hunters do not hesitate to use when attacking the ounce and other wild animals which, if not very formidable, are pretty numerous in these forests.

Torres had obviously little to fear from this meeting, and so he went on running toward the monkey's corpse.

But the young men, who were taking the same direction, had less ground to cover, and coming forward a few paces, found themselves face to face with Torres.

The latter had recovered his presence of mind.

"Many thanks, gentlemen," said he gayly, as he raised the brim of his hat; "in killing this wretched animal you have just done me a great service!"

The hunters looked at him inquiringly, not knowing what value to attach to his thanks.

Torres explained matters in a few words.

"You thought you had killed a monkey," said he, "but as it happens you have killed a thief!"

"If we have been of use to you," said the youngest of the two, "it was by accident, but we are none the less pleased to find that we have done some good."

And taking several steps to the rear, he bent over the guariba, and, not without an effort, withdrew the case from his stiffened hand.

"Doubtless that, sir, is what belongs to you?"

"The very thing," said Torres briskly, catching hold of the case and failing to repress a huge sigh of relief.

"Whom ought I to thank, gentlemen," said he, "for the service you have rendered me?"

"My friend, Manoel, assistant surgeon, Brazilian army," replied the young man.

"If it was I who shot the monkey, Benito," said Manoel, "it was you that pointed him out to me."

"In that case, sirs," replied Torres, "I am under an obligation to you both, as well to you, Mr. Manoel, as to you, Mr. -- "

"Benito Garral," replied Manoel.

The captain of the woods required great command over himself to avoid giving a jump when he heard this name, and more especially when the young man obligingly continued:

"My father, Joam Garral, has his farm about three miles from here. If you would like, Mr. -- "

"Torres," replied the adventurer.

"If you would like to accompany us there, Mr. Torres, you will be hospitably received."

"I do not know that I can," said Torres, who, surprised by this unexpected meeting, hesitated to make a start. "I fear in truth that I am not able to accept your offer. The occurrence I have just related to you has caused me to lose time. It is necessary for me to return at once to the Amazon - as I purpose descending thence to Para."

"Very well, Mr. Torres," replied Benito, "it is not unlikely that we shall see you again in our travels, for before a month has passed my father and all his family will have taken the same road as you."

"Ah!" said Torres sharply, "your father is thinking of recrossing the Brazilian frontier?"

"Yes, for a voyage of some months," replied Benito. "At least we hope to make him decide so. Don't we, Manoel?"

Manoel nodded affirmatively.

"Well, gentlemen," replied Torres, "it is very probable that we shall meet again on the road. But I cannot, much to my regret, accept your offer now. I thank you, nevertheless, and I consider myself as twice your debtor."

And having said so, Torres saluted the young men, who in turn saluted him, and set out on their way to the farm.

As for Torres he looked after them as they got further and further away, and when he had lost sight of them -

"Ah! he is about to recross the frontier!" said he, with a deep voice. "Let him recross it! and he will be still more at my mercy! Pleasant journey to you, Joam Garral!"

And having uttered these words the captain of the woods, making for the south so as to regain the left bank of the river by the shortest road, disappeared into the dense forest.

CHAPTER III

THE GARRAL FAMILY

THE VILLAGE of Iquitos is situated on the left bank
of the Amazon, near the seventy-fourth meridian, on
that portion of the great river which still bears the
name of the Marânon, and of which the bed separates
Peru from the republic of Ecuador. It is about fifty-five
leagues to the west of the Brazilian frontier.

Iquitos, like every other collection of huts, hamlet, or
village met with in the basin of the Upper Amazon,
was founded by the missionaries. Up to the
seventeenth year of the century the Iquito Indians, who
then formed the entire population, were settled in the
interior of the province at some distance from the river.
But one day the springs in their territory all dried up
under the influence of a volcanic eruption, and they
were obliged to come and take up their abode on the
left of the Marânon. The race soon altered through the
alliances which were entered into with the riverine
Indians, Ticunas, or Omaguas, mixed descent with a
few Spaniards, and to-day Iquitos has a population of
two or three families of half-breeds.

The village is most picturesquely grouped on a kind of
esplanade, and runs along at about sixty feet from the
river. It consists of some forty miserable huts, whose

thatched roofs only just render them worthy of the name of cottages. A stairway made of crossed trunks of trees leads up to the village, which lies hidden from the traveler's eyes until the steps have been ascended. Once at the top he finds himself before an inclosure admitting of slight defense, and consisting of many different shrubs and arborescent plants, attached to each other by festoons of lianas, which here and there have made their way abgove the summits of the graceful palms and banana-trees.

At the time we speak of the Indians of Iquitos went about in almost a state of nudity. The Spaniards and half-breeds alone were clothed, and much as they scorned their indigenous fellow-citizens, wore only a simple shirt, light cotton trousers, and a straw hat. All lived cheerlessly enough in the village, mixing little together, and if they did meet occasionally, it was only at such times as the bell of the mission called them to the dilapidated cottage which served them for a church.

But if existence in the village of Iquitos, as in most of the hamlets of the Upper Amazon, was almost in a rudimentary stage, it was only necessary to journey a league further down the river to find on the same bank a wealthy settlement, with all the elements of comfortable life.

This was the farm of Joam Garral, toward which our two young friends returned after their meeting with the captain of the woods.

There, on a bend of the stream, at the junction of the River Nanay, which is here about five hundred feet across, there had been established for many years this farm, homestead, or, to use the expression of the country, *"fazenda,"* then in the height of its prosperity. The Nanay with its left bank bounded it to the north for about a mile, and for nearly the same distance to the east it ran along the bank of the larger river. To the west some small rivulets, tributaries of the Nanay, and some lagoons of small extent, separated it from the savannah and the fields devoted to the pasturage of the cattle.

It was here that Joam Garral, in 1826, twenty-six years before the date when our story opens, was received by the proprietor of the fazenda.

This Portuguese, whose name was Magalhaës, followed the trade of timber-felling, and his settlement, then recently formed, extended for about half a mile along the bank of the river.

There, hospitable as he was, like all the Portuguese of the old race, Magalhaës lived with his daughter Yaquita, who after the death of her mother had taken charge of his household. Magalhaës was an excellent worker, inured to fatigue, but lacking education. If he understood the management of the few slaves whom he owned, and the dozen Indians whom he hired, he showed himself much less apt in the various external requirements of his trade. In truth, the establishment at Iquitos was not prospering, and the affairs of the Portuguese were getting somewhat embarrassed.

It was under these circumstances that Joam Garral, then twenty-two years old, found himself one day in the presence of Magalhaës. He had arrived in the country at the limit both of his strength and his resources. Magalhaës had found him half-dead with hunger and fatigue in the neighboring forest. The

Portuguese had an excellent heart; he did not ask the unknown where he came from, but what he wanted. The noble, high-spirited look which Joam Garral bore in spite of his exhaustion had touched him. He received him, restored him, and, for several days to begin with, offered him a hospitality which lasted for his life.

Under such conditions it was that Joam Garral was introduced to the farm at Iquitos.

Brazilian by birth, Joam Garral was without family or fortune. Trouble, he said, had obliged him to quit his country and abandon all thoughts of return. He asked his host to excuse his entering on his past misfortunes - misfortunes as serious as they were unmerited. What he sought, and what he wished, was a new life, a life of labor. He had started on his travels with some slight thought of entering a fazenda in the interior. He was educated, intelligent. He had in all his bearing that inexpressible something which tells you that the man is genuine and of frank and upright character. Magalhaës, quite taken with him, asked him to remain at the farm, where he would, in a measure, supply that which was wanting in the worthy farmer.

Joam Garral accepted the offer without hesitation. His intention had been to join a *"seringal,"* or caoutchouc concern, in which in those days a good workman could earn from five to six piastres a day, and could hope to become a master if he had any luck; but Magalhaës very truly observed that if the pay was good, work was only found in the seringals at harvest time - that is to say, during only a few months of the year - and this would not constitute the permanent position that a young man ought to wish for.

The Portuguese was right. Joam Garral saw it, and entered resolutely into the service of the fazenda, deciding to devote to it all his powers.

Magalhaës had no cause to regret his generous action. His business recovered. His wood trade, which extended by means of the Amazon up to Para, was soon considerably extended under the impulse of Joam Garral. The fazenda began to grow in proportion, and to spread out along the bank of the river up to its junction with the Nanay. A delightful residence was made of the house; it was raised a story, surrounded by a veranda, and half hidden under beautiful trees - mimosas, fig-sycamores, bauhinias, and paullinias, whose trunks were invisible beneath a network of scarlet-flowered bromelias and passion-flowers.

At a distance, behind huge bushes and a dense mass of arborescent plants, were concealed the buildings in which the staff of the fazenda were accommodated - the servants' offices, the cabins of the blacks, and the huts of the Indians. From the bank of the river, bordered with reeds and aquatic plants, the tree-encircled house was alone visible.

A vast meadow, laboriously cleared along the lagoons, offered excellent pasturage. Cattle abounded - a new source of profit in these fertile countries, where a herd doubles in four years, and where ten per cent. interest is earned by nothing more than the skins and the hides of the animals killed for the consumption of those who raise them! A few "sitios," or manioc and coffee plantations, were started in parts of the woods which were cleared. Fields of sugar-canes soon required the construction of a mill to crush the sacchariferous stalks destined to be used hereafter in the manufacture of molasses, tafia, and rum. In short, ten years after the arrival of Joam Garral at the farm at Iquitos the fazenda had become one of the richest establishments on the Upper Amazon. Thanks to the good management exercised by the young clerk over the works at home and the business abroad, its prosperity daily increased.

The Portuguese did not wait so long to acknowledge what he owed to Joam Garral. In order to recompense him in proportion to his merits he had from the first given him an interest in the profits of his business, and four years after his arrival he had made him a partner on the same footing as himself, and with equal shares.

But there was more that he had in store for him. Yaquita, his daughter, had, in this silent young man, so gentle to others, so stern to himself, recognized the sterling qualities which her father had done. She was in love with him, but though on his side Joam had not remained insensible to the merits and the beauty of this excellent girl, he was too proud and reserved to dream of asking her to marry him.

A serious incident hastened the solution.

Magalhaës was one day superintending a clearance and was mortally wounded by the fall of a tree. Carried home helpless to the farm, and feeling himself lost, he raised up Yaquita, who was weeping by his side, took her hand, and put it into that of Joam Garral, making him swear to take her for his wife.

"You have made my fortune," he said, "and I shall not die in peace unless by this union I know that the fortune of my daughter is assured."

"I can continue her devoted servant, her brother, her protector, without being her husband," Joam Garral had at first replied. "I owe you all, Magalhaës. I will never forget it, but the price you would pay for my endeavors is out of all proportion to what they are worth."

The old man insisted. Death would not allow him to wait; he demanded the promise, and it was made to him.

Yaquita was then twenty-two years old, Joam was twenty-six. They loved each other and they were married some hours before the death of Magalhaës, who had just strength left to bless their union.

It was under these circumstances that in 1830 Joam Garral became the new fazender of Iquitos, to the immense satisfaction of all those who composed the staff of the farm.

The prosperity of the settlement could not do otherwise than grow when these two minds were thus united.

A year after her marriage Yaquita presented her husband with a son, and, two years after, a daughter. Benito and Minha, the grandchildren of the old Portuguese, became worthy of their grandfather, children worthy of Joam and Yaquita.

The daughter grew to be one of the most charming of girls. She never left the fazenda. Brought up in pure and healthy surroundings, in the midst of the beauteous nature of the tropics, the education given to her by her mother, and the instruction received by her from her father, were ample. What more could she have learned in a convent at Manaos or Belem? Where would she have found better examples of the domestic virtues? Would her mind and feelings have been more delicately formed away from her home? If it was ordained that she was not to succeed her mother in the management of the fazenda, she was equal to any other position to which she might be called.

With Benito it was another thing. His father very wisely wished him to receive as solid and complete an education as could then be obtained in the large towns of Brazil. There was nothing which the rich fazender refused his son. Benito was possessed of a cheerful disposition, an active mind, a lively intelligence, and qualities of heart equal to those of his head. At the age of twelve he was sent into Para, to Belem, and there, under the direction of excellent professors, he acquired the elements of an education which could not but eventually make him a distinguished man. Nothing in literature, in the sciences, in the arts, was a stranger to him. He studied as if the fortune of his father would not allow him to remain idle. He was not among such as imagine that riches exempt men from work - he was one of those noble characters, resolute and just, who believe that nothing should diminish our natural obligation in this respect if we wish to be worthy of the name of men.

During the first years of his residence at Belem, Benito had made the acquaintance of Manoel Valdez. This young man, the son of a merchant in Para, was pursuing his studies in the same institution as Benito. The conformity of their characters and their tastes proved no barrier to their uniting in the closest of friendships, and they became inseparable companions.

Manoel, born in 1832, was one year older than Benito. He had only a mother, and she lived on the modest fortune which her husband had left her. When Manoel's preliminary studies were finished, he had taken up the subject of medicine. He had a passionate taste for that noble profession, and his intention was to enter the army, toward which he felt himself attracted.

At the time that we saw him with his friend Benito, Manoel Valdez had already obtained his first step, and he had come away on leave for some months to the fazenda, where he was accustomed to pass his holidays. Well-built, and of distinguished bearing, with a certain native pride which became him well, the young man was treated by Joam and Yaquita as another son. But if this quality of son made him the brother of Benito, the title was scarcely appreciated by him when Minha was concerned, for he soon became attached to the young girl by a bond more intimate than could exist between brother and sister.

In the year 1852 - of which four months had already passed before the commencement of this history - Joam Garral attained the age of forty-eight years. In that sultry climate, which wears men away so quickly, he had known how, by sobriety, self-denial, suitable living, and constant work, to remain untouched where others had prematurely succumbed. His hair, which he wore short, and his beard, which was full, had already grown gray, and gave him the look of a Puritan. The proverbial honesty of the Brazilian merchants and fazenders showed itself in his features, of which straightforwardness was the leading characteristic. His calm temperament seemed to indicate an interior fire, kept well under control. The fearlessness of his look denoted a deep-rooted strength, to which, when danger threatened, he could never appeal in vain.

But, notwithstanding one could not help remarking about this quiet man of vigorous health, with whom all things had succeeded in life, a depth of sadness which even the tenderness of Yaquita had not been able to subdue.

Respected by all, placed in all the conditions that would seem necessary to happiness, why was not this just man more cheerful and less reserved? Why did he seem to be happy for others and not for himself? Was this disposition attributable to some secret grief? Herein was a constant source of anxiety to his wife.

Yaquita was now forty-four. In that tropical country where women are already old at thirty she had learned the secret of resisting the climate's destructive influences, and her features, a little sharpened but still beautiful, retained the haughty outline of the Portuguese type, in which nobility of face unites so naturally with dignity of mind.

Benito and Minha responded with an affection unbounded and unceasing for the love which their parents bore them.

Benito was now aged twenty-one, and quick, brave, and sympathetic, contrasted outwardly with his friend Manoel, who was more serious and reflective. It was a great treat for Benito, after quite a year passed at Belem, so far from the fazenda, to return with his young friend to his home to see once more his father, his mother, his sister, and to find himself, enthusiastic hunter as he was, in the midst of these superb forests of the Upper Amazon, some of whose secrets remained after so many centuries still unsolved by man.

Minha was twenty years old. A lovely girl, brunette, and with large blue eyes, eyes which seemed to open into her very soul; of middle height, good figure, and winning grace, in every way the very image of Yaquita. A little more serious than her brother, affable, good-natured, and charitable, she was beloved by all. On this subject you could fearlessly interrogate the humblest servants of the fazenda. It was unnecessary to ask her brother's friend, Manoel Valdez, what he thought of her. He was too much interested in the question to have replied without a certain amount of partiality.

This sketch of the Garral family would not be complete, and would lack some of its features, were we not to mention the numerous staff of the fazenda.

In the first place, then, it behooves us to name an old negress, of some sixty years, called Cybele, free through the will of her master, a slave through her affection for him and his, and who had been the nurse of Yaquita. She was one of the family. She thee-ed and thou-ed both daughter and mother. The whole of this good creature's life was passed in these fields, in the middle of these forests, on that bank of the river which bounded the horizon of the farm. Coming as a child to Iquitos in the slave-trading times, she had never quitted the village; she was married there, and early a widow, had lost her only son, and remained in the service of Magalhaës. Of the Amazon she knew no more than what flowed before her eyes.

With her, and more specially attached to the service of Minha, was a pretty, laughing mulatto, of the same age as her mistress, to whom she was completely devoted. She was called Lina. One of those gentle creatures, a little spoiled, perhaps, to whom a good deal of familiarity is allowed, but who in return adore their mistresses. Quick, restless, coaxing, and lazy, she could do what she pleased in the house.

As for servants they were of two kinds - Indians, of whom there were about a hundred, employed always for the works of the fazenda, and blacks to about double the number, who were not yet free, but whose children were not born slaves. Joam Garral had herein preceded the Brazilian government. In this country, moreover, the negroes coming from Benguela, the Congo, or the Gold Coast were always treated with kindness, and it was not at the fazenda of Iquitos that one would look for those sad examples of cruelty which were so frequent on foreign plantations.

CHAPTER IV

HESITATION

MANOEL WAS in love with the sister of his friend Benito, and she was in love with him. Each was sensible of the other's worth, and each was worthy of the other.

When he was no longer able to mistake the state of his feelings toward Minha, Manoel had opened his heart to Benito.

"Manoel, my friend," had immediately answered the enthusiastic young fellow, "you could not do better than wish to marry my sister. Leave it to me! I will commence by speaking to the mother, and I think I can promise that you will not have to wait long for her consent."

Half an hour afterward he had done so.

Benito had nothing to tell his mother which she did not know; Yaquita had already divined the young people's secret.

Before ten minutes had elapsed Benito was in the presence of Minha. They had but to agree; there was no need for much eloquence. At the first words the

Jules Verne

head of the gentle girl was laid on her brother's shoulder, and the confession, "I am so happy!" was whispered from her heart.

The answer almost came before the question; that was obvious. Benito did not ask for more.

There could be little doubt as to Joam Garral's consent. But if Yaquita and her children did not at once speak to him about the marriage, it was because they wished at the same time to touch on a question which might be more difficult to solve. That question was, Where should the wedding take place?

Where should it be celebrated? In the humble cottage which served for the village church? Why not? Joam and Yaquita had there received the nuptial benediction of the Padre Passanha, who was then the curate of Iquitos parish. At that time, as now, there was no distinction in Brazil between the civil and religious acts, and the registers of the mission were sufficient testimony to a ceremony which no officer of the civil power was intrusted to attend to.

Joam Garral would probably wish the marriage to take place at Iquitos, with grand ceremonies and the attendance of the whole staff of the fazenda, but if such was to be his idea he would have to withstand a vigorous attack concerning it.

"Manoel," Minha said to her betrothed, "if I was consulted in the matter we should not be married here, but at Para. Madame Valdez is an invalid; she cannot visit Iquitos, and I should not like to become her daughter without knowing and being known by her. My mother agrees with me in thinking so. We should like to persuade my father to take us to Belem. Do you not think so?"

To this proposition Manoel had replied by pressing Minha's hand. He also had a great wish for his mother to be present at his marriage. Benito had approved the scheme without hesitation, and it was only necessary to persuade Joam Garral. And hence on this day the young men had gone out hunting in the woods, so as to leave Yaquita alone with her husband.

In the afternoon these two were in the large room of the house. Joam Garral, who had just come in, was half-reclining on a couch of plaited bamboos, when Yaquita, a little anxious, came and seated herself beside him.

To tell Joam of the feelings which Manoel entertained toward his daughter was not what troubled her. The happiness of Minha could not but be assured by the marriage, and Joam would be glad to welcome to his arms the new son whose sterling qualities he recognized and appreciated. But to persuade her husband to leave the fazenda Yaquita felt to be a very serious matter.

In fact, since Joam Garral, then a young man, had arrived in the country, he had never left it for a day. Though the sight of the Amazon, with its waters gently flowing to the east, invited him to follow its course; though Joam every year sent rafts of wood to Manaos, to Belem, and the seacoast of Para; though he had seen each year Benito leave after his holidays to return to his studies, yet the thought seemed never to have occurred to him to go with him.

The products of the farm, of the forest, and of the fields, the fazender sold on the spot. He had no wish, either with thought or look, to go beyond the horizon which bounded his Eden.

From this it followed that for twenty-five years Joam Garral had never crossed the Brazilian frontier, his wife and daughter had never set foot on Brazilian soil. The longing to see something of that beautiful country of which Benito was often talking was not wanting, nevertheless. Two or three times Yaquita had sounded her husband in the matter. But she had noticed that the thought of leaving the fazenda, if only for a few weeks, brought an increase of sadness to his face. His eyes would close, and in a tone of mild reproach he would answer:

"Why leave our home? Are we not comfortable here?"

And Yaquita, in the presence of the man whose active kindness and unchangeable tenderness rendered her so happy, had not the courage to persist.

This time, however, there was a serious reason to make it worth while. The marriage of Minha afforded an excellent opportunity, it being so natural for them to accompany her to Belem, where she was going to live with her husband. She would there see and learn to love the mother of Manoel Valdez. How could Joam Garral hesitate in the face of so praiseworthy a desire? Why, on the other hand, did he not participate in this desire to become acquainted with her who was to be the second mother of his child?

Yaquita took her husband's hand, and with that gentle voice which had been to him all the music of his life:

"Joam," she said, "I am going to talk to you about something which we ardently wish, and which will make you as happy as we are."

"What is it about, Yaquita?" asked Joam.

"Manoel loves your daughter, he is loved by her, and in this union they will find the happiness -- "

At the first words of Yaquita Joam Garral had risen, without being able to control a sudden start. His eyes were immediately cast down, and he seemed to designedly avoid the look of his wife.

"What is the matter with you?" asked she.

"Minha? To get married!" murmured Joam.

"My dear," said Yaquita, feeling somewhat hurt, "have you any objection to make to the marriage? Have you not for some time noticed the feelings which Manoel has entertained toward our daughter?"

"Yes; and a year since -- "

And Joam sat down without finishing his thoughts. By an effort of his will he had again become master of himself. The unaccountable impression which had been made upon him disappeared. Gradually his eyes returned to meet those of Yaquita, and he remained thoughtfully looking at her.

Yaquita took his hand.

"Joam," she said, "have I been deceived? Had you no idea that this marriage would one day take place, and that it would give her every chance of happiness?"

"Yes," answered Joam. "All! Certainly. But, Yaquita, this wedding - this wedding that we are both thinking of - when is it coming off? Shortly?"

"It will come off when you choose, Joam."

"And it will take place here - at Iquitos?"

This question obliged Yaquita to enter on the other matter which she had at heart. She did not do so, however, without some hesitation, which was quite intelligible.

"Joam," said she, after a moment's silence, "listen to me. Regarding this wedding, I have got a proposal which I hope you will approve of. Two or three times during the last twenty years I have asked you to take me and my daughter to the provinces of the Lower Amazon, and to Para, where we have never been. The cares of the fazenda, the works which have required your presence, have not allowed you to grant our request. To absent yourself even for a few days would then have injured your business. But now everything has been successful beyond your dreams, and if the hour of repose has not yet come for you, you can at least for a few weeks get away from your work."

Joam Garral did not answer, but Yaquita felt his hand tremble in hers, as though under the shock of some sorrowful recollection. At the same time a half-smile came to her husband's lips - a mute invitation for her to finish what she had begun.

"Joam," she continued, "here is an occasion which we

shall never see again in this life. Minha is going to be married away from us, and is going to leave us! It is the first sorrow which our daughter has caused us, and my heart quails when I think of the separation which is so near! But I should be content if I could accompany her to Belem! Does it not seem right to you, even in other respects that we should know her husband's mother, who is to replace me, and to whom we are about to entrust her? Added to this, Minha does not wish to grieve Madame Valdez by getting married at a distance from her. When we were married, Joam, if your mother had been alive, would you not have liked her to be present at your wedding?"

At these words of Yaquita Joam made a movement which he could not repress.

"My dear," continued Yaquita, "with Minha, with our two sons, Benito and Manoel, with you, how I should like to see Brazil, and to journey down this splendid river, even to the provinces on the seacoast through which it runs! It seems to me that the separation would be so much less cruel! As we came back we should revisit our daughter in her house with her second mother. I would not think of her as gone I knew not where. I would fancy myself much less a stranger to the doings of her life."

This time Joam had fixed his eyes on his wife and looked at her for some time without saying anything.

What ailed him? Why this hesitation to grant a request which was so just in itself - to say "Yes," when it would give such pleasure to all who belonged to him? His business affairs could not afford a sufficient reason. A few weeks of absence would not compromise matters to such a degree. His manager would be able to take his place without any hitch in the fazenda. And yet all this time he hesitated.

Yaquita had taken both her husband's hands in hers, and pressed them tenderly.

"Joam," she said, "it is not a mere whim that I am asking you to grant. No! For a long time I have thought over the proposition I have just made to you; and if you consent, it will be the realization of my most cherished desire. Our children know why I am now talking to you. Minha, Benito, Manoel, all ask this favor, that we should accompany them. We would all rather have the wedding at Belem than at Iquitos. It will be better for your daughter, for her establishment, for the position which she will take at Belem, that she should arrive with her people, and appear less of a stranger in the town in which she will spend most of her life."

Joam Garral leaned on his elbows. For a moment he hid his face in his hands, like a man who had to collect his thoughts before he made answer. There was evidently some hesitation which he was anxious to overcome, even some trouble which his wife felt but could not explain. A secret battle was being fought under that thoughtful brow. Yaquita got anxious, and almost reproached herself for raising the question. Anyhow, she was resigned to what Joam should decide. If the expedition would cost too much, she would silence her wishes; she would never more speak of leaving the fazenda, and never ask the reason for the inexplicable refusal.

Some minutes passed. Joam Garral rose. He went to

the door, and did not return. Then he seemed to give a last look on that glorious nature, on that corner of the world where for twenty years of his life he had met with all his happiness.

Then with slow steps he returned to his wife. His face bore a new expression, that of a man who had taken a last decision, and with whom irresolution had ceased.

"You are right," he said, in a firm voice. "The journey is necessary. When shall we start?"

"Ah! Joam! my Joam!" cried Yaquita, in her joy. "Thank you for me! Thank you for them!"

And tears of affection came to her eyes as her husband clasped her to his heart.

At this moment happy voices were heard outside at the door of the house.

Manoel and Benito appeared an instant after at the threshold, almost at the same moment as Minha entered the room.

"Children! your father consents!" cried Yaquita. "We are going to Belem!"

With a grave face, and without speaking a word, Joam Garral received the congratulations of his son and the kisses of his daughter.

"And what date, father," asked Benito, "have you fixed for the wedding?"

"Date?" answered Joam. "Date? We shall see. We will

fix it at Belem."

"I am so happy! I am so happy!" repeated Minha, as she had done on the day when she had first known of Manoel's request. "We shall now see the Amazon in all its glory throughout its course through the provinces of Brazil! Thanks, father!"

And the young enthusiast, whose imagination was already stirred, continued to her brother and to Manoel:

"Let us be off to the library! Let us get hold of every book and every map that we can find which will tell us anything about this magnificent river system! Don't let us travel like blind folks! I want to see everything and know everything about this king of the rivers of the earth!"

CHAPTER V

THE AMAZON

"THE LARGEST river in the whole world!" said Benito to Manoel Valdez, on the morrow.

They were sitting on the bank which formed the southern boundary of the fazenda, and looking at the liquid molecules passing slowly by, which, coming from the enormous range of the Andes, were on their road to lose themselves in the Atlantic Ocean eight hundred leagues away.

"And the river which carries to the sea the largest volume of water," replied Manoel.

"A volume so considerable," added Benito, "that it freshens the sea water for an immense distance from its mouth, and the force of whose current is felt by ships at eight leagues from the coast."

"A river whose course is developed over more than thirty degrees of latitude."

"And in a basin which from south to north does not comprise less than twenty-five degrees."

"A basin!" exclaimed Benito. "Can you call it a basin,

the vast plain through which it runs, the savannah which on all sides stretches out of sight, without a hill to give a gradient, without a mountain to bound the horizon?"

"And along its whole extent," continued Manoel, "like the thousand tentacles of some gigantic polyp, two hundred tributaries, flowing from north or south, themselves fed by smaller affluents without number, by the side of which the large rivers of Europe are but petty streamlets."

"And in its course five hundred and sixty islands, without counting islets, drifting or stationary, forming a kind of archipelago, and yielding of themselves the wealth of a kingdom!"

"And along its flanks canals, lagoons, and lakes, such as cannot be met with even in Switzerland, Lombardy, Scotland, or Canada."

"A river which, fed by its myriad tributaries, discharges into the Atlantic over two hundred and fifty millions of cubic meters of water every hour."

"A river whose course serves as the boundary of two republics, and sweeps majestically across the largest empire of South America, as if it were, in very truth, the Pacific Ocean itself flowing out along its own canal into the Atlantic."

"And what a mouth! An arm of the sea in which one island, Marajo, has a circumference of more than five hundred leagues!"

"And whose waters the ocean does not pond back

without raising in a strife which is phenomenal, a tide-race, or *'pororoca,'* to which the ebbs, the bores, and the eddies of other rivers are but tiny ripples fanned up by the breeze."

"A river which three names are scarcely enough to distinguish, and which ships of heavy tonnage, without any change in their cargoes, can ascend for more than three thousand miles from its mouth."

"A river which, by itself, its affluents, and subsidiary streams, opens a navigable commercial route across the whole of the south of the continent, passing from the Magdalena to the Ortequazza, from the Ortequazza to the Caqueta, from the Caqueta to the Putumayo, from the Putumayo to the Amazon! Four thousand miles of waterway, which only require a few canals to make the network of navigation complete!"

"In short, the biggest and most admirable river system which we have in the world."

The two young men were speaking in a kind of frenzy of their incomparable river. They were themselves children of this great Amazon, whose affluents, well worthy of itself, from the highways which penetrate Bolivia, Peru, Ecuador, New Grenada, Venezuela, and the four Guianas - English, French, Dutch and Brazilian.

What nations, what races, has it seen whose origin is lost in the far-distant past! It is one of the largest rivers of the globe. Its true source still baffles our explorers. Numbers of States still claim the honor of giving it birth. The Amazon was not likely to escape the inevitable fate, and Peru, Ecuador, and Colombia have for years disputed as to the honor of its glorious paternity.

To-day, however, there seems to be little doubt but that the Amazon rises in Peru, in the district of Huaraco, in the department of Tarma, and that it starts from the Lake of Lauricocha, which is situated between the eleventh and twelfth degree of south latitude.

Those who make the river rise in Bolivia, and descend form the mountains of Titicaca, have to prove that the true Amazon is the Ucayali, which is formed by the junction of the Paro and the Apurimac - an assertion which is now generally rejected.

At its departure from Lake Lauricocha the youthful river starts toward the northeast for a distance of five hundred and sixty miles, and does not strike to the west until it has received an important tributary - the Panta. It is called the Marañon in its journey through Colombia and Peru up to the Brazilian frontier - or, rather, the Maranhao, for Marañon is only the French rendering of the Portuguese name.

From the frontier of Brazil to Manaos, where the superb Rio Negro joins it, it takes the name of the Solimaës, or Solimoens, from the name of the Indian tribe Solimao, of which survivors are still found in the neighboring provinces. And, finally, from Manaos to the sea it is the Amasenas, or river of the Amazons, a name given it by the old Spaniards, the descendants of the adventurous Orellana, whose vague but enthusiastic stories went to show that there existed a tribe of female warriors on the Rio Nhamunda, one of the middle-sized affluents of the great river.

From its commencement the Amazon is recognizable as destined to become a magnificent stream. There are neither rapids nor obstacles of any sort until it reaches a defile where its course is slightly narrowed between two picturesque and unequal precipices. No falls are met with until this point is reached, where it curves to the eastward, and passes through the intermediary chain of the Andes. Hereabouts are a few waterfalls, were it not for which the river would be navigable from its mouth to its source. As it is, however, according the Humboldt, the Amazon is free for five-sixths of its length.

And from its first starting there is no lack of tributaries, which are themselves fed by subsidiary streams. There is the Chinchipa, coming from the northeast, on its left. On its right it is joined by the Chachapoyas, coming from the northeast. On the left we have the Marona and the Pastuca; and the Guallaga comes in from the right near the mission station of Laguna. On the left there comes the Chambyra and the Tigré, flowing from the northeast; and on the right the Huallaga, which joins the main stream twenty-eight hundred miles from the Atlantic, and can be ascended by steamboats for over two hundred miles into the very heart of Peru. To the right, again, near the mission of San Joachim d'Omaguas, just where the upper basin terminates, and after flowing majestically across the pampas of Sacramento, it receives the magnificent Ucayali, the great artery which, fed by numerous affluents, descends from Lake Chucuito, in the northeast of Arica.

Such are the principal branches above the village of Iquitos. Down the stream the tributaries become so considerable that the beds of most European rivers would fail to contain them. But the mouths of these auxiliary waters Joam Garral and his people will pass as they journey down the Amazon.

To the beauties of this unrivaled river, which waters the finest country in the world, and keeps along its whole course at a few degrees to the south of the equator, there is to be added another quality, possessed by neither the Nile, the Mississippi, nor the Livingstone - or, in other words, the old Congo-Zaira-Lualaba - and that is (although some ill-informed travelers have stated to the contrary) that the Amazon crosses a most healthy part of South America. Its basin is constantly swept by westerly winds. It is not a narrow valley surrounded by high mountains which border its banks, but a huge plain, measuring three hundred and fifty leagues from north to south, scarcely varied with a few knolls, whose whole extent the atmospheric currents can traverse unchecked.

Professor Agassiz very properly protested against the pretended unhealthiness o the climate of a country which is destined to become one of the most active of the world's producers. According to him, "a soft and gentle breeze is constantly observable, and produces an evaporation, thanks to which the temperature is kept down, and the sun does not give out heat unchecked. The constancy of this refreshing breeze renders the climate of the river Amazon agreeable, and even delightful."

The Abbé Durand has likewise testified that if the temperature does not drop below 25 degrees Centigrade, it never rises above 33 degrees, and this gives for the year a mean temperature of from 28 degrees to 29 degrees, with a range of only 8 degrees.

After such statements we are safe in affirming that the basin of the Amazon has none of the burning heats of countries like Asia and Africa, which are crossed by the same parallels.

The vast plain which serves for its valley is accessible over its whole extent to the generous breezes which come from off the Atlantic.

And the provinces to which the river has given its name have acknowledged right to call themselves the healthiest of a country which is one of the finest on the earth.

And how can we say that the hydrographical system of the Amazon is not known?

In the sixteenth century Orellana, the lieutenant of one of the brothers Pizarro, descended the Rio Negro, arrived on the main river in 1540, ventured without a guide across the unknown district, and, after eighteen months of a navigation of which is record is most marvelous, reached the mouth.

In 1636 and 1637 the Portuguese Pedro Texeira ascended the Amazon to Napo, with a fleet of forty-seven pirogues.

In 1743 La Condamine, after having measured an arc of the meridian at the equator, left his companions Bouguer and Godin des Odonais, embarked on the Chinchipe, descended it to its junction with the Marañon, reached the mouth at Napo on the 31st of July, just in time to observe an emersion of the first satellite of Jupiter - which allowed this "Humboldt of the eighteenth century" to accurately determine the latitude and longitude of the spot - visited the villages on both banks, and on the 6th of September arrived in front of the fort of Para. This immense journey had important results - not only was the course of the Amazon made out in scientific fashion, but it seemed almost certain that it communicated with the Orinoco.

Fifty-five years later Humboldt and Bonpland completed the valuable work of La Condamine, and drew up the map of the Manañon as far as Napo.

Since this period the Amazon itself and all its principal tributaries have been frequently visited.

In 1827 Lister-Maw, in 1834 and 1835 Smyth, in 1844 the French lieutenant in command of the "Boulonnaise," the Brazilian Valdez in 1840, the French "Paul Marcoy" from 1848 to 1860, the whimsical painter Biard in 1859, Professor Agassiz in 1865 and 1866, in 1967 the Brazilian engineer Franz Keller-Linzenger, and lastly, in 1879 Doctor Crevaux, have explored the course of the river, ascended many of its tributaries, and ascertained the navigability of its principal affluents.

But what has won the greatest honor for the Brazilian government is that on the 31st of July, 1857, after numerous frontier disputes between France and Brazil, about the Guiana boundary, the course of the Amazon was declared to be free and open to all flags; and, to make practice harmonize with theory, Brazil entered into negotiations with the neighboring powers for the exploration of every river-road in the basin of the Amazon.

To-day lines of well-found steamboats, which

correspond direct with Liverpool, are plying on the river from its mouth up to Manaos; others ascend to Iquitos; others by way of the Tapajoz, the Madeira, the Rio Negro, or the Purus, make their way into the center of Peru and Bolivia.

One can easily imagine the progress which commerce will one day make in this immense and wealthy area, which is without a rival in the world.

But to this medal of the future there is a reverse. No progress can be accomplished without detriment to the indigenous races.

In face, on the Upper Amazon many Indian tribes have already disappeared, among others the Curicicurus and the Sorimaos. On the Putumayo, if a few Yuris are still met with, the Yahuas have abandoned the district to take refuge among some of the distant tributaries, and the Maoos have quitted its banks to wander in their diminished numbers among the forests of Japura.

The Tunantins is almost depopulated, and there are only a few families of wandering Indians at the mouth of the Jurua. The Teffé is almost deserted, and near the sources of the Japur there remained but the fragments of the great nation of the Umaüa. The Coari is forsaken. There are but few Muras Indians on the banks of the Purus. Of the ancient Manaos one can count but a wandering party or two. On the banks of the Rio Negro there are only a few half-breeds, Portuguese and natives, where a few years ago twenty-four different nations had their homes.

Such is the law of progress. The Indians will disappear. Before the Anglo-Saxon race Australians and

Tasmanians have vanished. Before the conquerors of the Far West the North American Indians have been wiped out. One day perhaps the Arabs will be annihilated by the colonization of the French.

But we must return to 1852. The means of communication, so numerous now, did not then exist, and the journey of Joam Garral would require not less than four months, owing to the conditions under which it was made.

Hence this observation of Benito, while the two friends were watching the river as it gently flowed at their feet:

"Manoel, my friend, if there is very little interval between our arrival at Belem and the moment of our separation, the time will appear to you to be very short."

"Yes, Benito," said Manoel, "and very long as well, for Minha cannot by my wife until the end of the voyage."

CHAPTER VI

A FOREST ON THE GROUND

THE GARRAL family were in high glee. The magnificent journey on the Amazon was to be undertaken under conditions as agreeable as possible. Not only were the fazender and his family to start on a voyage for several months, but, as we shall see, he was to be accompanied by a part of the staff of the farm.

In beholding every one happy around him, Joam forgot the anxieties which appeared to trouble his life. From the day his decision was taken he had been another man, and when he busied himself about the preparations for the expedition he regained his former activity. His people rejoiced exceedingly at seeing him again at work. His moral self reacted against his physical self, and Joam again became the active, energetic man of his earlier years, and moved about once more as though he had spent his life in the open air, under the invigorating influences of forests, fields, and running waters.

Moreover, the few weeks that were to precede his departure had been well employed.

At this period, as we have just remarked, the course of the Amazon was not yet furrowed by the numberless steam vessels, which companies were only then thinking of putting into the river. The service was worked by individuals on their own account alone, and often the boats were only employed in the business of the riverside establishments.

These boats were either *"ubas,"* canoes made from the trunk of a tree, hollowed out by fire, and finished with the ax, pointed and light in front, and heavy and broad in the stern, able to carry from one to a dozen paddlers, and of three or four tons burden: *"egariteas,"* constructed on a larger scale, of broader design, and leaving on each side a gangway for the rowers: or *"jangada,"* rafts of no particular shape, propelled by a triangular sail, and surmounted by a cabin of mud and straw, which served the Indian and his family for a floating home.

These three kinds of craft formed the lesser flotilla of the Amazon, and were only suited for a moderate traffic of passengers or merchandise.

Larger vessels, however, existed, either *"vigilingas,"* ranging from eight up to ten tons, with three masts rigged with red sails, and which in calm weather were rowed by four long paddles not at all easy to work against the stream; or *"cobertas,"* of twenty tons burden, a kind of junk with a poop behind and a cabin down below, with two masts and square sails of unequal size, and propelled, when the wind fell, by six long sweeps which Indians worked from a forecastle.

But neither of these vessels satisfied Joam Garral. From the moment that he had resolved to descend the Amazon he had thought of making the most of the voyage by carrying a huge convoy of goods into Para.

From this point of view there was no necessity to descend the river in a hurry. And the determination to which he had come pleased every one, excepting, perhaps, Manoel, who would for very good reasons have preferred some rapid steamboat.

But though the means of transport devised by Joam were primitive in the extreme, he was going to take with him a numerous following and abandon himself to the stream under exceptional conditions of comfort and security.

It would be, in truth, as if a part of the fazenda of Iquitos had been cut away from the bank and carried down the Amazon with all that composed the family of the fazender - masters and servants, in their dwellings, their cottages, and their huts.

The settlement of Iquitos included a part of those magnificent forests which, in the central districts of South America, are practically inexhaustible.

Joam Garral thoroughly understood the management of these woods, which were rich in the most precious and diverse species adapted for joinery, cabinet work, ship building, and carpentry, and from them he annually drew considerable profits.

The river was there in front of him, and could it not be as safely and economically used as a railway if one existed? So every year Joam Garral felled some hundreds of trees from his stock and formed immense rafts of floating wood, of joists, beams, and slightly squared trunks, which were taken to Para in charge of capable pilots who were thoroughly acquainted with the depths of the river and the direction of its currents.

This year Joam Garral decided to do as he had done in preceding years. Only, when the raft was made up, he was going to leave to Benito all the detail of the trading part of the business. But there was no time to lose. The beginning of June was the best season to start, for the waters, increased by the floods of the upper basin, would gradually and gradually subside until the month of October.

The first steps had thus to be taken without delay, for the raft was to be of unusual proportions. It would be necessary to fell a half-mile square of the forest which was situated at the junction of the Nanay and the Amazon - that is to say, the whole river side of the fazenda, to form the enormous mass, for such were the *jangadas,* or river rafts, which attained the dimensions of a small island.

It was in this *jangada,* safer than any other vessel of the country, larger than a hundred *egariteas* or *vigilingas* coupled together, that Joam Garral proposed to embark with his family, his servants, and his merchandise.

"Excellent idea!" had cried Minha, clapping her hands, when she learned her father's scheme.

"Yes," said Yaquita, "and in that way we shall reach Belem without danger or fatigue."

"And during the stoppages we can have some hunting in the forests which line the banks," added Benito.

"Won't it take rather long?" observed Manoel; "could we not hit upon some quicker way of descending the Amazon?"

It would take some time, obviously, but the interested observation of the young doctor received no attention from any one.

Joam Garral then called in an Indian who was the principal manager of the fazenda.

"In a month," he said to him, "the jangada must be built and ready to launch."

"We'll set to work this very day, sir."

It was a heavy task. There were about a hundred Indians and blacks, and during the first fortnight in May they did wonders. Some people unaccustomed to these great tree massacres would perhaps have groaned to see giants many hundred years old fall in a few hours beneath the axes of the woodmen; but there was such a quantity on the banks of the river, up stream and down stream, even to the most distant points of the horizon, that the felling of this half-mile of forest would scarcely leave an appreciable void.

The superintendent of the men, after receiving the instructions of Joam Garral, had first cleared the ground of the creepers, brushwood, weeds, and arborescent plants which obstructed it. Before taking to the saw and the ax they had armed themselves with a felling-sword, that indispensable tool of every one who desires to penetrate the Amazonian forests, a large blade slightly curved, wide and flat, and two or three feet long, and strongly handled, which the natives wield with consummate address. In a few hours, with the help of the felling-sword, they had cleared the ground, cut down the underwood, and opened large gaps into the densest portions of the wood.

In this way the work progressed. The ground was cleared in front of the woodmen. The old trunks were divested of their clothing of creepers, cacti, ferns, mosses, and bromelias. They were stripped naked to the bark, until such time as the bark itself was stripped from off them.

Then the whole of the workers, before whom fled an innumerable crowd of monkeys who were hardly their superiors in agility, slung themselves into the upper branches, sawing off the heavier boughs and cutting down the topmost limbs, which had to be cleared away on the spot. Very soon there remained only a doomed forest, with long bare stems, bereft of their crowns, through which the sun luxuriantly rayed on to the humid soil which perhaps its shots had never before caressed.

There was not a single tree which could not be used for some work of skill, either in carpentry or cabinet-work. There, shooting up like columns of ivory ringed with brown, were wax-palms one hundred and twenty feet high, and four feet thick at their base; white chestnuts, which yield the three-cornered nuts; *"murichis,"* unexcelled for building purposes; *"barrigudos,"* measuring a couple of yards at the swelling, which is found at a few feet above the earth, trees with shining russet bark dotted with gray tubercles, each pointed stem of which supports a horizontal parasol; and *"bombax"* of superb stature, with its straight and smooth white stem. Among these magnificent specimens of the Amazonian flora there fell many *"quatibos"* whose rosy canopies towered above the neighboring trees, whose fruits are like little cups with rows of chestnuts ranged within, and whose wood of clear violet is specially in demand for ship-building.

And besides there was the ironwood; and more particularly the *"ibiriratea,"* nearly black in its skin, and so close grained that of it the Indians make their battle-axes; *"jacarandas,"* more precious than mahogany; *"cæsalpinas,"* only now found in the depths of the old forests which have escaped the woodman's ax; *"sapucaias,"* one hundred and fifty feet high, buttressed by natural arches, which, starting from three yards from their base, rejoin the tree some thirty feet up the stem, twining themselves round the trunk like the filatures of a twisted column, whose head expands in a bouquet of vegetable fireworks made up of the yellow, purple, and snowy white of the parasitic plants.

Three weeks after the work was begun not one was standing of all the trees which had covered the angle of the Amazon and the Nanay. The clearance was complete. Joam Garral had not even had to bestir himself in the demolition of a forest which it would take twenty or thirty years to replace. Not a stick of young or old wood was left to mark the boundary of a future clearing, not even an angle to mark the limit of the denudation. It was indeed a clean sweep; the trees were cut to the level of the earth, to wait the day when their roots would be got out, over which the coming spring would still spread its verdant cloak.

This square space, washed on its sides by the waters of the river and its tributary, was destined to be cleared, plowed, planted, and sown, and the following year fields of manioc, coffee-shrubs, sugar-canes, arrow-root, maize, and peanuts would occupy the ground so recently covered by the trees.

The last week of the month had not arrived when the trunks, classified according to their varieties and specific gravity, were symmetrically arranged on the bank of the Amazon, at the spot where the immense jangada was to be guilt - which, with the different habitations for the accommodation of the crew, would become a veritable floating village - to wait the time when the waters of the river, swollen by the floods, would raise it and carry it for hundreds of leagues to the Atlantic coast.

The whole time the work was going on Joam Garral had been engaged in superintending it. From the clearing to the bank of the fazenda he had formed a large mound on which the portions of the raft were disposed, and to this matter he had attended entirely himself.

Yaquita was occupied with Cybele with the preparations for the departure, though the old negress could not be made to understand why they wanted to go or what they hoped to see.

"But you will see things that you never saw before," Yaquita kept saying to her.

"Will they be better than what I see now?" was Cybele's invariable reply.

Minha and her favorite for their part took care of what more particularly concerned them. They were not prepar-ing for a simple voyage; for them it was a permanent departure, and there were a thousand details to look after for settling in the other country in which the young mulatto was to live with the mistress to whom she was so devotedly attached. Minha was a trifle sorrowful, but the joyous Lina was quite unaffected at leaving Iquitos. Minha Valdez would be the same to her as Minha Garral, and to check her spirits she would have to be separated from her mistress, and that was never thought of.

Benito had actively assisted his father in the work, which was on the point of completion. He commenced his apprenticeship to the trade of a fazender, which would probably one day become his own, as he was about to do that of a merchant on their descent of the river.

As for Manoel, he divided his time between the house, where Yaquita and her daughter were as busy as possible, and the clearing, to which Benito fetched him rather oftener than he thought convenient, and on the whole the division was very unequal, as may well be imagined.

CHAPTER VII

FOLLOWING A LIANA

IT WAS a Sunday, the 26th of May, and the young people had made up their minds to take a holiday. The weather was splendid, the heat being tempered by the refreshing breezes which blew from off the Cordilleras, and everything invited them out for an excursion into the country.

Benito and Manoel had offered to accompany Minha through the thick woods which bordered the right bank of the Amazon opposite the fazenda.

It was, in a manner, a farewell visit to the charming environs of Iquitos. The young men went equipped for the chase, but as sportsmen who had no intention of going far from their companions in pursuit of any game. Manoel could be trusted for that, and the girls - for Lina could not leave her mistress - went prepared for a walk, an excursion of two or three leagues being not too long to frighten them.

Neither Joam Garral nor Yaquita had time to go with them. For one reason the plan of the jangada was not yet complete, and it was necessary that its construction should not be interrupted for a day, and another was that Yaquita and Cybele, well seconded as they were by the domestics of the fazenda, had not an hour to lose.

Minha had accepted the offer with much pleasure, and so, after breakfast on the day we speak of, at about eleven o'clock, the two young men and the two girls met on the bank at the angle where the two streams joined. One of the blacks went with them. They all embarked in one of the ubas used in the service of the farm, and after having passed between the islands of Iquitos and Parianta, they reached the right bank of the Amazon.

They landed at a clump of superb tree-ferns, which were crowned, at a height of some thirty feet with a sort of halo made of the dainty branches of green velvet and the delicate lacework of the drooping fronds.

"Well, Manoel," said Minha, "it is for me to do the honors of the forest; you are only a stranger in these regions of the Upper Amazon. We are at home here, and you must allow me to do my duty, as mistress of the house."

"Dearest Minha," replied the young man, "you will be none the less mistress of your house in our town of Belem than at the fazenda of Iquitos, and there as here -- "

"Now, then," interrupted Benito, "you did not come here to exchange loving speeches, I imagine. Just forget for a few hours that you are engaged."

"Not for an hour - not for an instant!" said Manoel.

"Perhaps you will if Minha orders you?"

"Minha will not order me."

"Who knows?" said Lina, laughing.

"Lina is right," answered Minha, who held out her hand to Manoel. "Try to forget! Forget! my brother requires it. All is broken off! As long as this walk lasts we are not engaged: I am no more than the sister of Benito! You are only my friend!"

"To be sure," said Benito.

"Bravo! bravo! there are only strangers here," said the young mulatto, clapping her hands.

"Strangers who see each other for the first time," added the girl; "who meet, bow to -- "

"Mademoiselle!" said Manoel, turning to Minha.

"To whom have I the honor to speak, sir?" said she in the most serious manner possible.

"To Manoel Valdez, who will be glad if your brother will introduce me."

"Oh, away with your nonsense!" cried Benito. "Stupid idea that I had! Be engaged, my friends - be it as much as you like! Be it always!"

"Always!" said Minha, from whom the word escaped so naturally that Lina's peals of laughter redoubled.

A grateful glance from Manoel repaid Minha for the

imprudence of her tongue.

"Come along," said Benito, so as to get his sister out of her embarrassment; "if we walk on we shall not talk so much."

"One moment, brother," she said. "You have seen how ready I am to obey you. You wished to oblige Manoel and me to forget each other, so as not to spoil your walk. Very well; and now I am going to ask a sacrifice from you so that you shall not spoil mine. Whether it pleases you or not, Benito, you must promise me to forget -- "

"Forget what?"

"That you are a sportsman!"

"What! you forbid me to -- "

"I forbid you to fire at any of these charming birds - any of the parrots, caciques, or curucus which are flying about so happily among the trees! And the same interdiction with regard to the smaller game with which we shall have to do to-day. If any ounce, jaguar, or such thing comes too near, well -- "

"But -- " said Benito.

"If not, I will take Manoel's arm, and we shall save or lose ourselves, and you will be obliged to run after us."

"Would you not like me to refuse, eh?" asked Benito, looking at Manoel.

"I think I should!" replied the young man.

Jules Verne

"Well then - no!" said Benito; "I do not refuse; I will obey and annoy you. Come on!"

And so the four, followed by the black, struck under the splendid trees, whose thick foliage prevented the sun's rays from every reaching the soil.

There is nothing more magnificent than this part of the right bank of the Amazon. There, in such picturesque confusion, so many different trees shoot up that it is possible to count more than a hundred different species in a square mile. A forester could easily see that no woodman had been there with his hatchet or ax, for the effects of a clearing are visible for many centuries afterward. If the new trees are even a hundred years old, the general aspect still differs from what it was originally, for the lianas and other parasitic plants alter, and signs remain which no native can misunderstand.

The happy group moved then into the tall herbage, across the thickets and under the bushes, chatting and laughing. In front, when the brambles were too thick, the negro, felling-sword in hand, cleared the way, and put thousands of birds to flight.

Minha was right to intercede for the little winged world which flew about in the higher foliage, for the finest representations of tropical ornithology were there to be seen - green parrots and clamorous parakeets, which seemed to be the natural fruit of these gigantic trees; humming-birds in all their varieties, light-blue and ruby red; *"tisauras"* with long scissors-like tails, looking like detached flowers which the wind blew from branch to branch; blackbirds, with orange plumage bound with brown; golden-edged beccaficos; and *"sabias,"* black as crows; all united in a deafening concert of shrieks and whistles. The long beak of the toucan stood out against the golden clusters of the *"quiriris,"* and the treepeckers or woodpeckers of Brazil wagged their little heads, speckled all over with their purple spots. It was truly a scene of enchantment.

But all were silent and went into hiding when above the tops of the trees there grated like a rusty weathercock the *"alma de gato"* or "soul of the cat," a kind of light fawn-colored sparrow-hawk. If he proudly hooted, displaying in the air the long white plumes of his tail, he in his turn meekly took to flight when in the loftier heights there appeared the *"gaviao,"* the large white-headed eagle, the terror of the whole winged population of these woods.

Minha made Manoel admire the natural wonders which could not be found in their simplicity in the more civilized provinces of the east. He listened to her more with his eyes than his ears, for the cries and the songs of these thousands of birds were every now and then so penetrating that he was not able to hear what she said. The noisy laughter of Lina was alone sufficiently shrill to ring out with its joyous note above every kind of clucking, chirping, hooting, whistling, and cooing.

At the end of an hour they had scarcely gone a mile. As they left the river the trees assumed another aspect, and the animal life was no longer met with near the ground, but at from sixty to eighty feet above, where troops of monkeys chased each other along the higher branches. Here and there a few cones of the solar rays shot down into the underwood. In fact, in these tropical forests light does not seem to be necessary for their existence. The air is enough for the vegetable growth, whether it be large or small, tree or plant, and all the heat required for the development of their sap is derived not from the surrounding atmosphere, but from the bosom of the soil itself, where it is stored up as in an enormous stove.

And on the bromelias, grass plantains, orchids, cacti, and in short all the parasites which formed a little forest beneath the large one, many marvelous insects were they tempted to pluck as though they had been genuine blossoms - nestors with blue wings like shimmering watered silk, leilu butterflies reflexed with gold and striped with fringes of green, agrippina moths, ten inches long, with leaves for wings, maribunda bees, like living emeralds set in sockets of gold, and legions of lampyrons or pyrophorus coleopters, valagumas with breastplates of bronze, and green elytræ, with yellow light pouring from their eyes, who, when the night comes, illuminate the forest with their many-colored scintillations.

"What wonders!" repeated the enthusiastic girl.

"You are at home, Minha, or at least you say so," said Benito, "and that is the way you talk of your riches!"

"Sneer away, little brother!" replied Minha; "such beautiful things are only lent to us; is it not so, Manoel? They come from the hand of the Almighty and belong to the world!"

"Let Benito laugh on, Minha," said Manoel. "He hides it very well, but he is a poet himself when his time comes, and he admires as much as we do all these beauties of nature. Only when his gun is on his arm, good-by to poetry!"

"Then be a poet now," replied the girl.

"I am a poet," said Benito. "O! Nature-enchanting, etc."

We may confess, however, that in forbidding him to use his gun Minha had imposed on him a genuine privation. There was no lack of game in the woods, and several magnificent opportunities he had declined with regret.

In some of the less wooded parts, in places where the breaks were tolerably spacious, they saw several pairs of ostriches, of the species known as *"naudus,"* from four to five feet high, accompanied by their inseparable *"seriemas,"* a sort of turkey, infinitely better from an edible point of view than the huge birds they escort.

"See what that wretched promise costs me," sighed Benito, as, at a gesture from his sister, he replaced under his arm the gun which had instinctively gone up to his shoulder.

"We ought to respect the seriemas," said Manoel, "for they are great destroyers of the snakes."

"Just as we ought to respect the snakes," replied Benito, "because they eat the noxious insects, and just as we ought the insects because they live on smaller insects more offensive still. At that rate we ought to respect everything."

But the instinct of the young sportsman was about to be put to a still more rigorous trial. The woods became of a sudden full of game.

Swift stags and graceful roebucks scampered off beneath the bushes, and a well-aimed bullet would assuredly have stopped them. Here and there turkeys showed themselves with their milk and coffee-colored plumage; and peccaries, a sort of wild pig highly appreciated by lovers of venison, and agouties, which are the hares and rabbits of Central America; and tatous belonging to the order of edentates, with their scaly shells of patterns of mosaic.

And truly Benito showed more than virtue, and even genuine heroism, when he came across some tapirs, called "antas" in Brazil, diminutives of the elephant, already nearly undiscoverable on the banks of the Upper Amazon and its tributaries, pachyderms so dear to the hunters for their rarity, so appreciated by the gourmands for their meat, superior far to beef, and above all for the protuberance on the nape of the neck, which is a morsel fit for a king.

His gun almost burned his fingers, but faithful to his promise he kept it quiet.

But yet - and he cautioned his sister about this - the gun would go off in spite of him, and probably register a master-stroke in sporting annals, if within range there should come a *"tamandoa assa,"* a kind of large and very curious ant-eater.

Happily the big ant-eater did not show himself, neither did any panthers, leopards, jaguars, guepars, or cougars, called indifferently ounces in South America, and to whom it is not advisable to get too near.

"After all," said Benito, who stopped for an instant, "to walk is very well, but to walk without an object -- "

"Without an object!" replied his sister; "but our object is to see, to admire, to visit for the last time these forests of Central America, which we shall not find again in Para, and to bid them a fast farewell."

"Ah! an idea!"

It was Lina who spoke.

"An idea of Lina's can be no other than a silly one," said Benito, shaking his head.

"It is unkind, brother," said Minha, "to make fun of Lina when she has been thinking how to give our walk the object which you have just regretted it lacks."

"Besides, Mr. Benito, I am sure my idea will please you," replied the mulatto.

"Well, what is it?" asked Minha.

"You see that liana?"

And Lina pointed to a liana of the *"cipos"* kind, twisted round a gigantic sensitive mimosa, whose leaves, light as feathers, shut up at the least disturbance.

"Well?" said Benito.

"I proposed," replied Minha, "that we try to follow that liana to its very end."

"It is an idea, and it is an object!" observed Benito, "to follow this liana, no matter what may be the obstacles, thickets, underwood, rocks, brooks, torrents, to let nothing stop us, not even -"

"Certainly, you are right, brother!" said Minha; "Lina is a trifle absurd."

"Come on, then!" replied her brother; "you say that Lina is absurd so as to say that Benito is absurd to approve of it!"

"Well, both of you are absurd, if that will amuse you," returned Minha. "Let us follow the liana!"

"You are not afraid?" said Manoel.

"Still objections!" shouted Benito.

"Ah, Manoel! you would not speak like that if you were already on your way and Minha was waiting for you at the end."

"I am silent," replied Manoel; "I have no more to say. I obey. Let us follow the liana!"

And off they went as happy as children home for their holidays.

This vegetable might take them far if they determined to follow it to its extremity, like the thread of Ariadne, as far almost as that which the heiress of Minos used to lead her from the labyrinth, and perhaps entangle them more deeply.

It was in fact a creeper of the salses family, one of the cipos known under the name of the red *"japicanga,"* whose length sometimes measures several miles. But, after all, they could leave it when they liked.

The cipo passed from one tree to another without

breaking its continuity, sometimes twisting round the trunks, sometimes garlanding the branches, here jumping form a dragon-tree to a rosewood, then from a gigantic chestnut, the *"Bertholletia excelsa,"* to some of the wine palms, *"baccabas,"* whose branches have been appropriately compared by Agassiz to long sticks of coral flecked with green. Here round *"tucumas,"* or ficuses, capriciously twisted like centenarian olive-trees, and of which Brazil had fifty-four varieties; here round the kinds of euphorbias, which produce caoutchouc, *"gualtes,"* noble palm-trees, with slender, graceful, and glossy stems; and cacao-trees, which shoot up of their own accord on the banks of the Amazon and its tributaries, having different melas-tomas, some with red flowers and others ornamented with panicles of whitish berries.

But the halts! the shouts of cheating! when the happy company thought they had lost their guiding thread! For it was necessary to go back and disentangle it from the knot of parasitic plants.

"There it is!" said Lina, "I see it!"

"You are wrong," replied Minha; "that is not it, that is a liana of another kind."

"No, Lina is right!" said Benito.

"No, Lina is wrong!" Manoel would naturally return.

Hence highly serious, long-continued discussions, in which no one would give in.

Then the black on one side and Benito on the other would rush at the trees and clamber up to the branches encircled by the cipo so as to arrive at the true direction.

Now nothing was assuredly less easy in that jumble of knots, among which twisted the liana in the middle of bromelias, *"karatas,"* armed with their sharp prickles, orchids with rosy flowers and violet lips the size of gloves, and oncidiums more tangled than a skein of worsted between a kitten's paws.

And then when the liana ran down again to the ground the difficulty of picking it out under the mass of lycopods, large-leaved heliconias, rosy-tasseled calliandras, rhipsalas encircling it like the thread on an electric reel, between the knots of the large white ipomas, under the fleshy stems of the vanilla, and in the midst of the shoots and branchlets of the grenadilla and the vine.

And when the cipo was found again what shouts of joy, and how they resumed the walk for an instant interrupted!

For an hour the young people had already been advancing, and nothing had happened to warn them that they were approaching the end.

They shook the liana with vigor, but it would not give, and the birds flew away in hundreds, and the monkeys fled from tree to tree, so as to point out the way.

If a thicket barred the road the felling-sword cut a deep gap, and the group passed in. If it was a high rock, carpeted with verdure, over which the liana twisted like a serpent, they climbed it and passed on.

A large break now appeared. There, in the more open air, which is as necessary to it as the light of the sun, the tree of the tropics, *par excellence,* which, according to Humboldt, "accompanies man in the infancy of his civilization," the great provider of the inhabitant of the torrid zones, a banana-tree, was standing alone. The long festoon of the liana curled round its higher branches, moving away to the other side of the clearing, and disappeared again into the forest.

"Shall we stop soon?" asked Manoel.

"No; a thousand times no!" cried Benito, "not without having reached the end of it!"

"Perhaps," observed Minha, "it will soon be time to think of returning."

"Oh, dearest mistress, let us go on again!" replied Lina.

"On forever!" added Benito.

And they plunged more deeply into the forest, which, becoming clearer, allowed them to advance more easily.

Besides, the cipo bore away to the north, and toward the river. It became less inconvenient to follow, seeing that they approached the right bank, and it would be easy to get back afterward.

A quarter of an hour later they all stopped at the foot of a ravine in front of a small tributary of the Amazon. But a bridge of lianas, made of *"bejucos,"* twined together by their interlacing branches, crossed the stream. The cipo, dividing into two strings, served for a handrail, and passed from one bank to the other.

Benito, all the time in front, had already stepped on the swinging floor of this vegetable bridge.

Manoel wished to keep his sister back.

"Stay - stay, Minha!" he said, "Benito may go further if he likes, but let us remain here."

"No! Come on, come on, dear mistress!" said Lina. "Don't be afraid, the liana is getting thinner; we shall get the better of it, and find out its end!"

And, without hesitation, the young mulatto boldly ventured toward Benito.

"What children they are!" replied Minha. "Come along, Manoel, we must follow."

And they all cleared the bridge, which swayed above the ravine like a swing, and plunged again beneath the mighty trees.

But they had not proceeded for ten minutes along the interminable cipo, in the direction of the river, when they stopped, and this time not without cause.

"Have we got to the end of the liana?" asked Minha.

"No," replied Benito; "but we had better advance with care. Look!" and Benito pointed to the cipo which, lost in the branches of a high ficus, was agitated by violent shakings.

"What causes that?" asked Manoel.

"Perhaps some animal that we had better approach with a little circumspection!"

And Benito, cocking his gun, motioned them to let him go on a bit, and stepped about ten paces to the front.

Manoel, the two girls, and the black remained motionless where they were.

Suddenly Benito raised a shout, and they saw him rush toward a tree; they all ran as well.

Sight the most unforeseen, and little adapted to gratify the eyes!

A man, hanging by the neck, struggled at the end of the liana, which, supple as a cord, had formed into a slipknot, and the shakings came from the jerks into which he still agitated it in the last convulsions of his agony!

Benito threw himself on the unfortunate fellow, and with a cut of his hunting-knife severed the cipo.

The man slipped on to the ground. Manoel leaned over him, to try and recall him to life, if it was not too late.

"Poor man!" murmured Minha.

"Mr. Manoel! Mr. Manoel!" cried Lina. "He breathes again! His heart beats; you must save him."

"True," said Manoel, "but I think it was about time that we came up."

He was about thirty years old, a white, clothed badly

enough, much emaciated, and he seemed to have suffered a good deal.

At his feet were an empty flask, thrown on the ground, and a cup and ball in palm wood, of which the ball, made of the head of a tortoise, was tied on with a fiber.

"To hang himself! to hang himself!" repeated Lina, "and young still! What could have driven him to do such a thing?"

But the attempts of Manoel had not been long in bringing the luckless wight to life again, and he opened his eyes and gave an "ahem!" so vigorous and unexpected that Lina, frightened, replied to his cry with another.

"Who are you, my friend?" Benito asked him.

"An ex-hanger-on, as far as I see."

"But your name?"

"Wait a minute and I will recall myself," said he, passing his hand over his forehead. "I am known as Fragoso, at your service; and I am still able to curl and cut your hair, to shave you, and to make you comfortable according to all the rules of my art. I am a barber, so to speak more truly, the most desperate of Figaros."

"And what made you think of -- "

"What would you have, my gallant sir?" replied Fragoso, with a smile; "a moment of despair, which I would have duly regretted had the regrets been in another world! But eight hundred leagues of country to traverse, and not a coin in my pouch, was not very comforting! I had lost courage obviously."

To conclude, Fragoso had a good and pleasing figure, and as he recovered it was evident that he was of a lively disposition. He was one of those wandering barbers who travel on the banks of the Upper Amazon, going from village to village, and putting the resources of their art at the service of negroes, negresses, Indians and Indian women, who appreciate them very much.

But poor Fragoso, abandoned and miserable, having eaten nothing for forty hours, astray in the forest, had for an instant lost his head, and we know the rest.

"My friend," said Benito to him, "you will go back with us to the fazenda of Iquitos?"

"With pleasure," replied Fragoso; "you cut me down and I belong to you. I must somehow be dependent."

"Well, dear mistress, don't you think we did well to continue our walk?" asked Lina.

"That I do," returned the girl.

"Never mind," said Benito; "I never thought that we should finish by finding a man at the end of the cipo."

"And, above all, a barber in difficulties, and on the road to hang himself!" replied Fragoso.

The poor fellow, who was now wide awake, was told about what had passed. He warmly thanked Lina for the good idea she had had of following the liana, and they all started on the road to the fazenda, where Fragoso was received in a way that gave him neither wish nor want to try his wretched task again.

CHAPTER VIII

THE JANGADA

THE HALF-MILE square of forest was cleared. With the carpenters remained the task of arranging in the form of a raft the many venerable trees which were lying on the strand.

And an easy task it was. Under the direction of Joam Garral the Indians displayed their incomparable ingenuity. In everything connected with house-building or ship-building these natives are, it must be admitted, astonishing workmen. They have only an ax and a saw, and they work on woods so hard that the edge of their tools gets absolutely jagged; yet they square up trunks, shape beams out of enormous stems, and get out of them joists and planking without the aid of any machinery whatever, and, endowed with prodigious natural ability, do all these things easily with their skilled and patient hands.

The trees had not been launched into the Amazon to begin with; Joam Garral was accustomed to proceed in a different way. The whole mass of trunks was symmetrically arranged on a flat part of the bank, which he had already leveled up at the junction of the Nanay with the great river.

There it was that the jangada was to be built; thence it was that the Amazon was to float it when the time came for it to start for its destination.

And here an explanatory note is necessary in regard to the geography of this immense body of water, and more especially as relating to a singular phenomenon which the riverside inhabitants describe from personal observation.

The two rivers which are, perhaps, more extensive than the great artery of Brazil, the Nile and the Missouri-Mississippi, flow one from south to north across the African continent, the other from north to south through North America. They cross districts of many different latitudes, and consequently of many different climates.

The Amazon, on the contrary, is entirely comprised - at least it is from the point where it turns to the east, on the frontiers of Ecuador and Peru - between the second and fourth parallels of south latitude. Hence this immense river system is under the same climatic conditions during the whole of its course.

In these parts there are two distinct seasons during which rain falls. In the north of Brazil the rainy season is in September; in the south it occurs in March. Consequently the right-hand tributaries and the left-hand tributaries bring down their floods at half-yearly intervals, and hence the level of the Amazon, after reaching its maximum in June, gradually falls until October.

This Joam Garral knew by experience, and he intended to profit by the phenomenon to launch the jangada, after having built it in comfort on the river bank. In fact, between the mean and the higher level the height of the Amazon could vary as much as forty feet, and between the mean and the lower level as much as thirty feet. A difference of seventy feet like this gave the fazender all he required.

The building was commenced without delay. Along the huge bank the trunks were got into place according to their sizes and floating power, which of course had to be taken into account, as among these thick and heavy woods there were many whose specific gravity was but little below that of water.

The first layer was entirely composed of trunks laid side by side. A little interval had to be left between them, and they were bound together by transverse beams, which assured the solidity of the whole. *"Piaçaba"* ropes strapped them together as firmly as any chain cables could have done. This material, which consists of the ramicles of a certain palm-tree growing very abundantly on the river banks, is in universal use in the district. Piaçaba floats, resists immersion, and is cheaply made - very good reasons for causing it to be valuable, and making it even an article of commerce with the Old World.

Above this double row of trunks and beams were disposed the joists and planks which formed the floor of the jangada, and rose about thirty inches above the load water-line. The bulk was enormous, as we must confess when it is considered that the raft measured a thousand feet long and sixty broad, and thus had a superificies of sixty thousand square feet. They were, in fact, about to commit a whole forest to the Amazon.

The work of building was conducted under the immediate direction of Joam Garral. But when that part was finished the question of arrangement was submitted to the discussion of all, including even the gallant Fragoso.

Just a word as to what he was doing in his new situation at the fazenda.

The barber had never been so happy as since the day when he had been received by the hospitable family. Joam Garral had offered to take him to Para, on the road to which he was when the liana, according to his account, had seized him by the neck and brought him up with a round turn. Fragoso had accepted the offer, thanked him from the bottom of his heart, and ever since had sought to make himself useful in a thousand ways. He was a very intelligent fellow - what one might call a "double right-hander" - that is to say, he could do everything, and could do everything well. As merry as Lina, always singing, and always ready with some good-natured joke, he was not long in being liked by all.

But it was with the young mulatto that he claimed to have contracted the heaviest obligation.

"A famous idea that of yours, Miss Lina," he was constantly saying, "to play at 'following the liana!' It is a capital game even if you do not always find a poor chap of a barber at the end!"

"Quite a chance, Mr. Fragoso," would laughingly reply Lina; "I assure you, you owe me nothing!"

"What! nothing! I owe you my life, and I want it

prolonged for a hundred years, and that my recollection of the fact may endure even longer! You see, it is not my trade to be hanged! If I tried my hand at it, it was through necessity. But, on consideration, I would rather die of hunger, and before quite going off I should try a little pasturage with the brutes! As for this liana, it is a lien between us, and so you will see!"

The conversation generally took a joking turn, but at the bottom Fragoso was very grateful to the mulatto for having taken the initiative in his rescue, and Lina was not insensible to the attentions of the brave fellow, who was as straightforward, frank, and good-looking as she was. Their friendship gave rise to many a pleasant, "Ah, ah!" on the part of Benito, old Cybele, and others.

To return to the Jangada. After some discussion it was decided, as the voyage was to be of some months' duration, to make it as complete and comfortable as possible. The Garral family, comprising the father, mother, daughter, Benito, Manoel, and the servants, Cybele and Lina, were to live in a separate house. In addition to these, there were to go forty Indians, forty blacks, Fragoso, and the pilot who was to take charge of the navigation of the raft.

Though the crew was large, it was not more than sufficient for the service on board. To work the jangada along the windings of the river and between the hundreds of islands and islets which lay in its course required fully as many as were taken, for if the current furnished the motive power, it had nothing to do with the steering, and the hundred and sixty arms were no more than were necessary to work the long boathooks by which the giant raft was to be kept in mid-stream.

In the first place, then, in the hinder part of the jangada they built the master's house. It was arranged to contain several bedrooms and a large dining-hall. One of the rooms was destined for Joam and his wife, another for Lina and Cybele near those of their mistresses, and a third room for Benito and Manoel. Minha had a room away from the others, which was not by any means the least comfortably designed.

This, the principal house, was carefully made of weather-boarding, saturated with boiling resin, and thus rendered water-tight throughout. It was capitally lighted with windows on all sides. In front, the entrance-door gave immediate access to the common room. A light veranda, resting on slender bamboos, protected the exterior from the direct action of the solar rays. The whole was painted a light-ocher color, which reflected the heat instead of absorbing it, and kept down the temperature of the interior.

But when the heavy work, so to speak, had been completed, Minha intervened with:

"Father, now your care has inclosed and covered us, you must allow us to arrange our dwelling to please ourselves. The outside belongs to you, the inside to us. Mother and I would like it to be as though our house at the fazenda went with us on the journey, so as to make you fancy that we had never left Iquitos!"

"Do just as you like, Minha," replied Joam Garral, smiling in the sad way he often did.

"That will be nice!"

"I leave everything to your good taste."

"And that will do us honor, father. It ought to, for the sake of the splendid country we are going through - which is yours, by the way, and into which you are to enter after so many years' absence."

"Yes, Minha; yes," replied Joam. "It is rather as if we were returning from exile - voluntary exile! Do your best; I approve beforehand of what you do."

On Minha and Lina, to whom were added of their own free will Manoel on the one side and Fragoso on the other, devolved the care of decorating the inside of the house. With some imagination and a little artistic feeling the result was highly satisfactory.

The best furniture of the fazenda naturally found its place within, as after arriving in Para they could easily return it by one of the *igariteos*. Tables, bamboo easy-chairs, cane sofas, carved wood shelves, everything that constituted the charming furniture of the tropics, was disposed with taste about the floating home. No one is likely to imagine that the walls remained bare. The boards were hidden beneath hangings of most agreeable variety. These hangings were made of valuable bark, that of the *"tuturis,"* which is raised up in large folds like the brocades and damasks and softest and richest materials of our modern looms. On the floors of the rooms were jaguar skins, with wonderful spots, and thick monkey furs of exquisite fleeciness. Light curtains of the russet silk, produced by the *"sumauma,"* hung from the windows. The beds, enveloped in mosquito curtains, had their pillows, mattresses, and bolsters filled with that fresh and elastic substance which in the Upper Amazon is yielded by the bombax.

Throughout on the shelves and side-tables were little odds and ends, brought from Rio Janeiro or Belem, those most precious to Minha being such as had come from Manoel. What could be more pleasing in her eyes than the knickknacks given by a loving hand which spoke to her without saying anything?

In a few days the interior was completed, and it looked just like the interior of the fazenda. A stationary house under a lovely clump of trees on the borders of some beautiful river! Until it descended between the banks of the larger stream it would not be out of keeping with the picturesque landscape which stretched away on each side of it.

We may add that the exterior of the house was no less charming than the interior.

In fact, on the outside the young fellows had given free scope to their taste and imagination.

From the basement to the roof it was literally covered with foliage. A confused mass of orchids, bromelias, and climbing plants, all in flower, rooted in boxes of excellent soil hidden beneath masses of verdure. The trunk of some ficus or mimosa was never covered by a more startlingly tropical attire. What whimsical climbers - ruby red and golden yellow, with variegated clusters and tangled twigs - turned over the brackets, under the ridges, on the rafters of the roof, and across the lintels of the doors! They had brought them wholesale from the woods in the neighborhood of the fazenda. A huge liana bound all the parasites together; several times it made the round of the house, clinging on to every angle, encircling every projection, forking, uniting, it everywhere threw out its irregular branchlets, and allowed not a bit of the house to be seen beneath its enormous clusters of bloom.

As a delicate piece of attention, the author of which can be easily recognized, the end of the cipo spread out before the very window of the young mulatto, as though a long arm was forever holding a bouquet of fresh flowers across the blind.

To sum up, it was as charming as could be; and as Yaquita, her daughter, and Lina were content, we need say no more about it.

"It would not take much to make us plant trees on the jangada," said Benito.

"Oh, trees!" ejaculated Minha.

"Why not?" replied Manoel. "Transported on to this solid platform, with some good soil, I am sure they would do well, and we would have no change of climate to fear for them, as the Amazon flows all the time along the same parallel."

"Besides," said Benito, "every day islets of verdure, torn from the banks, go drifting down the river. Do they not pass along with their trees, bushes, thickets, rocks, and fields, to lose themselves in the Atlantic eight hundred leagues away? Why, then, should we not transform our raft into a floating garden?"

"Would you like a forest, miss?" said Fragoso, who stopped at nothing.

"Yes, a forest!" cried the young mulatto; "a forest with its birds and its monkeys -- "

"Its snakes, its jaguars!" continued Benito.

"Its Indians, its nomadic tribes," added Manoel, "and even its cannibals!"

"But where are you going to, Fragoso?" said Minha, seeing the active barber making a rush at the bank.

"To look after the forest!" replied Fragoso.

"Useless, my friend," answered the smiling Minha. "Manoel has given me a nosegay and I am quite content. It is true," she added, pointing to the house hidden beneath the flowers, "that he has hidden our house in his betrothal bouquet!"

CHAPTER IX

THE EVENING OF THE FIFTH OF JUNE

WHILE THE master's house was being constructed, Joam Garral was also busied in the arrangement of the out-buildings, comprising the kitchen, and offices in which provisions of all kinds were intended to be stored.

In the first place, there was an important stock of the roots of that little tree, some six or ten feet in height, which yields the manioc, and which form the principal food of the inhabitants of these inter-tropical countries. The root, very much like a long black radish, grows in clumps like potatoes. If it is not poisonous in Africa, it is certain that in South America it contains a more noxious juice, which it is necessary to previously get rid of by pressure. When this result is obtained, the root is reduced to flour, and is then used in many ways, even in the form of tapioca, according to the fancy of the natives.

On board the jangada there was a huge pile of this useful product destined for general consumption.

As for preserved meats, not forgetting a whole flock of sheep, kept in a special stable built in the front, they consisted principally of a quantity of the *"presunto"* hams of the district, which are of first-class quality; but the guns of the young fellows and of some of the Indians were reckoned on for additional supplies, excellent hunters as they were, to whom there was likely to be no lack of game on the islands and in the forests bordering on the stream. The river was expected to furnish its daily quota; prawns, which ought rather to be called crawfish; *"tambagus,"* the finest fish in the district, of a flavor superior to that of salmon, to which it is often compared; *"pirarucus"* with red scales, as large as sturgeons, which when salted are used in great quantities throughout Brazil; *"candirus,"* awkward to capture, but good to eat; *"piranhas,"* or devil-fish, striped with red bands, and thirty inches long; turtles large and small, which are counted by millions, and form so large a part of the food of the natives; some of every one of these things it was hoped would figure in turn on the tables of the master and his men.

And so each day shooting and fishing were to be regularly indulged in.

For beverages they had a good store of the best that country produced; *"caysuma"* or *"machachera,"* from the Upper and Lower Amazon, an agreeable liquor of slightly acidulated taste, which is distilled from the boiled root of the sweet manioc; *"beiju,"* from Brazil, a sort of national brandy, the *"chica"* of Peru; the *"mazato"* of the Ucayali, extracted from the boiled fruits of the banana-tree, pressed and fermented; *"guarana,"* a kind of paste made from the double almond of the *"paulliniasorbilis,"* a genuine tablet of chocolate so far as its color goes, which is reduced to a fine powder, and with the addition of water yields an excellent drink.

And this was not all. There is in these countries a species of dark violet wine, which is got from the juice of the palm, and the aromatic flavor of this *"assais"* is greatly appreciated by the Brazilans, and of it there were on board a respectable number of frasques (each holding a little more than half a gallon), which would probably be emptied before they arrived at Para.

The special cellar of the jangada did honor to Benito, who had been appointed its commander-in-chief. Several hundred bottles of sherry, port, and letubal recalled names dear to the earlier conquerors of South America. In addition, the young butler had stored away certain demijohns, holding half a dozen gallons each, of excellent *"tafia,"* a sugared brandy a trifle more pronounced in taste than the national *beiju*.

As far as tobacco was concerned, there was none of that coarse kind which usually contents the natives of the Amazonian basin. It all came direct from Villa Bella da Imperatriz - or, in other words, fro the district in which is grown the best tobacco in Central America.

The principal habitation, with its annexes - kitchen, offices, and cellars - was placed in the rear - or, let us say, stern of the craft - and formed a part reserved for the Garral family and their personal servants.

In the center the huts for the Indians and the blacks had been erected. The staff were thus placed under the same conditions as at the fazenda of Iquitos, and would always be able to work under the direction of the pilot.

To house the crew a good many huts were required, and these gave to the jangada the appearance of a small village got adrift, and, to tell the truth, it was a better built and better peopled village than many of those on the Upper Amazon.

For the Indians Joam Garral had designed regular cabins - huts without walls, with only light poles supporting the roof of foliage. The air circulated freely throughout these open constructions and swung the hammock suspended in the interior, and the natives, among whom were three or four complete families, with women and children, were lodged as if they were on shore.

The blacks here found their customary sheds. They differed from the cabins by being closed in on their four faces, of which only one gave access to the interior. The Indians, accustomed to live in the open air, free and untrammeled, were not able to accustom themselves to the imprisonment of the *ajoupas,* which agreed better with the life of the blacks.

In the bow regular warehouses had arisen, containing the goods which Joam Garral was carrying to Belem at the same time as the products of his forests.

There, in vast storerooms, under the direction of Benito, the rich cargo had been placed with as much order as if it had been carefully stowed away in a ship's hold.

In the first place, seven thousand arrobas of caoutchouc, each of about thirty pounds, composed the most precious part of the cargo, for every pound of it was worth from three to four francs. The jangada also took fifty hundredweight of sarsaparilla, a smilax which forms an important branch of foreign trade throughout the Amazon districts, and is getting rarer and rarer along the banks of the river, so that the natives are very careful to spare the stems when they gather them. Tonquin bans, known in Brazil under the name of *"cumarus,"* and used in the manufacture of certain essential oils; sassafras, from which is extracted a precious balsam for wounds; bales of dyeing plants, cases of several gums, and a quantity of precious woods, completed a well-adapted cargo for lucrative and easy sale in the provinces of Para.

Some may feel astonished that the number of Indians and Negroes embarked were only sufficient to work the raft, and that a larger number were not taken in case of an attack by the riverside Indians.

Such would have been useless. The natives of Central America are not to be feared in the least, and the times are quite changed since it was necessary to provide against their aggressions. The Indians along the river belong to peaceable tribes, and the fiercest of them have retired before the advancing civilization, and drawn further and further away from the river and its tributaries. Negro deserters, escaped from the penal colonies of Brazil, England, Holland, or France, are alone to be feared. But there are only a small number of these fugitives, they only move in isolated groups across the savannahs or the woods, and the jangada was, in a measure, secured from any attack on the parts of the backwoodsmen.

On the other hand, there were a number of settlements on the river - towns, villages, and missions. The immense stream no longer traverses a desert, but a basin which is being colonized day by day. Danger was not taken into consideration. There were no precautions against attacks. To conclude our description of the jangada, we have only to speak of one or two erections of different kinds which gave it a very picturesque aspect.

In the bow was the cabin of the pilot - we say in the bow, and not at the stern, where the helmsman is generally found. In navigating under such circumstances a rudder is of no use. Long oars have no effect on a raft of such dimensions, even when worked with a hundred sturdy arms. It was from the sides, by means of long boathooks or props thrust against the bed of the stream, that the jangada was kept in the current, and had its direction altered when going astray. By this means they could range alongside either bank, if they wished for any reason to come to a halt. Three or four ubas, and two pirogues, with the necessary rigging, were carried on board, and afforded easy communications with the banks. The pilot had to look after the channels of the river, the deviations of the current, the eddies which it was necessary to avoid, the creeks or bays which afforded favorable anchorage, and to do this he had to be in the bow.

If the pilot was the material director of this immense machine - for can we not justly call it so? - another personage was its spiritual director; this was Padre Passanha, who had charge of the mission at Iquitos.

A religious family, like that of Joam Garral's, had availed themselves enthusiastically of this occasion of taking him with them.

Padre Passanha, then aged seventy, was a man of great worth, full of evangelical fervor, charitable and good, and in countries where the representatives of religion are not always examples of the virtues, he stood out as the accomplished type of those great missionaries who have done so much for civilization in the interior of the most savage regions of the world.

For fifty years Padre Passanha had lived at Iquitos, in the mission of which he was the chief. He was loved by all, and worthily so. The Garral family held him in great esteem; it was he who had married the daughter of Farmer Magalhaës to the clerk who had been received at the fazenda. He had known the children from birth; he had baptized them, educated them, and hoped to give each of them the nuptial blessing.

The age of the padre did not allow of his exercising his important ministry any longer. The horn of retreat for him had sounded; he was about to be replaced at Iquitos by a younger missionary, and he was preparing to return to Para, to end his days in one of those convents which are reserved for the old servants of God.

What better occasion could offer than that of descending the river with the family which was as his own? They had proposed it to him, and he had accepted, and when arrived at Belem he was to marry the young couple, Minha and Manoel.

But if Padre Passanha during the course of the voyage was to take his meals with the family, Joam Garral desired to build for him a dwelling apart, and heaven knows what care Yaquita and her daughter took to make him comfortable! Assuredly the good old priest had never been so lodged in his modest parsonage!

The parsonage was not enough for Padre Passanha; he ought to have a chapel.

The chapel then was built in the center of the jangada, and a little bell surmounted it.

It was small enough, undoubtedly, and it could not hold the whole of the crew, but it was richly decorated, and if Joam Garral found his own house on the raft, Padre Passanha had no cause to regret the poverty-stricken church of Iquitos.

Such was the wonderful structure which was going down the Amazon. It was then on the bank waiting till the flood came to carry it away. From the observation and calculation of the rising it would seem as though there was not much longer to wait.

All was ready to date, the 5th of June.

The pilot arrived the evening before. He was a man about fifty, well up in his profession, but rather fond of drink. Such as he was, Joam Garral in large matters at different times had employed him to take his rafts to Belem, and he had never had cause to repent it.

It is as well to add that Araujo - that was his name - never saw better than when he had imbibed a few glasses of tafia; and he never did any work at all without a certain demijohn of that liquor, to which he paid frequent court.

The rise of the flood had clearly manifested itself for several days. From minute to minute the level of the river rose, and during the twenty-four hours which preceded the maximum the waters covered the bank on which the raft rested, but did not lift the raft.

As soon as the movement was assured, and there could

be no error as to the height to which the flood would rise, all those interested in the undertaking were seized with no little excitement. For if through some inexplicable cause the waters of the Amazon did not rise sufficiently to flood the jangada, it would all have to be built over again. But as the fall of the river would be very rapid it would take long months before similar conditions recurred.

On the 5th of June, toward the evening, the future passengers of the jangada were collected on a plateau which was about a hundred feet above the bank, and waited for the hour with an anxiety quite intelligible.

There were Yaquita, her daughter, Manoel Valdez, Padre Passanha, Benito, Lina, Fragoso, Cybele, and some of the servants, Indian or negro, of the fazenda.

Fragoso could not keep himself still; he went and he came, he ran down the bank and ran up the plateau, he noted the points of the river gauge, and shouted "Hurrah!" as the water crept up.

"It will swim, it will swim!" he shouted. "The raft which is to take us to Belem! It will float if all the cataracts of the sky have to open to flood the Amazon!"

Joam Garral was on the raft with the pilot and some of the crew. It was for him to take all the necessary measures at the critical moment. The jangada was moored to the bank with solid cables, so that it could not be carried away by the current when it floated off.

Quite a tribe from one hundred and fifty to two hundred Indians, without counting the population of the village, had come to assist at the interesting spectacle.

They were all keenly on the watch, and silence reigned over the impressionable crowd.

Toward five o'clock in the evening the water had reached a level higher than that of the night before - by more than a foot - and the bank had already entirely disappeared beneath the liquid covering.

A certain groaning arose among the planks of the enormous structure, but there was still wanting a few inches before it was quite lifted and detached from the ground.

For an hour the groanings increased. The joists grated on all sides. A struggle was going on in which little by little the trunks were being dragged from their sandy bed.

Toward half-past six cries of joy arose. The jangada floated at last, and the current took it toward the middle of the river, but, in obedience to the cables, it quietly took up its position near the bank at the moment that Padre Passanha gave it his blessing, as if it were a vessel launched into the sea whose destinies are in the hands of the Most High!

CHAPTER X

FROM IQUITOS TO PEVAS

ON THE 6th of June, the very next day, Joam Garral and his people bade good-by to the superintendent and the Indians and negroes who were to stay behind at the fazenda. At six o'clock in the morning the jangada received all its passengers, or rather inhabitants, and each of them took possession of his cabin, or perhaps we had better say his house.

The moment of departure had come. Araujo, the pilot, got into his place at the bow, and the crew, armed with their long poles, went to their proper quarters.

Joam Garral, assisted by Benito and Manoel, superintended the unmooring.

At the command of the pilot the ropes were eased off, and the poles applied to the bank so as to give the jangada a start. The current was not long in seizing it, and coasting the left bank, the islands of Iquitos and Parianta were passed on the right.

The voyage had commenced - where would it finish? In Para, at Belem, eight hundred leagues from this little Peruvian village, if nothing happened to modify the route. How would it finish? That was the secret of the future.

The weather was magnificent. A pleasant *"pampero"* tempered the ardor of the sun - one of those winds which in June or July come from off the Cordilleras, many hundred leagues away, after having swept across the huge plain of the Sacramento. Had the raft been provided with masts and sails she would have felt the effects of the breeze, and her speed would have been greater; but owing to the sinuosities of the river and its abrupt changes, which they were bound to follow, they had had to renounce such assistance.

In a flat district like that through which the Amazon flows, which is almost a boundless plain, the gradient of the river bed is scarcely perceptible. It has been calculated that between Tabatinga on the Brazilian frontier, and the source of this huge body of water, the difference of level does not exceed a decimeter in each league. There is no other river in the world whose inclination is so slight.

It follows from this that the average speed of the current cannot be estimated at more than two leagues in twenty-four hours, and sometimes, while the droughts are on, it is even less. However, during the period of the floods it has been known to increase to between thirty and forty kilometers.

Happily, it was under these latter conditions that the jangada was to proceed; but, cumbrous in its movements, it could not keep up to the speed of the current which ran past it. There are also to be taken into account the stoppages occasioned by the bends in the river, the numerous islands which had to be rounded, the shoals which had to be avoided, and the hours of halting, which were necessarily lost when the night was too dark to advance securely, so that we cannot allow more than twenty-five kilometers for each twenty-four hours.

In addition, the surface of the water is far from being completely clear. Trees still green, vegetable remains, islets of plants constantly torn from the banks, formed quite a flotilla of fragments carried on by the currents, and were so many obstacles to speedy navigation.

The mouth of the Nanay was soon passed, and lost to sight behind a point on the left bank, which, with its carpet of russet grasses tinted by the sun, formed a ruddy relief to the green forests on the horizon.

The jangada took the center of the stream between the numerous picturesque islands, of which there are a dozen between Iquitos and Pucalppa.

Araujo, who did not forget to clear his vision and his memory by an occasional application to his demijohn, maneuvered very ably when passing through this archipelago. At his word of command fifty poles from each side of the raft were raised in the air, and struck the water with an automatic movement very curious to behold.

While this was going on, Yaquita, aided by Lina and Cybele, was getting everything in order, and the Indian cooks were preparing the breakfast.

As for the two young fellows and Minha, they were walking up and down in company with Padre Passanha, and from time to time the lady stopped and watered the plants which were placed about the base of the dwelling-house.

"Well, padre," said Benito, "do you know a more agreeable way of traveling?"

"No, my dear boy," replied the padre; "it is truly traveling with all one's belongings."

"And without any fatigue," added Manoel; "we might do hundreds of thousands of miles in this way."

"And," said Minha, "you do not repent having taken passage with us? Does it not seem to you as if we were afloat on an island drifted quietly away from the bed of the river with its prairies and its trees? Only -- "

"Only?" repeated the padre.

"Only we have made the island with our own hands; it belongs to us, and I prefer it to all the islands of the Amazon. I have a right to be proud of it."

"Yes, my daughter; and I absolve you from your pride. Besides, I am not allowed to scold you in the presence of Manoel!"

"But, on the other hand," replied she, gayly, "you should teach Manoel to scold me when I deserve it. He is a great deal too indulgent to my little self."

"Well, then, dear Minha," said Manoel, "I shall profit by that permission to remind you -- "

"Of what?"

"That you were very busy in the library at the fazenda,

and that you promised to make me very learned about everything connected with the Upper Amazon. We know very little about it in Para, and here we have been passing several islands and you have not even told me their names!"

"What is the good of that?" said she.

"Yes; what is the good of it?" repeated Benito. "What can be the use of remembering the hundreds of names in the 'Tupi' dialect with which these islands are dressed out? It is enough to know them. The Americans are much more practical with their Mississippi islands; they number them -- "

"As they number the avenues and streets of their towns," replied Manoel. "Frankly, I don't care much for that numerical system; it conveys nothing to the imagination - Sixty-fourth Island or Sixty-fifth Island, any more than Sixth Street or Third Avenue. Don't you agree with me, Minha?"

"Yes, Manoel; though I am of somewhat the same way of thinking as my brother. But even if we do not know their names, the islands of our great river are truly splendid! See how they rest under the shadows of those gigantic palm-trees with their drooping leaves! And the girdle of reeds which encircles them through which a pirogue can with difficulty make its way! And the mangrove trees, whose fantastic roots buttress them to the bank like the claws of some gigantic crab! Yes, the islands are beautiful, but, beautiful as they are, they cannot equal the one we have made our own!"

"My little Minha is enthusiastic to-day," said the padre.

"Ah, padre! I am so happy to see everybody happy around me!"

At this moment the voice of Yaquita was heard calling Minha into the house.

The young girl smilingly ran off.

"You will have an amiable companion," said the padre.

"All the joy of the house goes away with you, my friend."

"Brave little sister!" said Benito, "we shall miss her greatly, and the padre is right. However, if you do not marry her, Manoel - there is still time - she will stay with us."

"She will stay with you, Benito," replied Manoel. "Believe me, I have a presentiment that we shall all be reunited!"

The first day passed capitally; breakfast, dinner, siesta, walks, all took place as if Joam Garral and his people were still in the comfortable fazenda of Iquitos.

During these twenty-four hours the mouths of the rivers Bacali, Chochio, Pucalppa, on the left of the stream, and those of the rivers Itinicari, Maniti, Moyoc, Tucuya, and the islands of this name on the right, were passed without accident. The night, lighted by the moon, allowed them to save a halt, and the giant raft glided peacefully on along the surface of the Amazon.

On the morrow, the 7th of June, the jangada breasted

the banks of the village of Pucalppa, named also New Oran. Old Oran, situated fifteen leagues down stream on the same left bank of the river, is almost abandoned for the new settlement, whose population consists of Indians belonging to the Mayoruna and Orejone tribes. Nothing can be more picturesque than this village with its ruddy-colored banks, its unfinished church, its cottages, whose chimneys are hidden amid the palms, and its two or three ubas half-stranded on the shore.

During the whole of the 7th of June the jangada continued to follow the left bank of the river, passing several unknown tributaries of no importance. For a moment there was a chance of her grounding on the easterly shore of the island of Sinicure; but the pilot, well served by the crew, warded off the danger and remained in the flow of the stream.

In the evening they arrived alongside a narrow island, called Napo Island, from the name of the river which here comes in from the north-northwest, and mingles its waters with those of the Amazon through a mouth about eight hundred yards across, after having watered the territories of the Coto and Orejone Indians.

It was on the morning of the 7th of June that the jangada was abreast the little island of Mango, which causes the Napo to split into two streams before falling into the Amazon.

Several years later a French traveler, Paul Marcoy, went out to examine the color of the waters of this tributary, which has been graphically compared to the cloudy greenish opal of absinthe. At the same time he corrected some of the measurements of La Condamine. But then the mouth of the Napo was sensibly increased by the floods and it was with a good deal of rapidity that its current, coming from the eastern slopes of Cotopaxi, hurried fiercely to mingle itself with the tawny waters of the Amazon.

A few Indians had wandered to the mouth of this river. They were robust in build, of tall stature, with shaggy hair, and had their noses pierced with a rod of palm, and the lobes of their ears lengthened to their shoulders by the weight of heavy rings of precious wood. Some women were with them. None of them showed any intention of coming on board. It is asserted that these natives are cannibals; but if that is true - and it is said of many of the riverine tribes - there must have been more evidence for the cannibalism than we get to-day.

Some hours later the village of Bella Vista, situated on a somewhat lower bank, appeared, with its cluster of magnificent trees, towering above a few huts roofed with straw, over which there drooped the large leaves of some medium-sized banana-trees, like the waters overflowing from a tazza.

Then the pilot, so as to follow a better current, which turned off from the bank, directed the raft toward the right side of the river, which he had not yet approached. The maneuver was not accomplished without certain difficulties, which were successfully overcome after a good many resorts to the demijohn.

This allowed them to notice in passing some of those numerous lagoons with black waters, which are distributed along the course of the Amazon, and which often have no communication with the river. One of these, bearing the name of the Lagoon of Oran, is of fair size, and receives the water by a large strait. In the middle of the stream are scattered several islands and two or three islets curiously grouped; and on the opposite bank Benito recognized the site of the ancient Oran, of which they could only see a few uncertain traces.

During two days the jangada traveled sometimes under the left bank, sometimes under the right, according to the condition of the current, without giving the least sign of grounding.

The passengers had already become used to this new life. Joam Garral, leaving to his son everything that referred to the commercial side of the expedition, kept himself principally to his room, thinking and writing. What he was writing about he told to nobody, not even Yaquita, and it seemed to have already assumed the importance of a veritable essay.

Benito, all observation, chatted with the pilot and acted as manager. Yaquita, her daughter, and Manoel, nearly always formed a group apart, discussing their future projects just as they had walked and done in the park of the fazenda. The life was, in fact, the same. Not quite, perhaps, to Benito, who had not yet found occasion to participate in the pleasures of the chase. If, however, the forests of Iquitos failed him with their wild beasts, agoutis, peccaries, and cabiais, the birds flew in flocks from the banks of the river and fearlessly perched on the jangada. When they were of such quality as to figure fairly on the table, Benito shot them; and, in the interest of all, his sister raised no objection; but if he came across any gray or yellow herons, or red or white ibises, which haunt the sides, he spared them through love for Minha. One single species of grebe, which is uneatable, found no grace in the eyes of the young merchant; this was the *"caiarara,"* as quick to dive as to swim or fly; a bird with a disagreeable cry, but whose down bears a high price in the different markets of the Amazonian basin.

At length, after having passed the village of Omaguas and the mouth of the Ambiacu, the jangada arrived at Pevas on the evening of the 11th of June, and was moored to the bank.

As it was to remain here for some hours before nightfall, Benito disembarked, taking with him the ever-ready Fragoso, and the two sportsmen started off to beat the thickets in the environs of the little place. An agouti and a cabiai, not to mention a dozen partridges, enriched the larder after this fortunate excursion. At Pevas, where there is a population of two hundred and sixty inhabitants, Benito would perhaps have done some trade with the lay brothers of the mission, who are at the same time wholesale merchants, but these had just sent away some bales of sarsaparilla and arrobas of caoutchouc toward the Lower Amazon, and their stores were empty.

The jangada departed at daybreak, and passed the little archipelago of the Iatio and Cochiquinas islands, after having left the village of the latter name on the right. Several mouths of smaller unnamed affluents showed themselves on the right of the river through the spaces between the islands.

Many natives, with shaved heads, tattooed cheeks and foreheads, carrying plates of metal in the lobes of their ears, noses, and lower lips, appeared for an instant on the shore. They were armed with arrows and blow tubes, but made no use of them, and did not even attempt to communicate with the jangada.

Jules Verne

CHAPTER XI

FROM PEVAS TO THE FRONTIER

DURING THE FEW days which followed nothing occurred worthy of note. The nights were so fine that the long raft went on its way with the stream without even a halt. The two picturesque banks of the river seemed to change like the panoramas of the theaters which unroll from one wing to another. By a kind of optical illusion it appeared as though the raft was motionless between two moving pathways.

Benito had no shooting on the banks, for no halt was made, but game was very advantageously replaced by the results of the fishing.

A great variety of excellent fish were taken - *"pacos,"* *"surubis,"* *"gamitanas,"* of exquisite flavor, and several of those large rays called *"duridaris,"* with rose-colored stomachs and black backs armed with highly poisonous darts. There were also collected by thousands those *"candirus,"* a kind of small silurus, of which many are microscopic, and which so frequently make a pincushion of the calves of the bather when he imprudently ventures into their haunts.

The rich waters of the Amazon were also frequented by many other aquatic animals, which escorted the jangada through its waves for whole hours together.

There were the gigantic *"pria-rucus,"* ten and twelve feet long, cuirassed with large scales with scarlet borders, whose flesh was not much appreciated by the natives. Neither did they care to capture many of the graceful dolphins which played about in hundreds, striking with their tails the planks of the raft, gamboling at the bow and stern, and making the water alive with colored reflections and spurts of spray, which the refracted light converted into so many rainbows.

On the 16th of June the jangada, after fortunately clearing several shallows in approaching the banks, arrived near the large island of San Pablo, and the following evening she stopped at the village of Moromoros, which is situated on the left side of the Amazon. Twenty-four hours afterward, passing the mouths of the Atacoari or Cocha - or rather the *"furo,"* or canal, which communicates with the lake of Cabello-Cocha on the right bank - she put in at the rising ground of the mission of Cocha. This was the country of the Marahua Indians, whose long floating hair, and mouths opening in the middle of a kind of fan made of the spines of palm-trees, six inches long, give them a cat-like look - their endeavor being, according to Paul Marcoy, to resemble the tiger, whose boldness, strength, and cunning they admire above everything. Several women came with these Marahuas, smoking cigars, but holding the lighted ends in their teeth. All of them, like the king of the Amazonian forests, go about almost naked.

The mission of Cocha was then in charge of a Franciscan monk, who was anxious to visit

Padre Passanha.

Joam Garral received him with a warm welcome, and offered him a seat at the dinner-table.

On that day was given a dinner which did honor to the Indian cook. The traditional soup of fragrant herbs; cake, so often made to replace bread in Brazil, composed of the flour of the manioc thoroughly impregnated with the gravy of meat and tomato jelly; poultry with rice, swimming in a sharp sauce made of vinegar and *"malagueta;"* a dish of spiced herbs, and cold cake sprinkled with cinnamon, formed enough to tempt a poor monk reduced to the ordinary meager fare of his parish. They tried all they could to detain him, and Yaquita and her daughter did their utmost in persuasion. But the Franciscan had to visit on that evening an Indian who was lying ill at Cocha, and he heartily thanked the hospitable family and departed, not without taking a few presents, which would be well received by the neophytes of the mission.

For two days Araujo was very busy. The bed of the river gradually enlarged, but the islands became more numerous, and the current, embarrassed by these obstacles, increased in strength. Great care was necessary in passing between the islands of Cabello-Cocha, Tarapote, and Cacao. Many stoppages had to be made, and occasionally they were obliged to pole off the jangada, which now and then threatened to run aground. Every one assisted in the work, and it was under these difficult circumstances that, on the evening of the 20th of June, they found themselves at Nuestra-Senora-di-Loreto.

Loreto is the last Peruvian town situated on the left

bank of the river before arriving at the Brazilian frontier. It is only a little village, composed of about twenty houses, grouped on a slightly undulating bank, formed of ocherous earth and clay.

It was in 1770 that this mission was founded by the Jesuit missionaries. The Ticuma Indians, who inhabit the territories on the north of the river, are natives with ruddy skins, bushy hair, and striped designs on their faces, making them look like the lacquer on a Chinese table. Both men and women are simply clothed, with cotton bands bound round their thighs and stomachs. They are now not more than two hundred in number, and on the banks of the Atacoari are found the last traces of a nation which was formerly so powerful under its famous chiefs.

At Loreto there also live a few Peruvian soldiers and two or three Portuguese merchants, trading in cotton stuffs, salt fish, and sarsaparilla.

Benito went ashore, to buy, if possible, a few bales of this smilax, which is always so much in demand in the markets of the Amazon. Joam Garral, occupied all the time in the work which gave him not a moment's rest, did not stir. Yaquita, her daughter, and Manoel also remained on board. The mosquitoes of Loreto have a deserved reputation for driving away such visitors as do not care to leave much of their blood with the redoubtable diptera.

Manoel had a few appropriate words to say about these insects, and they were not of a nature to encourage an inclination to brave their stings.

"They say that all the new species which infest the

banks of the Amazon collect at the village of Loreto. I believe it, but do not wish to confirm it. There, Minha, you can take your choice between the gray mosquito, the hairy mosquito, the white-clawed mosquito, the dwarf mosquito, the trumpeter, the little fifer, the urtiquis, the harlequin, the big black, and the red of the woods; or rather they make take their choice of you for a little repast, and you will come back hardly recognizable! I fancy these bloodthirsty diptera guard the Brazilian frontier considerably better than the poverty-stricken soldiers we see on the bank."

"But if everything is of use in nature," asked Minha, "what is the use of mosquitoes?"

"They minister to the happiness of entomologists," replied Manoel; "and I should be much embarrassed to find a better explanation."

What Manoel had said of the Loreto mosquitoes was only too true. When Benito had finished his business and returned on board, his face and hands were tattooed with thousands of red points, without counting some chigoes, which, in spite of the leather of his boots, had introduced themselves beneath his toes.

"Let us set off this very instant," said Benito, "or these wretched insects will invade us, and the jangada will become uninhabitable!"

"And we shall take them into Para," said Manoel, "where there are already quite enough for its own needs."

And so, in order not to pass even the night near the banks, the jangada pushed off into the stream.

On leaving Loreto the Amazon turns slightly toward the southwest, between the islands of Arava, Cuyari, and Urucutea. The jangada then glided along the black waters of the Cajaru, as they mingled with the white stream of the Amazon. After having passed this tributary on the left, it peacefully arrived during the evening of the 23d of June alongside the large island of Jahuma.

The setting of the sun on a clear horizon, free from all haze, announced one of those beautiful tropical nights which are unknown in the temperate zones. A light breeze freshened the air; the moon arose in the constelled depths of the sky, and for several hours took the place of the twilight which is absent from these latitudes. But even during this period the stars shone with unequaled purity. The immense plain seemed to stretch into the infinite like a sea, and at the extremity of the axis, which measures more than two hundred thousand millions of leagues, there appeared on the north the single diamond of the pole star, on the south the four brilliants of the Southern Cross.

The trees on the left bank and on the island of Jahuma stood up in sharp black outline. There were recognizable in the undecided *silhouettes* the trunks, or rather columns, of *"copahus,"* which spread out in umbrellas, groups of *"sandis,"* from which is extracted the thick and sugared milk, intoxicating as wine itself, and *"vignaticos"* eighty feet high, whose summits shake at the passage of the lightest currents of air. "What a magnificent sermon are these forests of the Amazon!" has been justly said. Yes; and we might add, "What a magnificent hymn there is in the nights of the tropics!"

The birds were giving forth their last evening notes - *"bentivis,"* who hang their nests on the bank-side reeds; *"niambus,"* a kind of partridge, whose song is composed of four notes, in perfect accord; *"kamichis,"* with their plaintive melody; kingfishers, whose call responds like a signal to the last cry of their congeners; *"canindes,"* with their sonorous trumpets; and red macaws, who fold their wings in the foliage of the *"jaquetibas,"* when night comes on to dim their glowing colors.

On the jangada every one was at his post, in the attitude of repose. The pilot alone, standing in the bow, showed his tall stature, scarcely defined in the earlier shadows. The watch, with his long pole on his shoulder, reminded one of an encampment of Tartar horsemen. The Brazilian flag hung from the top of the staff in the bow, and the breeze was scarcely strong enough to lift the bunting.

At eight o'clock the three first tinklings of the Angelus escaped from the bell of the little chapel. The three tinklings of the second and third verses sounded in their turn, and the salutation was completed in the series of more rapid strokes of the little bell.

However, the family after this July day remained sitting under the veranda to breathe the fresh air from the open.

It had been so each evening, and while Joam Garral, always silent, was contented to listen, the young people gayly chatted away till bedtime.

"Ah! our splendid river! our magnificent Amazon!" exclaimed the young girl, whose enthusiasm for the immense stream never failed.

"Unequaled river, in very truth," said Manoel; "and I do not understand all its sublime beauties. We are going down it, however, like Orellana and La Condamine did so many centuries ago, and I am not at all surprised at their marvelous descriptions."

"A little fabulous," replied Benito.

"Now, brother," said Minha seriously, "say no evil of our Amazon."

"To remind you that it has its legends, my sister, is to say no ill of it."

"Yes, that is true; and it has some marvelous ones," replied Minha.

"What legends?" asked Manoel. "I dare avow that they have not yet found their way into Para - or rather that, for my part, I am not acquainted with them."

"What, then do you learn in the Belem colleges?" laughingly asked Minha.

"I begin to perceive that they teach us nothing," replied Manoel.

"What, sir!" replied Minha, with a pleasant serious-ness, "you do not know, among other fables, that an enormous reptile called the 'minhocao,' sometimes visits the Amazon, and that the waters of the river rise or fall according as this serpent plunges in or quits them, so gigantic is he?"

"But have you ever seen this phenomenal minhocao?"

"Alas, no!" replied Lina.

"What a pity!" Fragoso thought it proper to add.

"And the 'Mae d'Aqua,'" continued the girl - "that proud and redoubtable woman whose look fascinates and drags beneath the waters of the river the imprudent ones who gaze a her."

"Oh, as for the 'Mae d'Aqua,' she exists!" cried the naïve Lina; "they say that she still walks on the banks, but disappears like a water sprite as soon as you approach her."

"Very well, Lina," said Benito; "the first time you see her just let me know."

"So that she may seize you and take you to the bottom of the river? Never, Mr. Benito!"

"She believes it!" shouted Minha.

"There are people who believe in the trunk of Manaos," said Fragoso, always ready to intervene on behalf of Lina.

"The 'trunk of Manaos'?" asked Manoel. "What about the trunk of Manaos?"

"Mr. Manoel," answered Fragoso, with comic gravity, "it appears that there is - or rather formerly was - a trunk of *'turuma,'* which every year at the same time descended the Rio Negro, stopping several days at Manaos, and going on into Para, halting at every port, where the natives ornamented it with little flags. Arrived at Belem, it came to a halt, turned back on its road, remounted the Amazon to the Rio Negro, and returned to the forest from which it had mysteriously started. One day somebody tried to drag it ashore, but the river rose in anger, and the attempt had to be given up. And on another occasion the captain of a ship harpooned it and tried to tow it along. This time again the river, in anger, broke off the ropes, and the trunk mysteriously escaped."

"What became of it?" asked the mulatto.

"It appears that on its last voyage, Miss Lina," replied Fragoso, "it mistook the way, and instead of going up the Negro it continued in the Amazon, and it has never been seen again."

"Oh, if we could only meet it!" said Lina.

"If we meet it," answered Benito, "we will put you on it! It will take you back to the mysterious forest, and you will likewise pass into the state of a legendary mind!"

"And why not?" asked the mulatto.

"So much for your legends," said Manoel; "and I think your river is worthy of them. But it has also its histories, which are worth something more. I know one, and if I were not afraid of grieving you - for it is a very sad one - I would relate it."

"Oh! tell it, by all means, Mr. Manoel," exclaimed Lina; "I like stories which make you cry!"

"What, do you cry, Lina?" said Benito.

"Yes, Mr. Benito; but I cry when laughing."

"Oh, well! let us save it, Manoel!"

"It is the history of a Frenchwoman whose sorrows rendered these banks memorable in the eighteenth century."

"We are listening," said Minha.

"Here goes, then," said Manoel. "In 1741, at the time of the expedition of the two Frenchmen, Bouguer and La Condamine, who were sent to measure a terrestrial degree on the equator, they were accompanied by a very distinguished astronomer, Godin des Odonais. Godin des Odonais set out then, but he did not set out alone, for the New World; he took with him his young wife, his children, his father-in-law, and his brother-in-law. The travelers arrived at Quito in good health. There commenced a series of misfortunes for Madame Odonais; in a few months she lost some of her children. When Godin des Odonais had completed his work, toward the end of the year 1759, he left Quito and started for Cayenne. Once arrived in this town he wanted his family to come to him, but war had been declared, and he was obliged to ask the Portuguese government for permission for a free passage for Madame Odonais and her people. What do you think? Many years passed before the permission could be given. In 1765 Godin des Odonais, maddened by the delay, resolved to ascend the Amazon in search of his wife at Quito; but at the moment of his departure a sudden illness stopped him, and he could not carry out his intention.

However, his application had not been useless, and Madame des Odonais learned at last that the king of Portugal had given the necessary permission, and prepared to embark and descend the river to her husband. At the same time an escort was ordered to be ready in the missions of the Upper Amazon. Madame des Odonais was a woman of great courage, as you will see presently; she never hesitated, and notwithstanding the dangers of such a voyage across the continent, she started."

"It was her duty to her husband, Manoel," said Yaquita, "and I would have done the same."

"Madame des Odonais," continued Manoel, "came to Rio Bamba, at the south of Quito, bringing her brother-in-law, her children, and a French doctor. Their endeavor was to reach the missions on the Brazilian frontier, where they hoped to find a ship and the escort. The voyage at first was favorable; it was made down the tributaries of the Amazon in a canoe. The difficulties, however, gradually increased with the dangers and fatigues of a country decimated by the smallpox. Of several guides who offered their services, the most part disappeared after a few days; one of them, the last who remained faithful to the travelers, was drowned in the Bobonasa, in endeavoring to help the French doctor. At length the canoe, damaged by rocks and floating trees, became useless. It was therefore necessary to get on shore, and there at the edge of the impenetrable forest they built a few huts of foliage. The doctor offered to go on in front with a negro who had never wished to leave Madame des Odonais. The two went off; they waited for them several days, but in vain. They never returned.

"In the meantime the victuals were getting exhausted. The forsaken ones in vain endeavored to descend the Bobonasa on a raft. They had to again take to the forest, and make their way on foot through the almost impenetrable undergrowth. The fatigues were too much for the poor folks! They died off one by one in spite of the cares of the noble Frenchwoman. At the end of a few days children, relations, and servants, were all dead!"

"What an unfortunate woman!" said Lina.

"Madame des Odonais alone remained," continued Manoel. "There she was, at a thousand leagues from the ocean which she was trying to reach! It was no longer a mother who continued her journey toward the river - the mother had lost her shildren; she had buried them with her own hands! It was a wife who wished to see her husband once again! She traveled night and day, and at length regained the Bobonasa. She was there received by some kind-hearted Indians, who took her to the missions, where the escort was waiting. But she arrived alone, and behind her the stages of the route were marked with graves! Madame des Odonais reached Loreto, where we were a few days back. From this Peruvian village she descended the Amazon, as we are doing at this moment, and at length she rejoined her husband after a separation of nineteen years."

"Poor lady!" said Minha.

"Above all, poor mother!" answered Yaquita.

At this moment Araujo, the pilot, came aft and said:

"Joam Garral, we are off the Ronde Island. We are

passing the frontier!"

"The frontier!" replied Joam.

And rising, he went to the side of the jangada, and looked long and earnestly at the Ronde Island, with the waves breaking up against it. Then his hand sought his forehead, as if to rid himself of some remembrance.

"The frontier!" murmured he, bowing his head by an involuntary movement.

But an instant after his head was raised, and his expression was that of a man resolved to do his duty to the last.

CHAPTER XII

FRAGOSO AT WORK

"BRAZA" (burning embers) is a word found in the Spanish language as far back as the twelfth century. It has been used to make the word "brazil," as descriptive of certain woods which yield a reddish dye. From this has come the name "Brazil," given to that vast district of South America which is crossed by the equator, and in which these products are so frequently met with. In very early days these woods were the object of considerable trade. Although correctly called *"ibirapitunga,"* from the place of production, the name of *"brazil"* stuck to them, and it has become that of the country, which seems like an immense heap of embers lighted by the rays of the tropical sun.

Brazil was from the first occupied by the Portuguese. About the commencement of the sixteenth century, Alvarez Cabral, the pilot, took possession of it, and although France and Holland partially established themselves there, it has remained Portuguese, and possesses all the qualities which distinguish that gallant little nation. It is to-day the largest state of South America, and has at its head the intelligent artist-king Dom Pedro.

"What is your privilege in the tribe?" asked Montaigne

of an Indian whom he met at Havre.

"The privilege of marching first to battle!" innocently answered the Indian.

War, we know, was for a long time the surest and most rapid vehicle of civilization. The Brazilians did what this Indian did: they fought, they defended their conquests, they enlarged them, and we see them marching in the first rank of the civilizing advance.

It was in 1824, sixteen years after the foundation of the Portugo-Brazilian Empire, that Brazil proclaimed its independence by the voice of Don Juan, whom the French armies had chased from Portugal.

It remained only to define the frontier between the new empire and that of its neighbor, Peru. This was no easy matter.

If Brazil wished to extend to the Rio Napo in the west, Peru attempted to reach eight degrees further, as far as the Lake of Ega.

But in the meantime Brazil had to interfere to hinder the kidnapping of the Indians from the Amazon, a practice which was engaged in much to the profit of the Hispano-Brazilian missions. There was no better method of checking this trade than that of fortifying the Island of the Ronde, a little above Tabatinga, and there establishing a post.

This afforded the solution, and from that time the frontier of the two countries passed through the middle of this island.

Above, the river is Peruvian, and is called the Marañon, as has been said. Below, it is Brazilian, and takes the name of the Amazon.

It was on the evening of the 25th of June that the jangada stopped before Tabatinga, the first Brazilian town situated on the left bank, at the entrance of the river of which it bears the name, and belonging to the parish of St. Paul, established on the right a little further down stream.

Joam Garral had decided to pass thirty-six hours here, so as to give a little rest to the crew. They would not start, therefore, until the morning of the 27th.

On this occasion Yaquita and her children, less likely, perhaps, than at Iquitos to be fed upon by the native mosquitoes, had announced their intention of going on ashore and visiting the town.

The population of Tabatinga is estimated at four hundred, nearly all Indians, comprising, no doubt, many of those wandering families who are never settled at particular spots on the banks of the Amazon or its smaller tributaries.

The post at the island of the Ronde has been abandoned for some years, and transferred to Tabatinga. It can thus be called a garrison town, but the garrison is only composed of nine soldiers, nearly all Indians, and a sergeant, who is the actual commandant of the place.

A bank about thirty feet high, in which are cut the steps of a not very solid staircase, forms here the curtain of the esplanade which carries the pigmy fort. The house of the commandant consists of a couple of huts placed in a square, and the soldiers occupy an oblong building a hundred feet away, at the foot of a large tree.

The collection of cabins exactly resembles all the villages and hamlets which are scattered along the banks of the river, although in them a flagstaff carrying the Brazilian colors does not rise above a sentry-box, forever destitute of its sentinel, nor are four small mortars present to cannonade on an emergency any vessel which does not come in when ordered.

As for the village properly so called, it is situated below, at the base of the plateau. A road, which is but a ravine shaded by focuses and miritis, leads to it in a few minutes. There, on a half-cracked hill of clay, stand a dozen houses, covered with the leaves of the *"boiassu"* palm placed round a central space.

All this is not very curious, but the environs of Tabatinga are charming, particularly at the mouth of the Javary, which is of sufficient extent to contain the Archipelago of the Aramasa Islands. Hereabouts are grouped many fine trees, and among them a large number of the palms, whose supple fibers are used in the fabrication of hammocks and fishing-nets, and are the cause of some trade. To conclude, the place is one of the most picturesque on the Upper Amazon.

Tabatinga is destined to become before long a station of some importance, and will no doubt rapidly develop, for there will stop the Brazilian steamers which ascend the river, and the Peruvian steamers which descend it. There they will tranship passengers and cargoes. It does not require much for an English or American village to become in a few years the center of considerable commerce.

The river is very beautiful along this part of its course. The influence of ordinary tides is not perceptible at Tabatinga, which is more than six hundred leagues from the Atlantic. But it is not so with the *"pororoca,"* that species of eddy which for three days in the height of the syzygies raises the waters of the Amazon, and turns them back at the rate of seventeen kilometers per hour. They say that the effects of this bore are felt up to the Brazilian frontier.

On the morrow, the 26th of June, the Garral family prepared to go off and visit the village. Though Joam, Benito, and Manoel had already set foot in a Brazilian town, it was otherwise with Yaquita and her daughter; for them it was, so to speak, a taking possession. It is conceivable, therefore, that Yaquita and Minha should attach some importance to the event.

If, on his part, Fragoso, in his capacity of wandering barber, had already run through the different provinces of South America, Lina, like her young mistress, had never been on Brazilian soil.

But before leaving the jangada Fragoso had sought Joam Garral, and had the following conversation with him.

"Mr. Garral," said he, "from the day when you received me at the fazenda of Iquitos, lodged, clothed, fed - in a word, took me in so hospitably - I have owed you -- "

"You owe me absolutely nothing, my friend," answered Joam, "so do not insist -- "

"Oh, do not be alarmed!" exclaimed Fragoso, "I am not going to pay it off! Let me add, that you took me on board the jangada and gave me the means of descending the river. But here we are, on the soil of Brazil, which, according to all probability, I ought never to have seen again. Without that liana -- "

"It is to Lina, and to Lina alone, that you should tender your thanks," said Joam.

"I know," said Fragoso, "and I will never forget what I owe here, any more than what I owe you."

"They tell me, Fragoso," continued Joam, "that you are going to say good-by, and intend to remain at Tabatinga."

"By no means, Mr. Garral, since you have allowed me to accompany you to Belem, where I hope at the least to be able to resume my old trade."

"Well, if that is your intention - what were you going to ask me?"

"I was going to ask if you saw any inconvenience in my working at my profession on our route. There is no necessity for my hand to rust; and, besides, a few handfuls of reis would not be so bad at the bottom of my pocket, more particularly if I had earned them. You know, Mr. Garral, that a barber who is also a hairdresser - and I hardly like to say a doctor, out of respect to Mr. Manoel - always finds customers in these Upper Amazon villages."

"Particularly among the Brazilians," answered Joam. "As for the natives -- "

"I beg pardon," replied Fragoso, "particularly among the natives. Ah! although there is no beard to trim - for nature has been very stingy toward them in that way - there are always some heads of hair to be dressed in the latest fashion. They are very fond of it, these savages, both the men and the women! I shall not be installed ten minutes in the square at Tabatinga, with my cup and ball in hand - the cup and ball I have brought on board, and which I can manage with pretty pleasantly - before a circle of braves and squaws will have formed around me. They will struggle for my favors. I could remain here for a month, and the whole tribe of the Ticunas would come to me to have their hair looked after! They won't hesitate to make the acquaintance of 'curling tongs' - that is what they will call me - if I revisit the walls of Tabatinga! I have already had two tries here, and my scissors and comb have done marvels! It does not do to return too often on the same track. The Indian ladies don't have their hair curled every day, like the beauties of our Brazilian cities. No; when it is done, it is done for year, and during the twelvemonth they will take every care not to endanger the edifice which I have raised - with what talent I dare not say. Now it is nearly a year since I was at Tabatinga; I go to find my monuments in ruin! And if it is not objectionable to you, Mr. Garral, I would render myself again worthy of the reputation which I have acquired in these parts, the question of reis, and not that of conceit, being, you understand, the principal."

"Go on, then, friend," replied Joam Garral laughingly; "but be quick! we can only remain a day at Tabatinga, and we shall start to-morrow at dawn."

"I will not lose a minute," answered Fragoso - "just

time to take the tools of my profession, and I am off."

"Off you go, Fragoso," said Joam, "and may the reis rain into your pocket!"

"Yes, and that is a proper sort of rain, and there can never be too much of it for your obedient servant."

And so saying Fragoso rapidly moved away.

A moment afterward the family, with the exception of Joam, went ashore. The jangada was able to approach near enough to the bank for the landing to take place without much trouble. A staircase, in a miserable state, cut in the cliff, allowed the visitors to arrive on the crest of the plateau.

Yaquita and her party were received by the commandant of the fort, a poor fellow who, however, knew the laws of hospitality, and offered them some breakfast in his cottage. Here and there passed and repassed several soldiers on guard, while on the threshold of the barrack appeared a few children, with their mothers of Ticuna blood, affording very poor specimens of the mixed race.

In place of accepting the breakfast of the sergeant, Yaquita invited the commandant and his wife to come and have theirs on board the jangada.

The commandant did not wait for a second invitation, and an appointment was made for eleven o'clock. In the meantime Yaquita, her daughter, and the young mulatto, accompanied by Manoel, went for a walk in the neighborhood, leaving Benito to settle with the commandant about the tolls - he being chief of the custom-house as well as of the military establishment.

That done, Benito, as was his wont, strolled off with his gun into the adjoining woods. On this occasion Manoel had declined to accompany him. Fragoso had left the jangada, but instead of mounting to the fort he had made for the village, crossing the ravine which led off from the right on the level of the bank. He reckoned more on the native custom of Tabatinga than on that of the garrison. Doubtless the soldiers' wives would not have wished better than to have been put under his hands, but the husbands scarcely cared to part with a few reis for the sake of gratifying the whims of their coquettish partners.

Among the natives it was quite the reverse. Husbands and wives, the jolly barber knew them well, and he knew they would give him a better reception.

Behold, then, Fragoso on the road, coming up the shady lane beneath the ficuses, and arriving in the central square of Tabatinga!

As soon as he set foot in the place the famous barber was signaled, recognized, surrounded. Fragoso had no big box, nor drum, nor cornet to attract the attention of his clients - not even a carriage of shining copper, with resplendent lamps and ornamented glass panels, nor a huge parasol, no anything whatever to impress the public, as they generally have at fairs. No; but Fragoso had his cup and ball, and how that cup and ball were manipulated between his fingers! With what address did he receive the turtle's head, which did for the ball, on the pointed end of the stick! With what grace did he make the ball describe some learned curve of which mathematicians have not yet calculated the value -

even those who have determined the wondrous curve of "the dog who follows his master!"

Every native was there - men, women, the old and the young, in their nearly primitive costume, looking on with all their eyes, listening with all their ears. The smiling entertainer, half in Portuguese, half in Ticunian, favored them with his customary oration in a tone of the most rollicking good humor. What he said was what is said by all the charlatans who place their services at the public disposal, whether they be Spanish Figaros or French perruqiers. At the bottom the same self-possession, the same knowledge of human weakness, the same description of threadbare witticisms, the same amusing dexterity, and, on the part of the natives, the same wide-mouth astonishment, the same curiosity, the same credulity as the simple folk of the civilized world.

It followed, then, that ten minutes later the public were completely won, and crowded round Fragoso, who was installed in a *"loja"* of the place, a sort of serving-bar to the inn.

The *loja* belonged to a Brazilian settled at Tabatinga. There, for a few vatems, which are the sols of the country, and worth about twenty reis, or half a dozen centimes each, the natives could get drinks of the crudest, and particularly assai, a liquor half-sold, half-liquid, made of the fruit of the palm-tree, and drunk from a *"coui"* or half-calabash in general use in this district of the Amazon.

And then men and women, with equal eagerness, took their places on the barber's stool. The scissors of Fragoso had little to do, for it was not a question of cutting these wealthy heads of hair, nearly all remarkable for their softness and their quality, but the use to which he could put his comb and the tongs, which were kept warming in the corner in a brasier.

And then the encouragements of the artist to the crowd!

"Look here! look here!" said he; "how will that do, my friends - if you don't sleep on the top of it! There you are, for a twelvemonth! and these are the latest novelties from Belem and Rio de Janeiro! The queen's maids of honor are not more cleverly decked out; and observe, I am not stingy with the pomade!"

No, he was not stingy with it. True, it was only a little grease, with which he had mixed some of the juices of a few flowers, but he plastered it on like cement!

And as to the names of the capillary edifices - for the monuments reared by the hands of Fragoso were of every order of architecture - buckles, rings, clubs, tresses, crimpings, rolls, corkscrews, curls, everything found there a place. Nothing false; no towers, no chignons, no shams! These head were not enfeebled by cuttings nor thinned by fallings-off, but were forests in all their native virginity! Fragoso, however, was not above adding a few natural flowers, two or three long fish-bones, and some fine bone or copper ornaments, which were brought him by the dandies of the district. Assuredly, the exquisites of the Directory would have envied the arrangement of these high-art coiffures, three and four stories high, and the great Leonard himself would have bowed before his transatlantic rival.

And then the vatems, the handfuls of reis - the only coins for which the natives of the Amazon exchange their goods - which rained into the pocket of Fragoso, and which he collected with evident satisfaction. But assuredly night would come before he could satisfy the demands of the customers, who were so constantly renewed. It was not only the population of Tabatinga which crowded to the door of the loja. The news of the arrival of Fragoso was not slow to get abroad; natives came to him from all sides: Ticunas from the left bank of the river, Mayorunas from the right bank, as well as those who live on the Cajuru and those who come from the villages of the Javary.

A long array of anxious ones formed itself in the square. The happy ones coming from the hands of Fragoso went proudly from one house to another, showed themselves off without daring to shake themselves, like the big children that they were.

It thus happened that when noon came the much-occupied barber had not had time to return on board, but had had to content himself with a little assai, some manioc flour, and turtle eggs, which he rapidly devoured between two applications of the curling-tongs.

But it was a great harvest for the innkeeper, as all the operations could not be conducted without a large absorption of liquors drawn from the cellars of the inn. In fact, it was an event for the town of Tabatinga, this visit of the celebrated Fragoso, barber in ordinary and extraordinary to the tribes of the Upper Amazon!

CHAPTER XIII

TORRES

AT FIVE O'CLOCK in the evening Fragoso was still there, and was asking himself if he would have to pass the night on the spot to satisfy the expectant crowd, when a stranger arrived in the square, and seeing all this native gathering, advanced toward the inn.

For some minutes the stranger eyed Fragoso attentively with some circumspection. The examination was obviously satisfactory, for he entered the loja.

He was a man about thirty-five years of age. He was dressed in a somewhat elegant traveling costume, which added much to his personal appearance. But his strong black beard, which the scissors had not touched for some time, and his hair, a trifle long, imperiously required the good offices of a barber.

"Good-day, friend, good-day!" said he, lightly striking Fragoso on the shoulder.

Fragoso turned round when he heard the words pronounced in pure Brazilian, and not in the mixed idiom of the natives.

"A compatriot?" he asked, without stopping the

twisting of the refractory mouth of a Mayouma head.

"Yes," answered the stranger. "A compatriot who has need of your services."

"To be sure! In a minute," said Fragoso. "Wait till I have finished with this lady!"

And this was done in a couple of strokes with the curling-tongs.

Although he was the last comer, and had no right to the vacant place, he sat down on the stool without causing any expostulation on the part of the natives who lost a turn.

Fragoso put down the irons for the scissors, and, after the manner of his brethren, said:

"What can I do for you, sir?"

"Cut my beard and my hair," answered the stranger.

"All right!" said Fragoso, inserting his comb into the mass of hair.

And then the scissors to do their work.

"And you come from far?" asked Fragoso, who could not work without a good deal to say.

"I have come from the neighborhood of Iquitos."

"So have I!" exclaimed Fragoso. "I have come down the Amazon from Iquitos to Tabatinga. May I ask your name?"

"No objection at all," replied the stranger. "My name is Torres."

When the hair was cut in the latest style Fragoso began to thin his beard, but at this moment, as he was looking straight into his face, he stopped, then began again, and then:

"Eh! Mr. Torres," said he; "I seem to know you. We must have seen each other somewhere?"

"I do not think so," quickly answered Torres.

"I am always wrong!" replied Fragoso, and he hurried on to finish his task.

A moment after Torres continued the conversation which this question of Fragoso had interrupted, with:

"How did you come from Iquitos?"

"From Iquitos to Tabatinga?"

"Yes."

"On board a raft, on which I was given a passage by a worthy fazender who is going down the Amazon with his family."

"A friend indeed!" replied Torres. "That is a chance, and if your fazender would take me -- "

"Do you intend, then, to go down the river?"

"Precisely."

"Into Para?"

"No, only to Manaos, where I have business."

"Well, my host is very kind, and I think he would cheerfully oblige you."

"Do you think so?"

"I might almost say I am sure."

"And what is the name of this fazender?" asked Torres carelessly.

"Joam Garral," answered Fragoso.

And at the same time he muttered to himself:

"I certainly have seen this fellow somewhere!"

Torres was not the man to allow a conversation to drop which was likely to interest him, and for very good reasons.

"And so you think Joam Garral would give me a passage?"

"I do not doubt it," replied Fragoso. "What he would do for a poor chap like me he would not refuse to do for a compatriot like you."

"Is he alone on board the jangada?"

"No," replied Fragoso. "I was going to tell you that he is traveling with all his family - and jolly people they are, I assure you. He is accompanied by a crew of

Indians and negroes, who form part of the staff at the fazenda."

"Is he rich?"

"Oh, certainly!" answered Fragoso - "very rich. Even the timber which forms the jangada, and the cargo it carries, constitute a fortune!"

"The Joam Garral and his whole family have just passed the Brazilian frontier?"

"Yes," said Fragoso; "his wife, his son, his daughter, and Miss Minha's betrothed."

"Ah! he has a daughter?" said Torres.

"A charming girl!"

"Going to get married?"

"Yes, to a brave young fellow," replied Fragoso - "an army surgeon in garrison at Belem, and the wedding is to take place as soon as we get to the end of the voyage."

"Good!" said the smiling Torres; "it is what you might call a betrothal journey."

"A voyage of betrothal, of pleasure, and of business!" said Fragoso. "Madame Yaquita and her daughter have never set foot on Brazilian ground; and as for Joam Garral, it is the first time he has crossed the frontier since he went to the farm of old Magalhaës."

"I suppose," asked Torres, "that there are some

servants with the family?"

"Of course," replied Fragoso - "old Cybele, on the farm for the last fifty years, and a pretty mulatto, Miss Lina, who is more of a companion than a servant to her mistress. Ah, what an amiable disposition! What a heart, and what eyes! And the ideas she has about everything, particularly about lianas - " Fragoso, started on this subject, would not have been able to stop himself, and Lina would have been the object of a good many enthusiastic declarations, had Torres not quitted the chair for another customer.

"What do I owe you?" asked he of the barber.

"Nothing," answered Fragoso. "Between compatriots, when they meet on the frontier, there can be no question of that sort."

"But," replied Torres, "I want to -- "

"Very well, we will settle that later on, on board the jangada."

"But I do not know that, and I do not like to ask Joam Garral to allow me -- "

"Do not hesitate!" exclaimed Fragoso; "I will speak to him if you would like it better, and he will be very happy to be of use to you under the circumstances."

And at that instant Manoel and Benito, coming into the town after dinner, appeared at the door of the loja, wishing to see Fragoso at work.

Torres turned toward them and suddenly said: "There

are two gentlemen I know - or rather I remember."

"You remember them!" asked Fragoso, surprised.

"Yes, undoubtedly! A month ago, in the forest of Iquitos, they got me out of a considerable difficulty."

"But they are Benito Garral and Manoel Valdez."

"I know. They told me their names, but I never expected to see them here."

Torres advanced toward the two young men, who looked at him without recognizing him.

"You do not remember me, gentlemen?" he asked.

"Wait a little," answered Benito; "Mr. Torres, if I remember aright; it was you who, in the forest of Iquitos, got into difficulties with a guariba?"

"Quite true, gentlemen," replied Torres. "For six weeks I have been traveling down the Amazon, and I have just crossed the frontier at the same time as you have."

"Very pleased to see you again," said Benito; "but you have not forgotten that you promised to come to the fazenda to my father?"

"I have not forgotten it," answered Torres.

"And you would have done better to have accepted my offer; it would have allowed you to have waited for our departure, rested from you fatigues, and descended with us to the frontier; so many days of walking saved."

"To be sure!" answered Torres.

"Our compatriot is not going to stop at the frontier," said Fragoso, "he is going on to Manaos."

"Well, then," replied Benito, "if you will come on board the jangada you will be well received, and I am sure my father will give you a passage."

"Willingly," said Torres; "and you will allow me to thank you in advance."

Manoel took no part in the conversation; he let Benito make the offer of his services, and attentively watched Torres, whose face he scarcely remembered. There was an entire want of frankness in the eyes, whose look changed unceasingly, as if he was afraid to fix them anywhere. But Manoel kept this impression to himself, not wishing to injure a compatriot whom they were about to oblige.

"Gentlemen," said Torres, "if you like, I am ready to follow you to the landing-place."

"Come, then," answered Benito.

A quarter of an hour afterward Torres was on board the jangada. Benito introduced him to Joam Garral, acquainting him with the circumstances under which they had previously met him, and asked him to give him a passage down to Manaos.

"I am happy, sir, to be able to oblige you," replied Joam.

"Thank you," said Torres, who at the moment of

putting forth his hand kept it back in spite of himself.

"We shall be off at daybreak to-morrow," added Joam Garral, "so you had better get your things on board."

"Oh, that will not take me long!" answered Torres; "there is only myself and nothing else!"

"Make yourself at home," said Joam Garral.

That evening Torres took possession of a cabin near to that of the barber. It was not till eight o'clock that the latter returned to the raft, and gave the young mulatto an account of his exploits, and repeated, with no little vanity, that the renown of the illustrious Fragoso was increasing in the basin of the Upper Amazon.

CHAPTER XIV

STILL DESCENDING

AT DAYBREAK on the morrow, the 27th of June, the cables were cast off, and the raft continued its journey down the river.

An extra passenger was on board. Whence came this Torres? No one exactly knew. Where was he going to? "To Manaos," he said. Torres was careful to let no suspicion of his past life escape him, nor of the profession that he had followed till within the last two months, and no one would have thought that the jangada had given refuge to an old captain of the woods. Joam Garral did not wish to mar the service he was rendering by questions of too pressing a nature.

In taking him on board the fazender had obeyed a sentiment of humanity. In the midst of these vast Amazonian deserts, more especially at the time when the steamers had not begun to furrow the waters, it was very difficult to find means of safe and rapid transit. Boats did not ply regularly, and in most cases the traveler was obliged to walk across the forests. This is what Torres had done, and what he would continue to have done, and it was for him unexpected good luck to have got a passage on the raft.

From the moment that Benito had explained under what conditions he had met Torres the introduction was complete, and he was able to consider himself as a passenger on an Atlantic steamer, who is free to take part in the general life if he cares, or free to keep himself a little apart if of an unsociable disposition.

It was noticed, at least during the first few days, that Torres did not try to become intimate with the Garral family. He maintained a good deal of reserve, answering if addressed, but never provoking a reply.

If he appeared more open with any one, it was with Fragoso. Did he not owe to this gay companion the idea of taking passage on board the raft? Many times he asked him about the position of the Garrals at Iquitos, the sentiments of the daughter for Manoel Valdez, and always discreetly. Generally, when he was not walking alone in the bow of the jangada, he kept to his cabin.

He breakfasted and dined with Joam Garral and his family, but he took little part in their conversation, and retired when the repast was finished.

During the morning the raft passed by the picturesque group of islands situated in the vast estuary of the Javary. This important affluent of the Amazon comes from the southwest, and from source to mouth has not a single island, nor a single rapid, to check its course. The mouth is about three thousand feet in width, and the river comes in some miles above the site formerly occupied by the town of the same name, whose possession was disputed for so long by Spaniards and Portuguese.

Up to the morning of the 30th of June there had been nothing particular to distinguish the voyage. Occasionally they met a few vessels gliding along by the banks attached one to another in such a way that a single Indian could manage the whole - *"navigar de bubina,"* as this kind of navigation is called by the people of the country, that is to say, "confidence navigation."

They had passed the island of Araria, the Archipelago of the Calderon islands, the island of Capiatu, and many others whose names have not yet come to the knowledge of geographers.

On the 30th of June the pilot signaled on the right the little village of Jurupari-Tapera, where they halted for two or three hours.

Manoel and Benito had gone shooting in the neighborhood, and brought back some feathered game, which was well received in the larder. At the same time they had got an animal of whom a naturalist would have made more than did the cook.

It was a creature of a dark color, something like a large Newfoundland dog.

"A great ant-eater!" exclaimed Benito, as he threw it on the deck of the jangada.

"And a magnificent specimen which would not disgrace the collection of a museum!" added Manoel.

"Did you take much trouble to catch the curious animal?" asked Minha.

"Yes, little sister," replied Benito, "and you were not

there to ask for mercy! These dogs die hard, and no less than three bullets were necessary to bring this fellow down."

The ant-eater looked superb, with his long tail and grizzly hair; with his pointed snout, which is plunged into the ant-hills whose insects form its principal food; and his long, thin paws, armed with sharp nails, five inches long, and which can shut up like the fingers of one's hand. But what a hand was this hand of the ant-eater! When it has got hold of anything you have to cut it off to make it let go! It is of this hand that the traveler, Emile Carrey, has so justly observed: "The tiger himself would perish in its grasp."

On the 2d of July, in the morning, the jangada arrived at the foot of San Pablo d'Olivença, after having floated through the midst of numerous islands which in all seasons are clad with verdure and shaded with magnificent trees, and the chief of which bear the names of Jurupari, Rita, Maracanatena, and Cururu Sapo. Many times they passed by the mouths of iguarapes, or little affluents, with black waters.

The coloration of these waters is a very curious phenomenon. It is peculiar to a certain number of these tributaries of the Amazon, which differ greatly in importance.

Manoel remarked how thick the cloudiness was, for it could be clearly seen on the surface of the whitish waters of the river.

"They have tried to explain this coloring in many ways," said he, "but I do not think the most learned have yet arrived at a satisfactory explanation."

"The waters are really black with a magnificent reflection of gold," replied Minha, showing a light, reddish-brown cloth, which was floating level with the jangada.

"Yes," said Manoel, "and Humboldt has already observed the curious reflection that you have; but on looking at it attentively you will see that it is rather the color of sepia which pervades the whole."

"Good!" exclaimed Benito. "Another phenomenon on which the *savants* are not agreed."

"Perhaps," said Fragoso, "they might ask the opinions of the caymans, dolphins, and manatees, for they certainly prefer the black waters to the others to enjoy themselves in."

"They are particularly attractive to those animals," replied Manoel, "but why it is rather embarrassing to say. For instance, is the coloration due to the hydrocarbons which the waters hold in solution, or is it because they flow through districts of peat, coal, and anthracite; or should we not rather attribute it to the enormous quantity of minute plants which they bear along? There is nothing certain in the matter. Under any circumstances, they are excellent to drink, of a freshness quite enviable for the climate, and without after-taste, and perfectly harmless. Take a little of the water, Minha, and drink it; you will find it all right."

The water is in truth limpid and fresh, and would advantageously replace many of the table-waters used in Europe. They drew several frasques for kitchen use.

It has been said that in the morning of the 2d of July

the jangada had arrived at San Pablo d'Olivença, where they turn out in thousands those long strings of beads which are made from the scales of the *"coco de piassaba."* This trade is here extensively followed. It may, perhaps, seem singular that the ancient lords of the country, Tupinambas and Tupiniquis, should find their principal occupation in making objects for the Catholic religion. But, after all, why not? These Indians are no longer the Indians of days gone by. Instead of being clothed in the national fashion, with a frontlet of macaw feathers, bow, and blow-tube, have they not adopted the American costume of white cotton trousers, and a cotton poncho woven by their wives, who have become thorough adepts in its manufacture?

San Pablo d'Olivença, a town of some importance, has not less than two thousand inhabitants, derived from all the neighboring tribes. At present the capital of the Upper Amazon, it began as a simple Mission, founded by the Portuguese Carmelites about 1692, and afterward acquired by the Jesuit missionaries.

From the beginning it has been the country of the Omaguas, whose name means "flat-heads," and is derived from the barbarous custom of the native mothers of squeezing the heads of their newborn children between two plates, so as to give them an oblong skull, which was then the fashion. Like everything else, that has changed; heads have re-taken their natural form, and there is not the slightest trace of the ancient deformity in the skulls of the chaplet-makers.

Every one, with the exception of Joam Garral, went ashore. Torres also remained on board, and showed no desire to visit San Pablo d'Olivença, which he did not, however, seem to be acquainted with.

Assuredly if the adventurer was taciturn he was not inquisitive.

Benito had no difficulty in doing a little bartering, and adding slightly to the cargo of the jangada. He and the family received an excellent reception from the principal authorities of the town, the commandant of the place, and the chief of the custom-house, whose functions did not in the least prevent them from engaging in trade. They even intrusted the young merchant with a few products of the country for him to dispose of on their account at Manaos and Belem.

The town is composed of some sixty houses, arranged on the plain which hereabouts crowns the river-bank. Some of the huts are covered with tiles - a very rare thing in these countries; but, on the other hand, the humble church, dedicated to St. Peter and St. Paul, has only a roof of straw, rather more appropriate for a stable of Bethlehem than for an edifice consecrated to religion in one of the most Catholic countries of the world.

The commandant, his lieutenant, and the head of the police accepted an invitation to dine with the family, and they were received by Joam Garral with the respect due to their rank.

During dinner Torres showed himself more talkative than usual. He spoke about some of his excursions into the interior of Brazil like a man who knew the country. But in speaking of these travels Torres did not neglect to ask the commandant if he knew Manaos, if his colleague would be there at this time, and if the judge, the first magistrate of the province, was accustomed to absent himself at this period of the hot season. It seemed that in putting this series of questions Torres looked at Joam Garral. It was marked enough for even Benito to notice it, not without surprise, and he observed that his father gave particular attention to the questions so curiously propounded by Torres.

The commandant of San Pablo d'Olivença assured the adventurer that the authorities were not now absent from Manaos, and he even asked Joam Garral to convey to them his compliments. In all probability the raft would arrive before the town in seven weeks, or a little later, say about the 20th or the 25th of August.

The guests of the fazender took leave of the Garral family toward the evening, and the following morning, that of the 3d of July, the jangada recommenced its descent of the river.

At noon they passed on the left the mouth of the Yacurupa. This tributary, properly speaking, is a true canal, for it discharges its waters into the Içá, which is itself an affluent of the Amazon.

A peculiar phenomenon, for the river displaces itself to feed its own tributaries!

Toward three o'clock in the afternoon the giant raft passed the mouth of the Jandiatuba, which brings its magnificent black waters from the southwest, and discharges them into the main artery by a mouth of four hundred meters in extent, after having watered the territories of the Culino Indians.

A number of islands were breasted - Pimaicaira,

Caturia, Chico, Motachina; some inhabited, others deserted, but all covered with superb vegetation, which forms an unbroken garland of green from one end of the Amazon to the other.

CHAPTER XV

THE CONTINUED DESCENT

ON THE EVENING of the 5th of July, the atmosphere had een oppressive since the morning and threatened approaching storms. Large bats of ruddy color skimmed with their huge wings the current of the Amazon. Among them could be distinguished the *"perros voladors,"* somber brown above and light-colored beneath, for which Minha, and particularly the young mulatto, felt an instinctive aversion.

These were, in fact, the horrible vampires which suck the blood of the cattle, and even attack man if he is imprudent enough to sleep out in the fields.

"Oh, the dreadful creatures!" cried Lina, hiding her eyes; "they fill me with horror!"

"And they are really formidable," added Minha; "are they not, Manoel?"

"To be sure - very formidable," answered he. "These vampires have a particular instinct which leads them to bleed you in the places where the blood most easily comes, and principally behind the ear. During the operation the continue to move their wings, and cause an agreeable freshness which renders the sleep of the sleeper more profound. They tell of people, unconsciously submitted to this hemorrhage for many hours, who have never awoke!"

"Talk no more of things like that, Manoel," said Yaquita, "or neither Minha nor Lina will dare sleep tonight."

"Never fear!" replied Manoel; "if necessary we will watch over them as they sleep."

"Silence!" said Benito.

"What is the matter?" asked Manoel.

"Do you not hear a very curious noise on that side?" continued Benito, pointing to the right bank.

"Certainly," answered Yaquita.

"What causes the noise?" asked Minha. "One would think it was shingle rolling on the beach of the islands."

"Good! I know what it is," answered Benito. "Tomorrow, at daybreak, there will be a rare treat for those who like fresh turtle eggs and little turtles!"

He was not deceived; the noise was produced by innumerable chelonians of all sizes, who were attracted to the islands to lay their eggs.

It is in the sand of the beach that these amphibians choose the most convenient places to deposit their eggs. The operation commences with sunset and finishes with the dawn.

At this moment the chief turtle had left the bed of the river to reconnoiter for a favorable spot; the others, collected in thousands, were soon after occupied in digging with their hind paddles a trench six hundred feet long, a dozen wide, and six deep. After laying their eggs they cover them with a bed of sand, which they beat down with their carapaces as if they were rammers.

This egg-laying operation is a grand affair for the riverine Indians of the Amazon and its tributaries. They watch for the arrival of the chelonians, and proceed to the extraction of the eggs to the sound of the drum; and the harvest is divided into three parts - one to the watchers, another to the Indians, a third to the state, represented by the captains of the shore, who, in their capacity of police, have to superintend the collection of the dues. To certain beaches which the decrease of the waters has left uncovered, and which have the privilege of attracting the greater number of turtles, there has been given the name of "royal beaches." When the harvest is gathered it is a holiday for the Indians, who give themselves up to games, dancing, and drinking; and it is also a holiday for the alligators of the river, who hold high revelry on the remains of the amphibians.

Turtles, or turtle eggs, are an object of very considerable trade throughout the Amazonian basin. It is these chelonians whom they "turn" - that is to say, put on their backs - when they come from laying their eggs, and whom they preserve alive, keeping them in palisaded pools like fish-pools, or attaching them to a stake by a cord just long enough to allow them to go and come on the land or under the water. In this way they always have the meat of these animals fresh.

They proceed differently with the little turtles which are just hatched. There is no need to pack them or tie them up. Their shell is still soft, their flesh extremely tender, and after they have cooked them they eat them just like oysters. In this form large quantities are consumed.

However, this is not the most general use to which the chelonian eggs are put in the provinces of Amazones and Para. The manufacture of *"manteigna de tartaruga,"* or turtle butter, which will bear comparison with the best products of Normandy or Brittany, does not take less every year that from two hundred and fifty to three hundred millions of eggs. But the turtles are innumerable all along the river, and they deposit their eggs on the sands of the beach in incalculable quantities. However, on account of the destruction caused not only by the natives, but by the water-fowl from the side, the urubus in the air, and the alligators in the river, their number has been so diminished that for every little turtle a Brazilian pataque, or about a franc, has to be paid.

On the morrow, at daybreak, Benito, Fragoso, and a few Indians took a pirogue and landed on the beach of one of the large islands which they had passed during the night. It was not necessary for the jangada to halt. They knew they could catch her up.

On the shore they saw the little hillocks which indicated the places where, that very night, each packet of eggs had been deposited in the trench in groups of from one hundred and sixty to one hundred and ninety. These there was no wish to get out. But an earlier laying had taken place two months before, the eggs had hatched under the action of the heat stored in the sand, and already several thousands of little turtles were running about the beach.

The hunters were therefore in luck. The pirogue was filled with these interesting amphibians, and they arrived just in time for breakfast. The booty was divided between the passengers and crew of the jangada, and if any lasted till the evening it did not last any longer.

In the morning of the 7th of July they were before San Jose de Matura, a town situated near a small river filled up with long grass, and on the borders of which a legend says that Indians with tails once existed.

In the morning of the 8th of July they caught sight of the village of San Antonio, two or three little houses lost in the trees at the mouth of the Iça, or Putumayo, which is about nine hundred meters wide.

The Putumayo is one of the most important affluents of the Amazon. Here in the sixteenth century missions were founded by the Spaniards, which were afterward destroyed by the Portuguese, and not a trace of them now remains.

Representatives of different tribes of Indians are found in the neighborhood, which are easily recognizable by the differences in their tattoo marks.

The Iça is a body of water coming from the east of the Pasto Mountains to the northeast of Quito, through the finest forests of wild cacao-trees. Navigable for a distance of a hundred and forty leagues for steamers of not greater draught than six feet, it may one day become one of the chief waterways in the west of America.

The bad weather was at last met with. It did not show itself in continual rains, but in frequent storms. These could not hinder the progress of the raft, which offered little resistance to the wind. Its great length rendered it almost insensible to the swell of the Amazon, but during the torrential showers the Garral family had to keep indoors. They had to occupy profitably these hours of leisure. They chatted together, communicated their observations, and their tongues were seldom idle.

It was under these circumstances that little by little Torres had begun to take a more active part in the conversation. The details of his many voyages throughout the whole north of Brazil afforded him numerous subjects to talk about. The man had certainly seen a great deal, but his observations were those of a skeptic, and he often shocked the straightforward people who were listening to him. It should be said that he showed himself much impressed toward Minha. But these attentions, although they were displeasing to Manoel, were not sufficiently marked for him to interfere. On the other hand, Minha felt for him an instinctive repulsion which she was at no pains to conceal.

On the 5th of July the mouth of the Tunantins appeared on the left bank, forming an estuary of some four hundred feet across, in which it pours its blackish waters, coming from the west-northwest, after having watered the territories of the Cacena Indians. At this spot the Amazon appears under a truly grandiose aspect, but its course is more than ever encumbered with islands and islets. It required all the address of the pilot to steer through the archipelago, going from one bank to another, avoiding the shallows, shirking the eddies, and maintaining the advance.

They might have taken the Ahuaty Parana, a sort of natural canal, which goes off a little below the mouth of the Tunantins, and re-enters the principal stream a hundred an twenty miles further on by the Rio Japura; but if the larger portion of this measures a hundred and fifty feet across, the narrowest is only sixty feet, and the raft would there have met with a difficulty.

On the 13th of July, after having touched at the island of Capuro, passed the mouth of the Jutahy, which, coming from the east-southeast, brings in its black waters by a mouth five hundred feet wide, and admired the legions of monkeys, sulphur-white in color, with cinnabar-red faces, who are insatiable lovers of the nuts produced by the palm-trees from which the river derives its name, the travelers arrived on the 18th of July before the little village of Fonteboa.

At this place the jangada halted for twelve hours, so as to give a rest to the crew.

Fonteboa, like most of the mission villages of the Amazon, has not escaped the capricious fate which, during a lengthened period, moves them about from one place to the other. Probably the hamlet has now finished with its nomadic existence, and has definitely become stationary. So much the better; for it is a charming place, with its thirty houses covered with foliage, and its church dedicated to Notre Dame de Guadaloupe, the Black Virgin of Mexico. Fonteboa has one thousand inhabitants, drawn from the Indians on both banks, who rear numerous cattle in the fields in the neighborhood. These occupations do not end here, for they are intrepid hunters, or, if they prefer it, intrepid fishers for the manatee.

On the morning of their arrival the young fellows assisted at a very interesting expedition of this nature. Two of these herbivorous cetaceans had just been signaled in the black waters of the Cayaratu, which comes in at Fonteboa. Six brown points were seen moving along the surface, and these were the two pointed snouts and four pinions of the lamantins.

Inexperienced fishermen would at first have taken these moving points for floating wreckage, but the natives of Fonteboa were not to be so deceived. Besides, very soon loud blowings indicated that the spouting animals were vigorously ejecting the air which had become useless for their breathing purposes.

Two ubas, each carrying three fishermen, set off from the bank and approached the manatees, who soon took flight. The black points at first traced a long furrow on the top of the water, and then disappeared for a time.

The fishermen continued their cautious advance. One of them, armed with a very primitive harpoon - a long nail at the end of a stick - kept himself in the bow of the boat, while the other two noiselessly paddled on. They waited till the necessity of breathing would bring the manatees up again. In ten minutes or thereabouts the animals would certainly appear in a circle more or less confined.

In fact, this time had scarcely elapsed before the black points emerged at a little distance, and two jets of air mingled with vapor were noiselessly shot forth.

The ubas approached, the harpoons were thrown at the same instant; one missed its mark, but the other struck one of the cetaceans near his tail.

It was only necessary to stun the animal, who rarely defends himself when touched by the iron of the harpoon. In a few pulls the cord brought him alongside the uba, and he was towed to the beach at the foot of the village.

It was not a manatee of any size, for it only measured about three feet long. These poor cetaceans have been so hunted that they have become very rare in the Amazon and its affluents, and so little time is left them to grow that the giants of the species do not now exceed seven feet. What are these, after manatees twelve and fifteen feet long, which still abound in the rivers and lakes of Africa?

But it would be difficult to hinder their destruction. The flesh of the manatee is excellent, superior even to that of pork, and the oil furnished by its lard, which is three inches thick, is a product of great value. When the meat is smoke-dried it keeps for a long time, and is capital food. If to this is added that the animal is easily caught, it is not to be wondered at that the species is on its way to complete destruction.

On the 19th of July, at sunrise, the jangada left Fonteboa, and entered between the two completely deserted banks of the river, and breasted some islands shaded with the grand forests of cacao-trees. The sky was heavily charged with electric cumuli, warning them of renewed storms.

The Rio Jurua, coming from the southwest, soon joins the river on the left. A vessel can go up it into Peru without encountering insurmountable obstacles among its white waters, which are fed by a great number of petty affluents.

"It is perhaps in these parts," said Manoel, "that we ought to look for those female warriors who so much astonished Orellana. But we ought to say that, like their predecessors, they do nor form separate tribes; they are simply the wives who accompany their husbands to the fight, and who, among the Juruas, have a great reputation for bravery."

The jangada continued to descend; but what a labyrinth the Amazon now appeared! The Rio Japura, whose mouth was forty-eight miles on ahead, and which is one of its largest tributaries, runs almost parallel with the river.

Between them were canals, iguarapes, lagoons, temporary lakes, an inextricable network which renders the hydrography of this country so difficult.

But if Araujo had no map to guide him, his experience served him more surely, and it was wonderful to see him unraveling the chaos, without ever turning aside from the main river.

In fact, he did so well that on the 25th of July, in the afternoon, after having passed before the village of Parani-Tapera, the raft was anchored at the entrance of the Lake of Ego, or Teffe, which it was useless to enter, for they would not have been able to get out of it again into the Amazon.

But the town of Ega is of some importance; it was worthy of a halt to visit it. It was arranged, therefore, that the jangada should remain on this spot till the 27th of July, and that on the morrow the large pirogue should take the whole family to Ega. This would give a rest, which was deservedly due to the hard-working crew of the raft.

The night passed at the moorings near a slightly rising shore, and nothing disturbed the quiet. A little sheet-lightning was observable on the horizon, but it came from a distant storm which did not reach the entrance to the lake.

CHAPTER XVI

EGA

AT SIX o'clock in the morning of the 20th of July, Yaquita, Minha, Lina, and the two young men prepared to leave the jangada.

Joam Garral, who had shown no intention of putting his foot on shore, had decided this time, at the request of the ladies of his family, to leave his absorbing daily work and accompany them on their excursion. Torres had evinced no desire to visit Ega, to the great satisfaction of Manoel, who had taken a great dislike to the man and only waited for an opportunity to declare it.

As to Fragoso, he could not have the same reason for going to Ega as had taken him to Tabatinga, which is a place of little importance compared to this.

Ega is a chief town with fifteen hundred inhabitants, and in it reside all those authorities which compose the administration of a considerable city - considerable for the country; that is to say, the military commandant, the chief of the police, the judges, the schoolmaster, and troops under the command of officers of all ranks.

With so many functionaries living in a town, with their wives and children, it is easy to see that hair-dressers would be in demand. Such was the case, and Fragoso would not have paid his expenses.

Doubtless, however, the jolly fellow, who could do no business in Ega, had thought to be of the party if Lina went with her mistress, but, just as they were leaving the raft, he resolved to remain, at the request of Lina herself.

"Mr. Fragoso!" she said to him, after taking him aside.

"Miss Lina?" answered Fragoso.

"I do not think that your friend Torres intends to go with us to Ega."

"Certainly not, he is going to stay on board, Miss Lina, but you wold oblige me by not calling him my friend!"

"But you undertook to ask a passage for him before he had shown any intention of doing so."

"Yes, and on that occasion, if you would like to know what I think, I made a fool of myself!"

"Quite so! and if you would like to know what I think, I do not like the man at all, Mr. Fragoso."

"Neither do I, Miss Lina, and I have all the time an idea that I have seen him somewhere before. But the remembrance is too vague; the impression, however, is far from being a pleasant one!"

"Where and when could you have met him? Cannot you call it to mind? It might be useful to know who he is and what he has been."

"No - I try all I can. How long was it ago? In what country? Under what circumstances? And I cannot hit upon it."

"Mr. Fragoso!"

"Miss Lina!"

"Stay on board and keep watch on Torres during our absence!"

"What? Not go with you to Ega, and remain a whole day without seeing you?"

"I ask you to do so!"

"Is it an order?"

"It is an entreaty!"

"I will remain!"

"Mr. Fragoso!"

"Miss Lina!"

"I thank you!"

"Thank me, then, with a good shake of the hand," replied Fragoso; "that is worth something."

Lina held out her hand, and Fragoso kept it for a few moments while he looked into her face. And that is the reason why he did not take his place in the pirogue, and became, without appearing to be, the guard upon Torres.

Did the latter notice the feelings of aversion with which he was regarded? Perhaps, but doubtless he had his reasons for taking no account of them.

A distance of four leagues separated the mooring-place from the town of Ega. Eight leagues, there and back, in a pirogue containing six persons, besides two negroes as rowers, would take some hours, not to mention the fatigue caused by the high temperature, though the sky was veiled with clouds.

Fortunately a lovely breeze blew from the northwest, and if it held would be favorable for crossing Lake Teffe. They could go to Ega and return rapidly without having to tack.

So the lateen sail was hoisted on the mast of the pirogue. Benito took the tiller, and off they went, after a last gesture from Lina to Fragoso to keep his eyes open.

The southern shore of the lake had to be followed to get to Ega.

After two hours the pirogue arrived at the port of this ancient mission founded by the Carmelites, which became a town in 1759, and which General Gama placed forever under Brazilian rule.

The passengers landed on a flat beach, on which were to be found not only boats from the interior, but a few of those little schooners which are used in the coasting-trade on the Atlantic seaboard.

When the two girls entered Ega they were at first much astonished.

"What a large town!" said Minha.

"What houses! what people!" replied Lina, whose eyes seemed to have expanded so that she might see better.

"Rather!" said Benito laughingly. "More than fifteen hundred inhabitants! Two hundred houses at the very least! Some of them with a first floor! And two or three streets! Genuine streets!"

"My dear Manoel!" said Minha, "do protect us against my brother! He is making fun of us, and only because he had already been in the finest towns in Amazones and Para!"

"Quite so, and he is also poking fun at his mother," added Yaquita, "for I confess I never saw anything equal to this!"

"Then, mother and sister, you must take great care that you do not fall into a trance when you get to Manaos, and vanish altogether when you reach Belem!"

"Never fear," answered Manoel; "the ladies will have been gently prepared for these grand wonders by visiting the principal cities of the Upper Amazon!"

"Now, Manoel," said Minha, "you are talking just like my brother! Are you making fun of us, too?"

"No, Minha, I assure you."

"Laugh on, gentlemen," said Lina, "and let us look around, my dear mistress, for it is very fine!"

Very fine! A collection of houses, built of mud,

whitewashed, and principally covered with thatch or palm-leaves; a few built of stone or wood, with verandas, doors, and shutters painted a bright green, standing in the middle of a small orchard of orange-trees in flower. But there were two or three public buildings, a barrack, and a church dedicated to St. Theresa, which was a cathedral by the side of the modest chapel at Iquitos. On looking toward the lake a beautiful panorama unfolded itself, bordered by a frame of cocoanut-trees and assais, which ended at the edge of the liquid level, and showed beyond the picturesque village of Noqueira, with its few small houses lost in the mass of the old olive-trees on the beach.

But for the two girls there was another cause of wonderment, quite feminine wonderment too, in the fashions of the fair Egans, not the primitive costume of the natives, converted Omaas or Muas, but the dress of true Brazilian ladies. The wives and daughters of the principal functionaries and merchants o the town pretentiously showed off their Parisian toilettes, a little out of date perhaps, for Ega is five hundred leagues away from Para, and this is itself many thousands of miles from Paris.

"Just look at those fine ladies in their fine clothes!"

"Lina will go mad!" exclaimed Benito.

"If those dresses were worn properly," said Minha, "they might not be so ridiculous!"

"My dear Minha," said Manoel, "with your simple gown and straw hat, you are better dressed than any one of these Brazilians, with their headgear and flying petticoats, which are foreign to their country and their race."

"If it pleases you to think so," answered Minha, "I do not envy any of them."

But they had come to see. They walked through the streets, which contained more stalls than shops; they strolled about the market-place, the rendezvous of the fashionable, who were nearly stifled in their European clothes; they even breakfasted at an hotel - it was scarcely an inn - whose cookery caused them to deeply regret the excellent service on the raft.

After dinner, at which only turtle flesh, served up in different forms, appeared, the Garral family went for the last time to admire the borders of the lake as the setting sun gilded it with its rays; then they rejoined their pirogue, somewhat disillusioned perhaps as to the magnificence of a town which one hour would give time enough to visit, and a little tired with walking about its stifling streets which were not nearly so pleasant as the shady pathways of Iquitos. The inquisitive Lina's enthusiasm alone had not been damped.

They all took their places in the pirogue. The wind remained in the northwest, and had freshened with the evening. The sail was hoisted. They took the same course as in the morning, across the lake fed by the black waters of the Rio Teffe, which, according to the Indians, is navigable toward the southwest for forty days' journey. At eight o'clock the priogue regained the mooring-place and hailed the jangada.

As soon as Lina could get Fragoso aside -

"Have you seen anything suspicious?" she inquired.

"Nothing, Miss Lina," he replied; "Torres has scarcely left his cabin, where he has been reading and writing."

"He did not get into the house or the dining-room, as I feared?"

"No, all the time he was not in his cabin he was in the bow of the raft."

"And what was he doing?"

"Holding an old piece of paper in his hand, consulting it with great attention, and muttering a lot of incomprehensible words."

"All that is not so unimportant as you think, Mr. Fragoso. These readings and writings and old papers have their interest! He is neither a professor nor a lawyer, this reader and writer!"

"You are right!"

"Still watch him, Mr. Fragoso!"

"I will watch him always, Miss Lina," replied Fragoso.

On the morrow, the 27th of July, at daybreak, Benito gave the pilot the signal to start.

Away between the islands, in the Bay of Arenapo, the mouth of the Japura, six thousand six hundred feet wide, was seen for an instant. This large tributary comes into the Amazon through eight mouths, as if it were pouring into some gulf or ocean. But its waters come from afar, and it is the mountains of the republic of Ecuador which start them on a course that there are no falls to break until two hundred and ten leagues from its junction with the main stream.

All this day was spent in descending to the island of Yapura, after which the river, less interfered with, makes navigation much easier. The current is not so rapid and the islets are easily avoided, so that there were no touchings or groundings.

The next day the jangada coasted along by vast beaches formed by undulating high domes, which served as the barriers of immense pasture grounds, in which the whole of the cattle in Europe could be raised and fed. These sand banks are considered to be the richest turtle grounds in the basin of the Upper Amazon.

On the evening of the 29th of July they were securely moored off the island of Catua, so as to pass the night, which promised to be dark.

On this island, as soon as the sun rose above the horizon, there appeared a party of Muras Indians, the remains of that ancient and powerful tribe, which formerly occupied more than a hundred leagues of the river bank between the Teffe and the Madeira.

These Indians went and came, watching the raft, which remained stationary. There were about a hundred of them armed with blow-tubes formed of a reed peculiar to these parts, and which is strengthened outside by the stem of a dwarf palm from which the pith has been extracted.

Joam Garral quitted for an instand the work which took up all his time, to warn his people to keep a good guard and not to provoke these Indians.

In truth the sides were not well matched. The Muras are remarkably clever at sending through their blow-tubes arrows which cause incurable wounds, even at a range of three hundred paces.

These arrows, made of the leaf of the *"coucourite"* palm, are feathered with cotton, and nine or ten inches long, with a point like a needle, and poisoned with *"curare."*

Curare, or *"wourah,"* the liquor "which kills in a whisper," as the Indians say, is prepared from the sap of one of the euphorbiaceæ and the juice of a bulbous strychnos, not to mention the paste of venomous ants and poisonous serpent fangs which they mix with it.

"It is indeed a terrible poison," said Manoel. "It attacks at once those nerves by which the movements are subordinated to the will. But the heart is not touched, and it does not cease to beat until the extinction of the vital functions, and besides no antidote is known to the poison, which commences by numbness of the limbs."

Very fortunately, these Muras made no hostile demonstrations, although they entertain a profound hatred toward the whites. They have, in truth, no longer the courage of their ancestors.

At nightfall a five-holed flute was heard behind the trees in the island, playing several airs in a minor key. Another flute answered. This interchange of musical phrases lasted for two or three minutes, and the Muras disappeared.

Fragoso, in an exuberant moment, had tried to reply by a song in his own fashion, but Lina had clapped her hand on his mouth, and prevented his showing off his insignificant singing talents, which he was so willingly lavish of.

On the 2d of August, at three o'clock in the afternoon, the raft arrived twenty leagues away from there at Lake Apoara, which is fed by the black waters of the river of the same name, and two days afterward, about five o'clock, it stopped at the entrance into Lake Coary.

This lake is one of the largest which communicates with the Amazon, and it serves as a reservoir for different rivers. Five or six affluents run into it, and there are stored and mixed up, and emerge by a narrow channel into the main stream.

After catching a glimpse of the hamlet of Tahua-Miri, mounted on its piles as on stilts, as a protection against inundation from the floods, which often sweep up over these low sand banks, the raft was moored for the night.

The stoppage was made in sight of the village of Coary, a dozen houses, considerably dilapidated, built in the midst of a thick mass of orange and calabash trees.

Nothing can be more changeable than the aspect of this village, for according to the rise or fall of the water the lake stretches away on all sides of it, or is reduced to a narrow canal, scarcely deep enough to communicate with the Amazon.

On the following morning, that of the 5th of August, they started at dawn, passing the canal of Yucura, belonging to the tangled system of lakes and furos of the Rio Zapura, and on the morning of the 6th of August they reached the entrance to Lake Miana.

No fresh incident occurred in the life on board, which proceeded with almost methodical regularity.

Fragoso, urged on by Lina, did not cease to watch Torres.

Many times he tried to get him to talk about his past life, but the adventurer eluded all conversation on the subject, and ended by maintaining a strict reserve toward the barber.

After catching a glimpse of the hamlet of Tahua-Miri, mounted on its piles as on stilts, as a protection against inundation from the floods, which often sweep up and over these low sand banks, the raft was moored for the night.

His intercourse with the Garral family remained the same. If he spoke little to Joam, he addressed himself more willingly to Yaquita and her daughter, and appeared not to notice the evident coolness with which he was received. They all agreed that when the raft arrived at Manaos, Torres should leave it, and that they would never speak of him again. Yaquita followed the advice of Padre Passanha, who counseled patience, but the good priest had not such an easy task in Manoel, who was quite disposed to put on shore the intruder who had been so unfortunately taken on to the raft.

The only thing that happened on this evening was the following:

A pirogue, going down the river, came alongside the jangada, after being hailed by Joam Garral.

"Are you going to Manaos?" asked he of the Indian who commanded and was steering her.

"Yes," replied he.

"When will you get there?"

"In eight days."

"Then you will arrive before we shall. Will you deliver a letter for me?"

"With pleasure."

"Take this letter, then, my friend, and deliver it at Manaos."

The Indian took the letter which Joam gave him, and a handful of reis was the price of the commission he had undertaken.

No members of the family, then gone into the house, knew anything of this. Torres was the only witness. He heard a few words exchanged between Joam and the Indian, and from the cloud which passed over his face it was easy to see that the sending of this letter considerably surprised him.

CHAPTER XVII

AN ATTACK

HOWEVER, if Manoel, to avoid giving rise to a violent scene on board, said nothing on the subject of Torres, he resolved to have an explanation with Benito.

"Benito," he began, after taking him to the bow of the jangada, "I have something to say to you."

Benito, generally so good-humored, stopped as he looked at Manoel, and a cloud came over his countenance.

"I know why," he said; "it is about Torres."

"Yes, Benito."

"And I also wish to speak to you."

"You have then noticed his attention to Minha?" said Manoel, turning pale.

"Ah! It is not a feeling of jealousy, though, that exasperates you against such a man?" said Benito quickly.

"No!" replied Manoel. "Decidedly not! Heaven forbid I

should do such an injury to the girl who is to become my wife. No, Benito! She holds the adventurer in horror! I am not thinking anything of that sort; but it distresses me to see this adventurer constantly obtruding himself by his presence and conversation on your mother and sister, and seeking to introduce himself into that intimacy with your family which is already mine."

"Manoel," gravely answered Benito, "I share your aversion for this dubious individual, and had I consulted my feelings I would already have driven Torres off the raft! But I dare not!"

"You dare not?" said Manoel, seizing the hand of his friend. "You dare not?"

"Listen to me, Manoel," continued Benito. "You have observed Torres well, have you not? You have remarked his attentions to my sister! Nothing can be truer! But while you have been noticing that, have you not seen that this annoying man never keeps his eyes off my father, no matter if he is near to him or far from him, and that he seems to have some spiteful secret intention in watching him with such unaccountable persistency?"

"What are you talking about, Benito? Have you any reason to think that Torres bears some grudge against Joam Garral?"

"No! I think nothing!" replied Benito; "it is only a presentiment! But look well at Torres, study his face with care, and you will see what an evil grin he has whenever my father comes into his sight."

"Well, then," exclaimed Manoel, "if it is so, Benito, the more reason for clearing him out!"

"More reason - or less reason," replied Benito. "Manoel, I fear - what? I know not - but to force my father to get rid of Torres would perhaps be imprudent! I repeat it, I am afraid, though no positive fact enables me to explain my fear to myself!"

And Benito seemed to shudder with anger as he said these words.

"Then," said Manoel, "you think we had better wait?"

"Yes; wait, before doing anything, but above all things let us be on our guard!"

"After all," answered Manoel, "in twenty days we shall be at Manaos. There Torres must stop. There he will leave us, and we shall be relieved of his presence for good! Till then we must keep our eyes on him!"

"You understand me, Manoel?" asked Benito.

"I understand you, my friend, my brother!" replied Manoel, "although I do not share, and cannot share, your fears! What connection can possibly exist between your father and this adventurer? Evidently your father has never seen him!"

"I do not say that my father knows Torres," said Benito; "but assuredly it seems to me that Torres knows my father. What was the fellow doing in the neighborhood of the fazenda when we met him in the forest of Iquitos? Why did he then refuse the hospitality which we offered, so as to afterward manage to force himself on us as our traveling companion? We arrive at Tabatinga, and there he is as if he was waiting for us! The probability is that these meetings were in pursuance of a preconceived plan. When I see the shifty, dogged look of Torres, all this crowds on my mind. I do not know! I am losing myself in things that defy explanation! Oh! why did I ever think of offering to take him on board this raft?"

"Be calm, Benito, I pray you!"

"Manoel!" continued Benito, who seemed to be powerless to contain himself, "think you that if it only concerned me - this man who inspires us all with such aversion and disgust - I should not hesitate to throw him overboard! But when it concerns my father, I fear lest in giving way to my impressions I may be injuring my object! Something tells me that with this scheming fellow there may be danger in doing anything until he has given us the right - the right and the duty - to do it. In short, on the jangada, he is in our power, and if we both keep good watch over my father, we can spoil his game, no matter how sure it may be, and force him to unmask and betray himself! Then wait a little longer!"

The arrival of Torres in the bow of the raft broke off the conversation. Torres looked slyly at the two young men, but said not a word.

Benito was not deceived when he said that the adventurer's eyes were never off Joam Garral as long as he fancied he was unobserved.

No! he was not deceived when he said that Torres' face grew evil when he looked at his father!

By what mysterious bond could these two men - one nobleness itself, that was self-evident - be connected with each other?

Such being the state of affairs it was certainly difficult for Torres, constantly watched as he was by the two young men, by Fragoso and Lina, to make a single movement without having instantly to repress it. Perhaps he understood the position. If he did, he did not show it, for his manner changed not in the least.

Satisfied with their mutual explanation, Manoel and Benito promised to keep him in sight without doing anything to awaken his suspicions.

During the following days the jangada passed on the right the mouths of the rivers Camara, Aru, and Yuripari, whose waters instead of flowing into the Amazon run off to the south to feed the Rio des Purus, and return by it into the main river. At five o'clock on the evening of the 10th of August they put into the island of Cocos.

They there passed a *"seringal."* This name is applied to a caoutchouc plantation, the caoutchouc being extracted from the *"seringueira"* tree, whose scientific name is *siphonia elastica.*

It is said that, by negligence or bad management, the number of these trees is decreasing in the basin of the Amazon, but the forests of seringueira trees are still very considerable on the banks of the Madeira, Purus, and other tributaries.

There were here some twenty Indians collecting and working the caoutchouc, an operation which principally takes place during the months of May, June, and July.

After having ascertained that the trees, well prepared by the river floods which have bathed their stems to a height of about four feet, are in good condition for the harvest, the Indians are set to work.

Incisions are made into the alburnum of the seringueiras; below the wound small pots are attached, which twenty-four hours suffice to fill with a milky sap. It can also be collected by means of a hollow bamboo, and a receptacle placed on the ground at the foot of the tree.

The sap being obtained, the Indians, to prevent the separation of its peculiar resins, fumigate it over a fire of the nuts of the assai palm. By spreading out the sap on a wooden scoop, and shaking it in the smoke, its coagulation is almost immediately obtained; it assumes a grayish-yellow tinge and solidifies. The layers formed in succession are detached from the scoop, exposed to the sun, hardened, and assume the brownish color with which we are familiar. The manufacture is then complete.

Benito, finding a capital opportunity, bought from the Indians all the caoutchouc stored in their cabins, which, by the way, are mostly built on piles. The price he gave them was sufficiently remunerative, and they were highly satisfied.

Four days later, on the 14th of August, the jangada passed the mouths of the Purus.

This is another of the large affluents of the Amazon,

and seems to possess a navigable course, even for large ships, of over five hundred leagues. It rises in the southwest, and measures nearly five thousand feet across at its junction with the main river. After winding beneath the shade of ficuses, tahuaris, nipa palms, and cecropias, it enters the Amazon by five mouths.

Hereabouts Araujo the pilot managed with great ease. The course of the river was but slightly obstructed with islands, and besides, from one bank to another its width is about two leagues.

The current, too, took along the jangada more steadily, and on the 18th of August it stopped at the village of Pasquero to pass the night.

The sun was already low on the horizon, and with the rapidity peculiar to these low latitudes, was about to set vertically, like an enormous meteor.

Joam Garral and his wife, Lina, and old Cybele, were in front of the house.

Torres, after having for an instant turned toward Joam as if he would speak to him, and prevented perhaps by the arrival of Padre Passanha, who had come to bid the family good-night, had gone back to his cabin.

The Indians and the negroes were at their quarters along the sides. Araujo, seated at the bow, was watching the current which extended straight away in front of him.

Manoel and Benito, with their eyes open, but chatting and smoking with apparent indifference, walked about the central part of the craft awaiting the hour of repose.

All at once Manoel stopped Benito with his hand and said:

"What a queer smell! Am I wrong? Do you not notice it?"

"One would say that it was the odor of burning musk!" replied Benito. "There ought to be some alligators asleep on the neighboring beach!"

"Well, nature has done wisely in allowing them so to betray themselves."

"Yes," said Benito, "it is fortunate, for they are sufficiently formidable creatures!"

Often at the close of the day these saurians love to stretch themselves on the shore, and install themselves comfortably there to pass the night. Crouched at the opening of a hole, into which they have crept back, they sleep with the mouth open, the upper jaw perpendicularly erect, so as to lie in wait for their prey. To these amphibians it is but sport to launch themselves in its pursuit, either by swimming through the waters propelled by their tails or running along the bank with a speed no man can equal.

It is on these huge beaches that the caymans are born, live, and die, not without affording extraordinary examples of longevity. Not only can the old ones, the centenarians, be recognized by the greenish moss which carpets their carcass and is scattered over their protuberances, but by their natural ferocity, which increases with age. As Benito said, they are formidable creatures, and it is fortunate that their attacks can be guarded against.

Suddenly cries were heard in the bow.

"Caymans! caymans!"

Manoel and Benito came forward and looked.

Three large saurians, from fifteen to twenty feet long, had managed to clamber on to the platform of the raft.

"Bring the guns! Bring the guns!" shouted Benito, making signs to the Indians and the blacks to get behind.

"Into the house!" said Manoel; "make haste!"

And in truth, as they could not attack them at once, the best thing they could do was to get into shelter without delay.

It was done in an instant. The Garral family took refuge in the house, where the two young men joined them. The Indians and the negroes ran into their huts and cabins. As they were shutting the door:

"And Minha?" said Manoel.

"She is not there!" replied Lina, who had just run to her mistress' room.

"Good heavens! where is she?" exclaimed her mother, and they all shouted at once:

"Himha! Minha!"

No reply.

"There she is, on the bow of the jangada!" said Benito.

"Minha!" shouted Manoel.

The two young men, and Fragoso and Joam Garral, thinking no more of danger, rushed out of the house, guns in hand.

Scarcely were they outside when two of the alligators made a half turn and ran toward them.

A dose of buckshot to the head, close to the eye, from Benito, stopped one of the monsters, who, mortally wounded, writhed in frightful convulsions and fell on his side.

But the second still lived, and came on, and there was no way of avoiding him.

The huge alligator tore up to Joam Garral, and after knocking him over with a sweep of his tail, ran at him with open jaws.

At this moment Torres rushed from the cabin, hatchet in hand, and struck such a terrific blow that its edge sunk into the jaw of the cayman and left him defenseless.

Blinded by the blood, the animal flew to the side, and, designedly or not, fell over and was lost in the stream.

"Minha! Minha!" shouted Manoel in distraction, when he got to the bow of the jangada.

Suddenly she came into view. She had taken refuge in the cabin of Araujo, and the cabin had just been upset by a powerful blow from the third alligator. Minha was flying aft, pursued by the monster, who was not six feet away from her.

Minha fell.

A second shot from Benito failed to stop the cayman. He only struck the animal's carapace, and the scales flew to splinters but the ball did not penetrate.

Manoel threw himself at the girl to raise her, or to snatch her from death! A side blow from the animal's tail knocked him down too.

Minha fainted, and the mouth of the alligator opened to crush her!

And then Fragoso jumped in to the animal, and thrust in a knife to the very bottom of his throat, at the risk of having his arm snapped off by the two jaws, had they quickly closed.

Fragoso pulled out his arm in time, but he could not avoid the chock of the cayman, and was hurled back into the river, whose waters reddened all around.

"Fragoso! Fragoso!" shrieked Lina, kneeling on the edge of the raft.

A second afterward Fragoso reappeared on the surface of the Amazon - safe and sound.

But, at the peril of his life he had saved the young girl, who soon came to. And as all hands were held out to him - Manoel's, Yaquita's, Minha's, and Lina's, and he did not know what to say, he ended by squeezing the hands of the young mulatto.

However, though Fragoso had saved Minha, it was assuredly to the intervention of Torres that Joam Garral owed his safety.

It was not, therefore, the fazender's life that the adventurer wanted. In the face of this fact, so much had to be admitted.

Manoel said this to Benito in an undertone.

"That is true!" replied Benito, embarrassed. "You are right, and in a sense it is one cruel care the less! Nevertheless, Manoel, my suspicions still exist! It is not always a man's worst enemy who wishes him dead!"

Joam Garral walked up to Torres.

"Thank you, Torres!" he said, holding out his hand. The adventurer took a step or two backward without replying.

"Torres," continued Joam, "I am sorry that we are arriving at the end of our voyage, and that in a few days we must part! I owe you -- "

"Joam Garral!" answered Torres, "you owe me nothing! Your life is precious to me above all things! But if you will allow me - I have been thinking - in place of stopping at Manaos, I will go on to Belem. Will you take me there?"

Joam Garral replied by an affirmative nod.

In hearing this demand Benito in an unguarded moment was about to intervene, but Manoel stopped him, and the young man checked himself, though not without a violent effort.

CHAPTER XVIII

THE ARRIVAL DINNER

IN THE MORNING, after a night which was scarcely sufficient to calm so much excitement, they unmoored from the cayman beach and departed. Before five days, if nothing interfered with their voyage, the raft would reach the port of Manaos.

Minha had quite recovered from her fright, and her eyes and smiles thanked all those who had risked their lives for her.

As for Lina, it seemed as though she was more grateful to the brave Fragoso than if it was herself that he had saved.

"I will pay you back, sooner or later, Mr. Fragoso," said she, smiling.

"And how, Miss Lina?"

"Oh! You know very well!"

"Then if I know it, let it be soon and not late!" replied the good-natured fellow.

And from this day it began to be whispered about that

Jules Verne

the charming Lina was engaged to Fragoso, that their marriage would take place at the same time as that of Minha and Manoel, and that the young couple would remain at Belem with the others.

"Capital! capital!" repeated Fragoso unceasingly; "but I never thought Para was such a long way off!"

As for Manoel and Benito, they had had a long conversation about what had passed. There could be no question about obtaining from Joam Garral the dismissal of his rescuer.

"Your life is precious to me above all things!" Torres had said.

This reply, hyperbolical and enigmatical at the time, Benito had heard and remembered.

In the meantime the young men could do nothing. More than ever they were reduced to waiting - to waiting not for four or five days, but for seven or eight weeks - that is to say, for whatever time it would take for the raft to get to Belem.

"There is in all this some mystery that I cannot understand," said Benito.

"Yes, but we are assured on one point," answered Manoel. "It is certain that Torres does not want your father's life. For the rest, we must still watch!"

It seemed that from this day Torres desired to keep himself more reserved. He did not seek to intrude on the family, and was even less assiduous toward Minha. There seemed a relief in the situation of which all, save perhaps Joam Garral, felt the gravity.

On the evening of the same day they left on the right the island of Baroso, formed by a furo of that name, and Lake Manaori, which is fed by a confused series of petty tributaries.

The night passed without incident, though Joam Garral had advised them to watch with great care.

On the morrow, the 20th of August, the pilot, who kept near the right bank on account of the uncertain eddies on the left, entered between the bank and the islands.

Beyond this bank the country was dotted with large and small lakes, much as those of Calderon, Huarandeina, and other black-watered lagoons. This water system marks the approach of the Rio Negro, the most remarkable of all the tributaries of the Amazon. In reality the main river still bore the name of the Solimoens, and it is only after the junction of the Rio Negro that it takes the name which has made it celebrated among the rivers of the globe.

During this day the raft had to be worked under curious conditions.

The arm followed by the pilot, between Calderon Island and the shore, was very narrow, although it appeared sufficiently large. This was owing to a great portion of the island being slightly above the mean level, but still covered by the high flood waters. On each side were massed forests of giant trees, whose summits towered some fifty feet above the ground, and joining one bank to the other formed an immense cradle.

On the left nothing could be more picturesque than this flooded forest, which seemed to have been planted in the middle of a lake. The stems of the trees arose from the clear, still water, in which every interlacement of their boughs was reflected with unequaled purity. They were arranged on an immense sheet of glass, like the trees in miniature on some table *epergne*, and their reflection could not be more perfect. The difference between the image and the reality could scarcely be described. Duplicates of grandeur, terminated above and below by a vast parasol of green, they seemed to form two hemispheres, inside which the jangada appeared to follow one of the great circles.

It had been necessary to bring the raft under these boughs, against which flowed the gentle current of the stream. It was impossible to go back. Hence the task of navigating with extreme care, so as to avoid the collisions on either side.

In this all Araujo's ability was shown, and he was admirably seconded by his crew. The trees of the forest furnished the resting-places for the long poles which kept the jangada in its course. The least blow to the jangada would have endangered the complete demolition of the woodwork, and caused the loss, if not of the crew, of the greater part of the cargo.

"It is truly very beautiful," said Minha, "and it would be very pleasant for us always to travel in this way, on this quiet water, shaded from the rays of the sun."

"At the same time pleasant and dangerous, dear Minha," said Manoel. "In a pirogue there is doubtless nothing to fear in sailing here, but on a huge raft of wood better have a free course and a clear stream."

"We shall be quite through the forest in a couple of hours," said the pilot.

"Look well at it, then!" said Lina. "All these beautiful things pass so quickly! Ah! dear mistress! do you see the troops of monkeys disporting in the higher branches, and the birds admiring themselves in the pellucid water!"

"And the flowers half-opened on the surface," replied Minha, "and which the current dandles like the breeze!"

"And the long lianas, which so oddly stretch from one tree to another!" added the young mulatto.

"And no Fragoso at the end of them!" said Lina's betrothed. "That was rather a nice flower you gathered in the forest of Iquitos!"

"Just behold the flower - the only one in the world," said Lina quizzingly; "and, mistress! just look at the splendid plants!"

And Lina pointed to the nymphæas with their colossal leaves, whose flowers bear buds as large as cocoanuts. Then, just where the banks plunged beneath the waters, there were clumps of *"mucumus,"* reeds with large leaves, whose elastic stems bend to give passage to the pirogues and close again behind them. There was there what would tempt any sportsman, for a whole world of aquatic birds fluttered between the higher clusters, which shook with the stream.

Ibises half-lollingly posed on some old trunk, and gray herons motionless on one leg, solemn flamingoes who

Jules Verne

from a distance looked like red umbrellas scattered in the foliage, and phenicopters of every color, enlivened the temporary morass.

And along the top of the water glided long and swiftly-swimming snakes, among them the formidable gymnotus, whose electric discharges successively repeated paralyze the most robust of men or animals, and end by dealing death. Precautions had to be taken against the *"sucurijus"* serpents, which, coiled round the trunk of some tree, unroll themselves, hang down, seize their prey, and draw it into their rings, which are powerful enough to crush a bullock. Have there not been met with in these Amazonian forests reptiles from thirty to thirty-five feet long? and even, according to M. Carrey, do not some exist whose length reaches forty-seven feet, and whose girth is that of a hogshead?

Had one of these sucurijus, indeed, got on to the raft he would have proved as formidable as an alligator.

Very fortunately the travelers had to contend with neither gymnotus nor sucuriju, and the passage across the submerged forest, which lasted about two hours, was effected without accident.

Three days passed. They neared Manaos. Twenty-four hours more and the raft would be off the mouth of the Rio Negro, before the capital of the province of Amazones.

In fact, on the 23d of August, at five o'clock in the evening, they stopped at the southern point of Muras Island, on the right bank of the stream. They only had to cross obliquely for a few miles to arrive at the port, but the pilot Araujo very properly would not risk it on that day, as night was coming on. The three miles which remained would take three hours to travel, and to keep to the course of the river it was necessary, above all things, to have a clear outlook.

This evening the dinner, which promised to be the last of this first part of the voyage, was not served without a certain amount of ceremony. Half the journey on the Amazon had been accomplished, and the task was worthy of a jovial repast. It was fitting to drink to the health of Amazones a few glasses of that generous liquor which comes from the coasts of Oporto and Setubal. Besides, this was, in a way, the betrothal dinner of Fragoso and the charming Lina - that of Manoel and Minha had taken place at the fazenda of Iquitos several weeks before. After the young master and mistress, it was the turn of the faithful couple who were attached to them by so many bonds of gratitude.

So Lina, who was to remain in the service of Minha, and Fragoso, who was about to enter into that of Manoel Valdez, sat at the common table, and even had the places of honor reserved for them.

Torres, naturally, was present at the dinner, which was worthy of the larder and kitchen of the jangada.

The adventurer, seated opposite to Joam Garral, who was always taciturn, listened to all that was said, but took no part in the conversation. Benito quietly and attentively watched him. The eyes of Torres, with a peculiar expression, constantly sought his father. One would have called them the eyes of some wild beast trying to fascinate his prey before he sprang on it.

Manoel talked mostly with Minha. Between whiles his

eyes wandered to Torres, but he acted his part more successfully than Benito in a situation which, if it did not finish at Manaos, would certainly end at Belem.

The dinner was jolly enough. Lina kept it going with her good humor, Fragoso with his witty repartees.

The Padre Passanha looked gayly round on the little world he cherished, and on the two young couples which his hands would shortly bless in the waters of Para.

"Eat, padre," said Benito, who joined in the general conversation; "do honor to this betrothal dinner. You will want some strength to celebrate both marriages at once!"

"Well, my dear boy," replied Passanha, "seek out some lovely and gentle girl who wishes you well, and you will see that I can marry you at the same time!"

"Well answered, padre!" exclaimed Manoel. "Let us drink to the coming marriage of Benito."

"We must look out for some nice young lady at Belem," said Minha. "He should do what everybody else does."

"To the wedding of Mr. Benito!" said Fragoso, "who ought to wish all the world to marry him!"

"They are right, sir," said Yaquita. "I also drink to your marriage, and may you be as happy as Minha and Manoel, and as I and your father have been!"

"As you always will be, it is to be hoped," said Torres,

drinking a glass of port without having pledged anybody. "All here have their happiness in their own hands."

It was difficult to say, but this wish, coming from the adventurer, left an unpleasant impression.

Manoel felt this, and wishing to destroy its effect, "Look here, padre," said he, "while we are on this subject, are there not any more couples to betroth on the raft?"

"I do not know," answered Padre Passanha, "unless Torres - you are not married, I believe?"

"No; I am, and always shall be, a bachelor."

Benito and Manoel thought that while thus speaking Torres looked toward Minha.

"And what should prevent you marrying?" replied Padre Passanha; "at Belem you could find a wife whose age would suit yours, and it would be possible perhaps for you to settle in that town. That would be better than this wandering life, of which, up to the present, you have not made so very much."

"You are right, padre," answered Torres; "I do not say no. Besides the example is contagious. Seeing all these young couples gives me rather a longing for marriage. But I am quite a stranger in Belem, and, for certain reasons, that would make my settlement more difficult."

"Where do you come from, then?" asked Fragoso, who always had the idea that he had already met

Torres somewhere.

"From the province of Minas Geraes."

"And you were born - - "

"In the capital of the diamond district, Tijuco."

Those who had seen Joam Garral at this moment would have been surprised at the fixity of his look which met that of Torres.

CHAPTER XIX

ANCIENT HISTORY

BUT THE CONVERSATION was continued by Fragoso, who immediately rejoined:

"What! you come from Tijuco, from the very capital of the diamond district?"

"Yes," said Torres. "Do you hail from that province?"

"No! I come from the Atlantic seaboard in the north of Brazil," replied Fragoso.

"You do not know this diamond country, Mr. Manoel?" asked Torres.

A negative shake of the head from the young man was the only reply.

"And you, Mr. Benito," continued Torres, addressing the younger Garral, whom he evidently wished to join in the conversation; "you have never had curiosity enough to visit the diamond arraval?"

"Never," dryly replied Benito.

"Ah! I should like to see that country," said Fragoso,

who unconsciously played Torres' game. "It seems to me I should finish by picking up a diamond worth something considerable."

"And what would you do with this diamond worth something considerable, Fragoso?" queried Lina.

"Sell it!"

"Then you would get rich all of a sudden!"

"Very rich!"

"Well, if you had been rich three months ago you would never have had the idea of - that liana!"

"And if I had not had that," exclaimed Fragoso, "I should not have found a charming little wife who - well, assuredly, all is for the best!"

"You see, Fragoso," said Minha, "when you marry Lina, diamond takes the place of diamond, and you do not lose by the change!"

"To be sure, Miss Minha," gallantly replied Fragoso; "rather I gain!"

There could be no doubt that Torres did not want the subject to drop, for he went on with:

"It is a fact that at Tijuco sudden fortunes are realized enough to turn any man's head! Have you heard tell of the famous diamond of Abaete, which was valued at more than two million contos of reis? Well, this stone, which weighed an ounce, came from the Brazilian mines! And they were three convicts - yes! three men sentenced to transportation for life - who found it by chance in the River Abaete, at ninety leagues from Terro de Frio."

"At a stroke their fortune was made?" asked Fragoso.

"No," replied Torres; "the diamond was handed over to the governor-general of the mines. The value of the stone was recognized, and King John VI., of Portugal, had it cut, and wore it on his neck on great occasions. As for the convicts, they got their pardon, but that was all, and the cleverest could not get much of an income out of that!"

"You, doubtless?" said Benito very dryly.

"Yes - I? Why not?" answered Torres. "Have you ever been to the diamond district?" added he, this time addressing Joam Garral.

"Never!" said Joam, looking straight at him.

"That is a pity!" replied he. "You should go there one day. It is a very curious place, I assure you. The diamond valley is an isolated spot in the vast empire of Brazil, something like a park of a dozen leagues in circumference, which in the nature of its soil, its vegetation, and its sandy rocks surrounded by a circle of high mountains, differs considerably from the neighboring provinces. But, as I have told you, it is one of the richest places in the world, for from 1807 to 1817 the annual return was about eighteen thousand carats. Ah! there have been some rare finds there, not only for the climbers who seek the precious stone up to the very tops of the mountains, but also for the smugglers who fraudulently export it. But the work in the mines is not so pleasant, and the two thousand negroes employed in that work by the government are obliged even to divert the watercourses to get at the diamantiferous sand. Formerly it was easier work."

"In short," said Fragoso, "the good time has gone!"

"But what is still easy is to get the diamonds in scoundrel-fashion - that is, by theft; and - stop! in 1826, when I was about eight years old, a terrible drama happened at Tijuco, which showed that criminal would recoil from nothing if they could gain a fortune by one bold stroke. But perhaps you are not interested?"

"On the contrary, Torres; go on," replied Joam Garral, in a singularly calm voice.

"So be it," answered Torres. "Well, the story is about stealing diamonds, and a handful of those pretty stones is worth a million, sometimes two!"

And Torres, whose face expressed the vilest sentiments of cupidity, almost unconsciously made a gesture of opening and shutting his hand.

"This is what happened," he continued. "At Tijuco it is customary to send off in one delivery the diamonds collected during the year. They are divided into two lots, according to their size, after being sorted in a dozen sieves with holes of different dimensions. These lots are put into sacks and forwarded to Rio de Janeiro; but as they are worth many millions you may imagine they are heavily escorted. A workman chosen by the superintendent, four cavalrymen from the district regiment, and ten men on foot, complete the convoy.

They first make for Villa Rica, where the commandant puts his seal on the sacks, and then the convoy continues its journey to Rio de Janeiro. I should add that, for the sake of precaution, the start is always kept secret. Well, in 1826, a young fellow named Dacosta, who was about twenty-two or twenty-three years of age, and who for some years had been employed at Tijuco in the offices of the governor-general, devised the following scheme. He leagued himself with a band of smugglers, and informed them of the date of the departure of the convoy. The scoundrels took their measures accordingly. They were numerous and well armed. Close to Villa Rica, during the night of the 22d of January, the gang suddenly attacked the diamond escort, who defended themselves bravely, but were all massacred, with the exception of one man, who, seriously wounded, managed to escape and bring the news of the horrible deed. The workman was not spared any more than the soldiers. He fell beneath he blows of the thieves, and was doubtless dragged away and thrown over some precipice, for his body was never found."

"And this Dacosta?" asked Joam Garral.

"Well, his crime did not do him much good, for suspicion soon pointed toward him. He was accused of having got up the affair. In vain he protested that he was innocent. Thanks to the situation he held, he was in a position to know the date on which the convoy's departure was to take place. He alone could have informed the smugglers. He was charged, arrested, tried, and sentenced to death. Such a sentence required his execution in twenty-four hourse."

"Was the fellow executed?" asked Fragoso.

"No," replied Torres; "they shut him up in the prison at Villa Rica, and during the night, a few hours only before his execution, whether alone or helped by others, he managed to escape."

"Has this young man been heard of since?" asked Joam Garral.

"Never," replied Torres. "He probably left Brazil, and now, in some distant land, lives a cheerful life with the proceeds of the robbery which he is sure to have realized."

"Perhaps, on the other hand, he died miserably!" answered Joam Garral.

"And, perhaps," added Padre Passanha, "Heaven caused him to feel remorse for his crime."

Here they all rose from the table, and, having finished their dinner, went out to breathe the evening air. The sun was low on the horizon, but an hour had still to elapse before nightfall.

"These stories are not very lively," said Fragoso, "and our betrothal dinner was best at the beginning."

"But it was your fault, Fragoso," answered Lina.

"How my fault?"

"It was you who went on talking about the district and the diamonds, when you should not have done so."

"Well, that's true," replied Fragoso; "but I had no idea we were going to wind up in that fashion."

"You are the first to blame!"

"And the first to be punished, Miss Lina; for I did not hear you laugh all through the dessert."

The whole family strolled toward the bow of the jangada. Manoel and Benito walked one behind the other without speaking. Yaquita and her daughter silently followed, and all felt an unaccountable impression of sadness, as if they had a presentiment of some coming calamity.

Torres stepped up to Joam Garral, who, with bowed head, seemed to be lost in thought, and putting his hand on his shoulder, said, "Joam Garral, may I have a few minutes' conversation with you?"

Joam looked at Torres.

"Here?" he asked.

"No; in private."

"Come, then."

They went toward the house, entered it, and the door was shut on them.

It would be difficult to depict what every one felt when Joam Garral and Torres disappeared. What could there be in common between the adventurer and the honest fazender of Iquitos? The menace of some frightful misfortune seemed to hang over the whole family, and they scarcely dared speak to each other.

"Manoel!" said Benito, seizing his friend's arm,

"whatever happens, this man must leave us tomorrow at Manaos."

"Yes! it is imperative!" answered Manoel.

"And if through him some misfortune happens to my father - I shall kill him!"

CHAPTER XX

BETWEEN THE TWO MEN

FOR A MOMENT, alone in the room, where none could see or hear them, Joam Garral and Torres looked at each other without uttering a word. Did the adventurer hesitate to speak? Did he suspect that Joam Garral would only reply to his demands by a scornful silence?

Yes! Probably so. So Torres did not question him. At the outset of the conversation he took the affirmative, and assumed the part of an accuser.

"Joam," he said, "your name is not Garral. Your name is Dacosta!"

At the guilty name which Torres thus gave him, Joam Garral could not repress a slight shudder.

"You are Joam Dacosta," continued Torres, "who, twenty-five years ago, were a clerk in the governor-general's office at Tijuco, and you are the man who was sentenced to death in this affair of the robbery and murder!"

No response from Joam Garral, whose strange tranquillity surprised the adventurer. Had he made a mistake in accusing his host? No! For Joam Garral made no start at the terrible accusations. Doubtless he wanted to know to what Torres was coming.

"Joam Dacosta, I repeat! It was you whom they sought for this diamond affair, whom they convicted of crime and sentenced to death, and it was you who escaped from the prison at Villa Rica a few hours before you should have been executed! Do you not answer?"

Rather a long silence followed this direct question which Torres asked. Joam Garral, still calm, took a seat. His elbow rested on a small table, and he looked fixedly at his accuser without bending his head.

"Will you reply?" repeated Torres.

"What reply do you want from me?" said Joam quietly.

"A reply," slowly answered Torres, "that will keep me from finding out the chief of the police at Manaos, and saying to him, 'A man is there whose identity can easily be established, who can be recognized even after twenty-five years' absence, and this man was the instigator of the diamond robbery at Tijuco. He was the accomplice of the murderers of the soldiers of the escort; he is the man who escaped from execution; he is Joam Garral, whose true name is Joam Dacosta.'"

"And so, Torres," said Joam Garral, "I shall have nothing to fear from you if I give the answer you require?"

"Nothing, for neither you nor I will have any interest in talking about the matter."

"Neither you nor I?" asked Joam Garral. "It is not with money, then, that your silence is to be bought?"

"No! No matter how much you offered me!"

"What do you want, then?"

"Joam Garral," replied Torres, "here is my proposal. Do not be in a hurry to reply by a formal refusal. Remember that you are in my power."

"What is this proposal?" asked Joam.

Torres hesitated for a moment.

The attitude of this guilty man, whose life he held in his hands, was enough to astonish him. He had expected a stormy discussion and prayers and tears. He had before him a man convicted of the most heinous of crimes, and the man never flinched.

At length, crossing his arms, he said:

"You have a daughter! - I like her - and I want to marry her!"

Apparently Joam Garral expected anything from such a man, and was as quiet as before.

"And so," he said, "the worthy Torres is anxious to enter the family of a murderer and a thief?"

"I am the sole judge of what it suits me to do," said Torres. "I wish to be the son-in-law of Joam Garral, and I will."

"You ignore, then, that my daughter is going to marry Manoel Valdez?"

"You will break it off with Manoel Valdez!"

"And if my daughter declines?"

"If you tell her all, I have no doubt she would consent," was the impudent answer.

"All?"

"All, if necessary. Between her own feelings and the honor of her family and the life of her father she would not hesitate."

"You are a consummate scoundrel, Torres," quietly said Joam, whose coolness never forsook him.

"A scoundrel and a murderer were made to understand each other."

At these words Joam Garral rose, advanced to the adventurer, and looking him straight in the face, "Torres," he said, "if you wish to become one of the family of Joam Dacosta, you ought to know that Joam Dacosta was innocent of the crime for which he was condemned."

"Really!"

"And I add," replied Joam, "that you hold the proof of his innocence, and are keeping it back to proclaim it on the day when you marry his daughter."

"Fair play, Joam Garral," answered Torres, lowering

his voice, "and when you have heard me out, you will see if you dare refuse me your daughter!"

"I am listening, Torres."

"Well," said the adventurer, half keeping back his words, as if he was sorry to let them escape from his lips, "I know you are innocent! I know it, for I know the true culprit, and I am in a position to prove your innocence."

"And the unhappy man who committed the crime?"

"Is dead."

"Dead!" exclaimed Joam Garral; and the word made him turn pale, in spite of himself, as if it had deprived him of all power of reinstatement.

"Dead," repeated Torres; "but this man, whom I knew a long time after his crime, and without knowing that he was a convict, had written out at length, in his own hand, the story of this affair of the diamonds, even to the smallest details. Feeling his end approaching, he was seized with remorse. He knew where Joam Dacosta had taken refuge, and under what name the innocent man had again begun a new life. He knew that he was rich, in the bosom of a happy family, but he knew also that there was no happiness for him. And this happiness he desired to add to the reputation to which he was entitled. But death came - he intrusted to me, his companion, to do what he could no longer do. He gave me the proofs of Dacosta's innocence for me to transmit them to him, and he died."

"The man's name?" exclaimed Joam Garral, in a tone

he could not control.

"You will know it when I am one of your family."

"And the writing?"

Joam Garral was ready to throw himself on Torres, to search him, to snatch from him the proofs of his innocence.

"The writing is in a safe place," replied Torres, "and you will not have it until your daughter has become my wife. Now will you still refuse me?"

"Yes," replied Joam, "but in return for that paper the half of my fortune is yours."

"The half of your fortune?" exclaimed Torres; "agreed, on condition that Minha brings it to me at her marriage."

"And it is thus that you respect the wishes of a dying man, of a criminal tortured by remorse, and who has charge you to repair as much as he could the evil which he had done?"

"It is thus."

"Once more, Torres," said Joam Garral, "you are a consummate scoundrel."

"Be it so."

"And as I am not a criminal we were not made to understand one another."

"And your refuse?"

"I refuse."

"It will be your ruin, then, Joam Garral. Everything accuses you in the proceedings that have already taken place. You are condemned to death, and you know, in sentences for crimes of that nature, the government is forbidden the right of commuting the penalty. Denounced, you are taken; taken, you are executed. And I will denounce you."

Master as he was of himself, Joam could stand it no longer. He was about to rush on Torres.

A gesture from the rascal cooled his anger.

"Take care," said Torres, "your wife knows not that she is the wife of Joam Dacosta, your children do not know they are the children of Joam Dacosta, and you are not going to give them the information."

Joam Garral stopped himself. He regained his usual command over himself, and his features recovered their habitual calm.

"This discussion has lasted long enough," said he, moving toward the door, "and I know what there is left for me to do."

"Take care, Joam Garral!" said Torres, for the last time, for he could scarcely believe that his ignoble attempt at extortion had collapsed.

Joam Garral made him no answer. He threw back the door which opened under the veranda, made a sign to

Torres to follow him, and they advanced toward the center of the jangada, where the family were assembled.

Benito, Manoel, and all of them, under a feeling of deep anxiety, had risen. They could see that the bearing of Torres was still menacing, and that the fire of anger still shone in his eyes.

In extraordinary contrast, Joam Garral was master of himself, and almost smiling.

Both of them stopped before Yaquita and her people. Not one dared to say a word to them.

It was Torres who, in a hollow voice, and with his customary impudence, broke the painful silence.

"For the last time, Joam Garral," he said, "I ask you for a last reply!"

"And here is my reply."

And addressing his wife:

"Yaquita," he said, "peculiar circumstances oblige me to alter what we have formerly decided as to the marriage of Minha and Manoel."

"At last!" exclaimed Torres.

Joam Garral, without answering him, shot at the adventurer a glance of the deepest scorn.

But at the words Manoel had felt his heart beat as if it would break.

The girl arose, ashy pale, as if she would seek shelter by the side of her mother. Yaquita opened her arms to protect, to defend her.

"Father," said Benito, who had placed himself between Joam Garral and Torres, "what were you going to say?"

"I was going to say," answered Joam Garral, raising his voice, "that to wait for our arrival in Para for the wedding of Minha and Manoel is to wait too long. The marriage will take place here, not later than to-morrow, on the jangada, with the aid of Padre Passanha, if, after a conversation I am about to have with Manoel, he agrees with me to defer it no longer."

"Ah, father, father!" exclaimed the young man.

"Wait a little before you call me so, Manoel," replied Joam, in a tone of unspeakable suffering.

Here Torres, with crossed arms, gave the whole family a look of inconceivable insolence.

"So that is you last word?" said he, extending his hand toward Joam Garral

"No, that is not my last word."

"What is it, then?"

"This, Torres. I am master here. You will be off, if you please, and even if you do not please, and leave the jangada at this very instant!"

"Yes, this instant!" exclaimed Benito, "or I will throw

you overboard."

Torres shrugged his shoulders.

"No threats," he said; "they are of no use. It suits me also to land, and without delay. But you will remember me, Joam Garral. We shall not be long before we meet."

"If it only depends on me," answered Joam Garral, "we shall soon meet, and rather sooner, perhaps, than you will like. To-morrow I shall be with Judge Ribeiro, the first magistrate of the province, whom I have advised of my arrival at Manaos. If you dare, meet me there!"

"At Judge Ribeiro's?" said Torres, evidently disconcerted.

"At Judge Ribeiro's," answered Joam Garral.

And then, showing the pirogue to Torres, with a gesture of supreme contempt Joam Garral ordered four of his people to land him without delay on the nearest point of the island.

The scoundrel at last disappeared.

The family, who were still appalled, respected the silence of its chief; but Fragoso, comprehending scarce half the gravity of the situation, and carried away by his customary vivacity, came up to
Joam Garral.

"If the wedding of Miss Minha and Mr. Manoel is to take place to-morrow on the raft -- "

"Yours shall take place at the same time," kindly answered Joam Garral.

And making a sign to Manoel, he retired to his room with him.

The interview between Joam and Manoel had lasted for half an hour, and it seemed a century to the family, when the door of the room was reopened.

Manoel came out alone; his face glowed with generous resolution.

Going up to Yaquita, he said, "My mother!" to Minha he said, "My wife!" and to Benito he said, "My brother!" and, turning toward Lina and Fragoso, he said to all, "To-morrow!"

He knew all that had passed between Joam Garral and Torres. He knew that, counting on the protection of Judge Ribeiro, by means of a correspondence which he had had with him for a year past without speaking of it to his people, Joam Garral had at last succeeded in clearing himself and convincing him of his innocence. He knew that Joam Garral had boldly undertaken the voyage with the sole object of canceling the hateful proceedings of which he had been the victim, so as not to leave on his daughter and son-in-law the weight of the terrible situation which he had had to endure so long himself.

Yes, Manoel knew all this, and, further, he knew that Joam Garral - or rather Joam Dacosta - was innocent, and his misfortunes made him even dearer and more devoted to him. What he did not know was that the material proof of the innocence of the fazender existed, and that this proof was in the hands of Torres. Joam Garral wished to reserve for the judge himself the use of this proof, which, if the adventurer had spoken truly, would demonstrate his innocence.

Manoel confined himself, then, to announcing that he was going to Padre Passanha to ask him to get things ready for the two weddings.

Next day, the 24th of August, scarcely an hour before the ceremony was to take place, a large pirogue came off from the left bank of the river and hailed the jangada. A dozen paddlers had swiftly brought it from Manaos, and with a few men it carried the chief of the police, who made himself known and came on board.

At the moment Joam Garral and his family, attired for the ceremony, were coming out of the house.

"Joam Garral?" asked the chief of the police.

"I am here," replied Joam.

"Joam Garral," continued the chief of the police, "you have also been Joam Dacosta; both names have been borne by the same man - I arrest you!"

At these words Yaquita and Minha, struck with stupor, stopped without any power to move.

"My father a murderer?" exclaimed Benito, rushing toward Joam Garral.

By a gesture his father silenced him.

"I will only ask you one question," said Joam with firm

voice, addressing the chief of police. "Has the warrant in virtue of which you arrest me been issued against me by the justice at Manaos - by Judge Ribeiro?"

"No," answered the chief of the police, "it was given to me, with an order for its immediate execution, by his substitute. Judge Ribeiro was struck with apoplexy yesterday evening, and died during the night at two o'clock, without having recovered his consciousness."

"Dead!" exclaimed Joam Garral, crushed for a moment by the news - "dead! dead!"

But soon raising his head, he said to his wife and children, "Judge Ribeiro alone knew that I was innocent, my dear ones. The death of the judge may be fatal to me, but that is no reason for me to despair."

And, turning toward Manoel, "Heaven help us!" he said to him; "we shall see if truth will come down to the earth from Above."

The chief of the police made a sign to his men, who advanced to secure Joam Garral.

"But speak, father!" shouted Benito, mad with despair; "say one word, and we shall contest even by force this horrible mistake of which you are the victim!"

"There is no mistake here, my son," replied Joam Garral; "Joam Dacosta and Joam Garral are one. I am in truth Joam Dacosta! I am the honest man whom a legal error unjustly doomed to death twenty-five years ago in the place of the true culprit! That I am quite innocent I swear before Heaven, once for all, on your heads, my children, and on the head of your mother!"

"All communication between you and yours is now forbidden," said the chief of the police. "You are my prisoner, Joam Garral, and I will rigorously execute my warrant."

Joam restrained by a gesture his dismayed children and servants.

"Let the justice of man be done while we wait for the justice of God!"

And with his head unbent, he stepped into the pirogue.

It seemed, indeed, as though of all present Joam Garral was the only one whom this fearful thunderbolt, which had fallen so unexpectedly on his head, had failed to overwhelm.

PART II - THE CRYPTOGRAM

CHAPTER I

MANAOS

THE TOWN of Manaos is in 3° 8' 4" south latitude, and 67° 27' west longitude, reckoning from the Paris meridian. It is some four hundred and twenty leagues from Belem, and about ten miles from the *embouchure* of the Rio Negro.

Manaos is not built on the Amazon. It is on the left bank of the Rio Negro, the most important and remarkable of all the tributaries of the great artery of Brazil, that the capital of the province, with its picturesque group of private houses and public buildings, towers above the surrounding plain.

The Rio Negro, which was discovered by the Spaniard Favella in 1645, rises in the very heart of the province of Popayan, on the flanks of the mountains which separate Brazil from New Grenada, and it communicates with the Orinoco by two of its affluents, the Pimichin and the Cassiquary.

After a noble course of some seventeen hundred miles it mingles its cloudy waters with those of the Amazon through a mouth eleven hundred feet wide, but such is its vigorous influx that many a mile has to be completed before those waters lose their distinctive character. Hereabouts the ends of both its banks trend off and form a huge bay fifteen leagues across, extending to the islands of Anavilhanas; and in one of its indentations the port of Manaos is situated. Vessels of all kinds are there collected in great numbers, some moored in the stream awaiting a favorable wind, others under repair up the numerous *iguarapes,* or canals, which so capriciously intersect the town, and give it its slightly Dutch appearance.

With the introduction of steam vessels, which is now rapidly taking place, the trade of Manaos is destined to increase enormously. Woods used in building and furniture work, cocoa, caoutchouc, coffee, sarsaparilla, sugar-canes, indigo, muscado nuts, salt fish, turtle butter, and other commodities, are brought here from all parts, down the innumerable streams into the Rio Negro from the west and north, into the Madeira from the west and south, and then into the Amazon, and by it away eastward to the coast of the Atlantic.

Manaos was formerly called Moura, or Barra de Rio Negro. From 1757 to 1804 it was only part of the captaincy which bears the name of the great river at whose mouth it is placed; but since 1826 it has been the capital of the large province of Amazones, borrowing its latest name from an Indian tribe which formerly existed in these parts of equatorial America.

Careless travelers have frequently confounded it with the famous Manoa, a city of romance, built, it was reported, near the legendary lake of Parima - which would seem to be merely the Upper Branco, a tributary of the Rio Negro. Here was the Empire of El Dorado, whose monarch, if we are to believe the fables of the district, was every morning covered with powder of gold, there being so much of the precious metal abounding in this privileged locality that it was swept up with the very dust of the streets. This assertion, however, when put to the test, was disproved, and with extreme regret, for the auriferous deposits which had deceived the greedy scrutiny of the gold-seekers turned out to be only worthless flakes of mica!

In short, Manaos has none of the fabulous splendors of the mythical capital of El Dorado. It is an ordinary town of about five thousand inhabitants, and of these at least three thousand are in government employ. This fact is to be attributed to the number of its public buildings, which consist of the legislative chamber, the government house, the treasury, the post-office, and the custom-house, and, in addition, a college founded in 1848, and a hospital erected in 1851. When with these is also mentioned a cemetery on the south side of a hill, on which, in 1669, a fortress, which has since been demolished, was thrown up against the pirates of the Amazon, some idea can be gained as to the importance of the official establishments of the city. Of religious buildings it would be difficult to find more than two, the small Church of the Conception and the Chapel of Notre Dame des Remedes, built on a knoll which overlooks the town. These are very few for a town of Spanish origin, though to them should perhaps be added the Carmelite Convent, burned down in 1850, of which only the ruins remain. The population of Manaos does not exceed the number above given, and after reckoning the public officials and soldiers, is principally made of up Portuguese and Indian merchants belonging to the different tribes of the Rio Negro.

Three principal thoroughfares of considerable irregularity run through the town, and they bear names highly characteristic of the tone of thought prevalent in these parts - God-the-Father Street, God-the-Son Street, and God-the-Holy Ghost Street!

In the west of the town is a magnificent avenue of centenarian orange trees which were carefully respected by the architects who out of the old city made the new. Round these principal thoroughfares is interwoven a perfect network of unpaved alleys, intersected every now and then by four canals, which are occasionally crossed by wooden bridges. In a few places these iguarapes flow with their brownish waters through large vacant spaces covered with straggling weeds and flowers of startling hues, and here and there are natural squares shaded by magnificent trees, with an occasional white-barked sumaumeira shooting up, and spreading out its large dome-like parasol above its gnarled branches.

The private houses have to be sought for among some hundreds of dwellings, of very rudimentary type, some roofed with tiles, others with interlaced branches of the palm-tree, and with prominent miradors, and projecting shops for the most part tenanted by Portuguese traders.

And what manner of people are they who stroll on to the fashionable promenade from the public buildings and private residences? Men of good appearance, with black cloth coats, chimney-pot hats, patent-leather boots, highly-colored gloves, and diamond pins in their necktie bows; and women in loud, imposing toilets, with flounced dressed and headgear of the latest style; and Indians, also on the road to Europeanization in a way which bids fair to destroy every bit of local color in this central portion of the district of the Amazon!

Such is Manaos, which, for the benefit of the reader, it was necessary to sketch. Here the voyage of the giant raft, so tragically interrupted, had just come to a pause in the midst of its long journey, and here will be unfolded the further vicissitudes of the mysterious history of the fazender of Iquitos.

CHAPTER II

THE FIRST MOMENTS

SCARCELY HAD the pirogue which bore off Joam Garral, or rather Joam Dacosta - for it is more convenient that he should resume his real name - disappeared, than Benito stepped up to Manoel.

"What is it you know?" he asked.

"I know that your father is innocent! Yes, innocent!" replied Manoel, "and that he was sentenced to death twenty-three years ago for a crime which he never committed!"

"He has told you all about it, Manoel?"

"All about it," replied the young man. "The noble fazender did not wish that any part of his past life should be hidden from him who, when he marries his daughter, is to be his second son."

"And the proof of his innocence my father can one day produce?"

"That proof, Benito, lies wholly in the twenty-three years of an honorable and honored life, lies entirely in the bearing of Joam Dacosta, who comes forward to say to justice, 'Here am I! I do not care for this false existence any more. I do not care to hide under a name which is not my true one! You have condemned an innocent man! Confess your errors and set matters right.'"

"And when my father spoke like that, you did not hesitate for a moment to believe him?"

"Not for an instant," replied Manoel.

The hands of the two young fellows closed in a long and cordial grasp.

Then Benito went up to Padre Passanha.

"Padre," he said, "take my mother and sister away to their rooms. Do not leave them all day. No one here doubts my father's innocence - not one, you know that! To-morrow my mother and I will seek out the chief of the police. They will not refuse us permission to visit the prison. No! that would be too cruel. We will see my father again, and decide what steps shall be taken to procure his vindication."

Yaquita was almost helpless, but the brave woman, though nearly crushed by this sudden blow, arose. With Yaquita Dacosta it was as with Yaquita Garral. She had not a doubt as to the innocence of her husband. The idea even never occurred to her that Joam Dacosta had been to blame in marrying her under a name which was not his own. She only thought of the life of happiness she had led with the noble man who had been injured so unjustly. Yes! On the morrow she would go to the gate of the prison, and never leave it until it was opened!

Padre Passanha took her and her daughter, who could not restrain her tears, and the three entered the house.

The two young fellows found themselves alone.

"And now," said Benito, "I ought to know all that my father has told you."

"I have nothing to hide from you."

"Why did Torres come on board the jangada?"

"To see to Joam Dacosta the secret of his past life."

"And so, when we first met Torres in the forest of Iquitos, his plan had already been formed to enter into communication with my father?"

"There cannot be a doubt of it," replied Manoel. "The scoundrel was on his way to the fazenda with the idea of consummating a vile scheme of extortion which he had been preparing for a long time."

"And when he learned from us that my father and his whole family were about to pass the frontier, he suddenly changed his line of conduct?"

"Yes. Because Joam Dacosta once in Brazilian territory became more at his mercy than while within the frontiers of Peru. That is why we found Torres at Tabatinga, where he was waiting in expectation of our arrival."

"And it was I who offered him a passage on the raft!" exclaimed Benito, with a gesture of despair.

"Brother," said Manoel, "you need not reproach yourself. Torres would have joined us sooner or later. He was not the man to abandon such a trail. Had we lost him at Tabatinga, we should have found him at Manaos."

"Yes, Manoel, you are right. But we are not concerned with the past now. We must think of the present. An end to useless recriminations! Let us see!" And while speaking, Benito, passing his hand across his forehead, endeavored to grasp the details of the strange affair.

"How," he asked, "did Torres ascertain that my father had been sentenced twenty-three years back for this abominable crime at Tijuco?"

"I do not know," answered Manoel, "and everything leads me to think that your father did not know that."

"But Torres knew that Garral was the name under which Joam Dacosta was living?"

"Evidently."

"And he knew that it was in Peru, at Iquitos, that for so many years my father had taken refuge?"

"He knew it," said Manoel, "but how he came to know it I do not understand."

"One more question," continued Benito. "What was the proposition that Torres made to my father during the short interview which preceded his expulsion?"

"He threatened to denounce Joam Garral as being Joam Dacosta, if he declined to purchase his silence."

"And at what price?"

"At the price of his daughter's hand!" answered Manoel unhesitatingly, but pale with anger.

"The scoundrel dared to do that!" exclaimed Benito.

"To this infamous request, Benito, you saw the reply that your father gave."

"Yes, Manoel, yes! The indignant reply of an honest man. He kicked Torres off the raft. But it is not enough to have kicked him out. No! That will not do for me. It was on Torres' information that they came here and arrested my father; is not that so?"

"Yes, on his denunciation."

"Very well," continued Benito, shaking his fist toward the left bank of the river, "I must find out Torres. I must know how he became master of the secret. He must tell me if he knows the real author of this crime. He shall speak out. And if he does not speak out, I know what I shall have to do."

"What you will have to do is for me to do as well!" added Manoel, more coolly, but not less resolutely.

"No! Manoel, no, to me alone!"

"We are brothers, Benito," replied Manoel. "The right of demanding an explanation belongs to us both."

Benito made no reply. Evidently on that subject his decision was irrevocable.

At this moment the pilot Araujo, who had been observing the state of the river, came up to them.

"Have you decided," he asked, "if the raft is to remain at her moorings at the Isle of Muras, or to go on to the port of Manaos?"

The question had to be decided before nightfall, and the sooner it was settled the better.

In fact, the news of the arrest of Joam Dacosta ought already to have spread through the town. That it was of a nature to excite the interest of the population of Manaos could scarcely be doubted. But would it provoke more than curiosity against the condemned man, who was the principal author of the crime of Tijuco, which had formerly created such a sensation? Ought they not to fear that some popular movement might be directed against the prisoner? In the face of this hypothesis was it not better to leave the jangada moored near the Isle of Muras on the right bank of the river at a few miles from Manaos?

The pros and cons of the question were well weighed.

"No!" at length exclaimed Benito; "to remain here would look as though we were abandoning my father and doubting his innocence - as though we were afraid to make common cause with him. We must go to Manaos, and without delay."

"You are right," replied Manoel. "Let us go."

Araujo, with an approving nod, began his preparations for leaving the island. The maneuver necessitated a good deal of care. They had to work the raft slantingly across the current of the Amazon, here doubled in force by that of the Rio Negro, and to make for the *embouchure* of the tributary about a dozen miles down on the left bank.

The ropes were cast off from the island. The jangada, again started on the river, began to drift off diagonally. Araujo, cleverly profiting by the bendings of the current, which were due to the projections of the banks, and assisted by the long poles of his crew, succeeded in working the immense raft in the desired direction.

In two hours the jangada was on the other side of the Amazon, a little above the mouth of the Rio Negro, and fairly in the current which was to take it to the lower bank of the vast bay which opened on the left side of the stream.

At five o'clock in the evening it was strongly moored alongside this bank, not in the port of Manaos itself, which it could not enter without stemming a rather powerful current, but a short mile below it.

The raft was then in the black waters of the Rio Negro, near rather a high bluff covered with cecropias with buds of reddish-brown, and palisaded with stiff-stalked reeds called *"froxas,"* of which the Indians make some of their weapons.

A few citizens were strolling about the bank. A feeling of curiosity had doubtless attracted them to the anchorage of the raft. The news of the arrest of Joam Dacosta had soon spread about, but the curiosity of the Manaens did not outrun their discretion, and they were very quiet.

Benito's intention had been to land that evening, but Manoel dissuaded him.

"Wait till to-morrow," he said; "night is approaching, and there is no necessity for us to leave the raft."

"So be it! To-morrow!" answered Benito.

And here Yaquita, followed by her daughter and Padre Passanha, came out of the house. Minha was still weeping, but her mother's face was tearless, and she had that look of calm resolution which showed that the wife was now ready for all things, either to do her duty or to insist on her rights.

Yaquita slowly advanced toward Manoel.

"Manoel," she said, "listen to what I have to say, for my conscience commands me to speak as I am about to do."

"I am listening," replied Manoel.

Yaquita, looking him straight in the face, continued: "Yesterday, after the interview you had with Joam Dacosta, my husband, you came to me and called me - mother! You took Minha's hand, and called her - your wife! You then knew everything, and the past life of Joam Dacosta had been disclosed to you."

"Yes," answered Manoel, "and heaven forbid I should have had any hesitation in doing so!"

"Perhaps so," replied Yaquita; "but then Joam Dacosta had not been arrested. The position is not now the same. However innocent he may be, my husband is in the hands of justice; his past life has been publicly proclaimed. Minha is a convict's daughter."

"Minha Dacosta or Minha Garral, what matters it to me?" exclaimed Manoel, who could keep silent no longer.

"Manoel!" murmured Minha.

And she would certainly have fallen had not Lina's arm supported her.

"Mother, if you do not wish to kill her," said Manoel, "call me your son!"

"My son! my child!"

It was all Yaquita could say, and the tears, which she restrained with difficulty, filled her eyes.

And then they all re-entered the house. But during the long night not an hour's sleep fell to the lot of the unfortunate family who were being so cruelly tried.

CHAPTER III

RETROSPECTIVE

JOAM DACOSTA had relied entirely on Judge Albeiro, and his death was most unfortunate.

Before he was judge at Manaos, and chief magistrate in the province, Ribeiro had known the young clerk at the time he was being prosecuted for the murder in the diamond arrayal. He was then an advocate at Villa Rica, and he it was who defended the prisoner at the trial. He took the cause to heart and made it his own, and from an examination of the papers and detailed information, and not from the simple fact of his position in the matter, he came to the conclusion that his client was wrongfully accused, and that he had taken not the slightest part in the murder of the escort or the theft of the diamonds - in a word, that Joam Dacosta was innocent.

But, notwithstanding this conviction, notwithstanding his talent and zeal, Ribeiro was unable to persuade the jury to take the same view of the matter. How could he remove so strong a presumption? If it was not Joam Dacosta, who had every facility for informing the scoundrels of the convoy's departure, who was it? The official who accompanied the escort had perished with the greater part of the soldiers, and suspicion could not point against him. Everything agreed in distinguishing Dacosta as the true and only author of the crime.

Ribeiro defended him with great warmth and with all his powers, but he could not succeed in saving him. The verdict of the jury was affirmative on all the questions. Joam Dacosta, convicted of aggravated and premeditated murder, did not even obtain the benefit of extenuating circumstances, and heard himself condemned to death.

There was no hope left for the accused. No commutation of the sentence was possible, for the crime was committed in the diamond arrayal. The condemned man was lost. But during the night which preceded his execution, and when the gallows was already erected, Joam Dacosta managed to escape from the prison at Villa Rica. We know the rest.

Twenty years later Ribeiro the advocate became the chief justice of Manaos. In the depths of his retreat the fazender of Iquitos heard of the change, and in it saw a favorable opportunity for bringing forward the revision of the former proceedings against him with some chance of success. He knew that the old convictions of the advocate would be still unshaken in the mind of the judge. He therefore resolved to try and rehabilitate himself. Had it not been for Ribeiro's nomination to the chief justiceship in the province of Amazones, he might perhaps have hesitated, for he had no new material proof of his innocence to bring forward. Although the honest man suffered acutely, he might still have remained hidden in exile at Iquitos, and still have asked for time to smother the remembrances of the horrible occurrence, but something was urging him to act in the matter without delay.

In fact, before Yaquita had spoken to him, Joam Dacosta had noticed that Manoel was in love with his daughter.

The union of the young army doctor and his daughter was in every respect a suitable one. It was evident to Joam that some day or other he would be asked for her hand in marriage, and he did not wish to be obliged to refuse.

But then the thought that his daughter would have to marry under a name which did not belong to her, that Manoel Valdez, thinking he was entering the family of Garral, would enter that of Dacosta, the head of which was under sentence of death, was intolerable to him. No! The wedding should not take place unless under proper conditions! Never!

Let us recall what had happened up to this time. Four years after the young clerk, who eventually became the partner of Magalhaës, had arrived at Iquitos, the old Portuguese had been taken back to the farm mortally injured. A few days only were left for him to live. He was alarmed at the thought that his daughter would be left alone and unprotected; but knowing that Joam and Yaquita were in love with each other, he desired their union without delay.

Joam at first refused. He offered to remain the protector or the servant of Yaquita without becoming her husband. The wish of the dying Magalhaës was so urgent that resistance became impossible. Yaquita put her hand into the hand of Joam, and Joam did not withdraw it.

Yes! It was a serious matter! Joam Dacosta ought to

have confessed all, or to have fled forever from the house in which he had been so hospitably received, from the establishment of which he had built up the prosperity! Yes! To confess everything rather than to give to the daughter of his benefactor a name which was not his, instead of the name of a felon condemned to death for murder, innocent though he might be!

But the case was pressing, the old fazender was on the point of death, his hands were stretched out toward the young people! Joam was silent, the marriage took place, and the remainder of his life was devoted to the happiness of the girl he had made his wife.

"The day when I confess everything," Joam repeated, "Yaquita will pardon everything! She will not doubt me for an instant! But if I ought not to have deceived her, I certainly will not deceive the honest fellow who wishes to enter our family by marrying Mina! No! I would rather give myself up and have done with this life!"

Many times had Joam thought of telling his wife about his past life. Yes! the avowal was on his lips whenever she asked him to take her into Brazil, and with her and her daughter descend the beautiful Amazon river. He knew sufficient of Yaquita to be sure that her affection for him would not thereby be diminished in the least. But courage failed him!

And this is easily intelligible in the face of the happiness of the family, which increased on every side. This happiness was his work, and it might be destroyed forever by his return.

Such had been his life for those long years; such had

been the continuous source of his sufferings, of which he had kept the secret so well; such had been the existence of this man, who had no action to be ashamed of, and whom a great injustice compelled to hide away from himself!

But at length the day arrived when there could no longer remain a doubt as to the affection which Manoel bore to Minha, when he could see that a year would not go by before he was asked to give his consent to her marriage, and after a short delay he no longer hesitated to proceed in the matter.

A letter from him, addressed to Judge Ribeiro, acquainted the chief justice with the secret of the existence of Joam Dacosta, with the name under which he was concealed, with the place where he lived with his family, and at the same time with his formal intention of delivering himself up to justice, and taking steps to procure the revision of the proceedings, which would either result in his rehabilitation or in the execution of the iniquitous judgment delivered at Villa Rica.

What were the feelings which agitated the heart of the worthy magistrate? We can easily divine them. It was no longer to the advocate that the accused applied; it was to the chief justice of the province that the convict appealed. Joam Dacosta gave himself over to him entirely, and did not even ask him to keep the secret.

Judge Ribeiro was at first troubled about this unexpected revelation, but he soon recovered himself, and scrupulously considered the duties which the position imposed on him. It was his place to pursue criminals, and here was one who delivered himself into his hands. This criminal, it was true, he had defended;

he had never doubted but that he had been unjustly condemned; his joy had been extreme when he saw him escape by flight from the last penalty; he had even instigated and facilitated his flight! But what the advocate had done in the past could the magistrate do in the present?

"Well, yes!" had the judge said, "my conscience tells me not to abandon this just man. The step he is taking is a fresh proof of his innocence, a moral proof, even if he brings me others, which may be the most convincing of all! No! I will not abandon him!"

From this day forward a secret correspondence took place between the magistrate and Joam Dacosta. Ribeiro at the outset cautioned his client against compromising himself by any imprudence. He had again to work up the matter, again to read over the papers, again to look through the inquiries. He had to find out if any new facts had come to light in the diamond province referring to so serious a case. Had any of the accomplices of the crime, of the smugglers who had attacked the convoy, been arrested since the attempt? Had any confessions or half-confessions been brought forward? Joam Dacosta had done nothing but protest his innocence from the very first. But that was not enough, and Judge Ribeiro was desirous of finding in the case itself the clue to the real culprit.

Joam Dacosta had accordingly been prudent. He had promised to be so. But in all his trials it was an immense consolation for him to find his old advocate, though now a chief justice, so firmly convinced that he was not guilty. Yes! Joam Dacosta, in spite of his condemnation, was a victim, a martyr, an honest man to whom society owed a signal reparation! And when the magistrate knew the past career of the fazender of Iquitos since his sentence, the position of his family, all that life of devotion, of work, employed unceasingly for the happiness of those belonging to him, he was not only more convinced but more affected, and determined to do all that he could to procure the rehabilitation of the felon of Tijuco.

For six months a correspondence had passed between these two men.

One day, the case being pressing, Joam Dacosta wrote to Judge Ribeiro:

"In two months I will be with you, in the power of the chief justice of the province!"

"Come, then," replied Ribeiro.

The jangada was then ready to go down the river. Joam Dacosta embarked on it with all his people. During the voyage, to the great astonishment of his wife and son, he landed but rarely, as we know. More often he remained shut up on his room, writing, working, not at his trading accounts, but, without saying anything about it, at a kind of memoir, which he called "The History of My Life," and which was meant to be used in the revision of the legal proceedings.

Eight days before his new arrest, made on account of information given by Torres, which forestalled and perhaps would ruin his prospects, he intrusted to an Indian on the Amazon a letter, in which he warned Judge Ribeiro of his approaching arrival.

The letter was sent and delivered as addressed, and the

magistrate only waited for Joam Dacosta to commence on the serious undertaking which he hoped to bring to a successful issue.

During the night before the arrival of the raft at Manaos Judge Ribeiro was seized with an attack of apoplexy. But the denunciation of Torres, whose scheme of extortion had collapsed in face of the noble anger of his victim, had produced its effect. Joam Dacosta was arrested in the bosom of his family, and his old advocate was no longer in this world to defend him!

Yes, the blow was terrible indeed. His lot was cast, whatever his fate might be; there was no going back for him! And Joam Dacosta rose from beneath the blow which had so unexpectedly struck him. It was not only his own honor which was in question, but the honor of all who belonged to him.

CHAPTER IV

MORAL PROOFS

THE WARRANT against Joam Dacosta, alias Joam Garral, had been issued by the assistant of Judge Ribeiro, who filled the position of the magistrate in the province of Amazones, until the nomination of the successor of the late justice.

This assistant bore the name of Vicente Jarriquez. He was a surly little fellow, whom forty years' practice in criminal procedure had not rendered particularly friendly toward those who came before him. He had had so many cases of this sort, and tried and sentenced so many rascals, that a prisoner's innocence seemed to him *à priori* inadmissable. To be sure, he did not come to a decision unconscientiously; but his conscience was strongly fortified and was not easily affected by the circumstances of the examination or the arguments for the defense. Like a good many judges, he thought but little of the indulgence of the jury, and when a prisoner was brought before him, after having passed through the sieve of inquest, inquiry, and examination, there was every presumption in his eyes that the man was quite ten times guilty.

Jarriquez, however, was not a bad man. Nervous, fidgety, talkative, keen, crafty, he had a curious look about him, with his big head on his little body; his ruffled hair, which would not have disgraced the judge's wig of the past; his piercing gimlet-like eyes, with their expression of surprising acuteness; his prominent nose, with which he would assuredly have gesticulated had it been movable; his ears wide open, so as to better catch all that was said, even when it was out of range of ordinary auditory apparatus; his fingers unceasingly tapping the table in front of him, like those of a pianist practicing on the mute; and his body so long and his legs so short, and his feet perpetually crossing and recrossing, as he sat in state in his magistrate's chair.

In private life, Jarriquez, who was a confirmed old bachelor, never left his law-books but for the table which he did not despise; for chess, of which he was a past master; and above all things for Chinese puzzles, enigmas, charades, rebuses, anagrams, riddles, and such things, with which, like more than one European justice - thorough sphinxes by taste as well as by profession - he principally passed his leisure.

It will be seen that he was an original, and it will be seen also how much Joam Dacosta had lost by the death of Judge Ribeiro, inasmuch as his case would come before this not very agreeable judge.

Moreover, the task of Jarriquez was in a way very simple. He had either to inquire nor to rule; he had not even to regulate a discussion nor to obtain a verdict, neither to apply the articles of the penal code nor to pronounce a sentence. Unfortunately for the fazender, such formalities were no longer necessary; Joam Dacosta had been arrested, convicted, and sentenced twenty-three years ago for the crime at Tijuco; no limitation had yet affected his sentence. No demand in commutation of the penalty could be introduced, and no appeal for mercy could be received. It was only necessary then to establish his identity, and as soon as the order arrived from Rio Janeiro justice would have to take its course.

But in the nature of things Joam Dacosta would protest his innocence; he would say he had been unjustly condemned. The magistrate's duty, notwithstanding the opinions he held, would be to listen to him. The question would be, what proofs could the convict offer to make good his assertions? And if he was not able to produce them when he appeared before his first judges, was he able to do so now?

Herein consisted all the interest of the examination. There would have to be admitted the fact of a defaulter, prosperous and safe in a foreign country, leaving his refuge of his own free will to face the justice which his past life should have taught him to dread, and herein would be one of those rare and curious cases which ought to interest even a magistrate hardened with all the surroundings of forensic strife. Was it impudent folly on the part of the doomed man of Tijuco, who was tired of his life, or was it the impulse of a conscience which would at all risks have wrong set right? The problem was a strange one, it must be acknowledged.

On the morrow of Joam Dacosta's arrest, Judge Jarriquez made his way to the prison in God-the-Son Street, where the convict had been placed. The prison was an old missionary convent, situated on the bank of one of the principal iguarapes of the town. To the voluntary prisoners of former times there had succeeded in this building, which was but little adapted for the purpose, the compulsory prisoners of to-day. The room occupied by Joam Dacosta was nothing like one of those sad little cells which form part of our modern penitentiary system: but an old monk's room, with a barred window without shutters, opening on to an uncultivated space, a bench in one corner, and a kind of pallet in the other. It was from this apartment that Joam Dacosta, on this 25th of August, about eleven o'clock in the morning, was taken and brought into the judge's room, which was the old common hall of the convent.

Judge Jarriquez was there in front of his desk, perched on his high chair, his back turned toward the window, so that his face was in shadow while that of the accused remained in full daylight. His clerk, with the indifference which characterizes these legal folks, had taken his seat at the end of the table, his pen behind his ear, ready to record the questions and answers.

Joam Dacosta was introduced into the room, and at a sign from the judge the guards who had brought him withdrew.

Judge Jarriquez looked at the accused for some time. The latter, leaning slightly forward and maintaining a becoming attitude, neither careless nor humble, waited with dignity for the questions to which he was expected to reply.

"Your name?" said Judge Jarriquez.

"Joam Dacosta."

"Your age?"

"Fifty-two."

"Where do you live?"

"In Peru, at the village of Iquitos."

"Under what name?"

"Under that of Garral, which is that of my mother."

"And why do you bear that name?"

"Because for twenty-three years I wished to hide myself from the pursuit of Brazilian justice."

The answers were so exact, and seemed to show that Joam Dacosta had made up his mind to confess everything concerning his past and present life, that Judge Jarriquez, little accustomed to such a course, cocked up his nose more than was usual to him.

"And why," he continued, "should Brazilian justice pursue you?"

"Because I was sentenced to death in 1826 in the diamond affair at Tijuco."

"You confess then that you are Joam Dacosta?"

"I am Joam Dacosta."

All this was said with great calmness, and as simply as possible. The little eyes of Judge Jarriquez, hidden by their lids, seemed to say:

"Never came across anything like this before."

He had put the invariable question which had hitherto brought the invariable reply from culprits of every category protesting their innocence. The fingers of the judge began to beat a gentle tattoo on the table.

"Joam Dacosta," he asked, "what were you doing at Iquitos?"

"I was a fazender, and engaged in managing a farming establishment of considerable size."

"It was prospering?"

"Greatly prospering."

"How long ago did you leave your fazenda?"

"About nine weeks."

"Why?"

"As to that, sir," answered Dacosta, "I invented a pretext, but in reality I had a motive."

"What was the pretext?"

"The responsibility of taking into Para a large raft, and a cargo of different products of the Amazon."

"Ah! and what was the real motive of your departure?"

And in asking this question Jarriquez said to himself:

"Now we shall get into denials and falsehoods."

"The real motive," replied Joam Dacosta, in a firm

voice, "was the resolution I had taken to give myself up to the justice of my country."

"You give yourself up!" exclaimed the judge, rising from his stool. "You give yourself up of your own free will?"

"Of my own free will."

"And why?"

"Because I had had enough of this lying life, this obligation to live under a false name, of this impossibility to be able to restore to my wife and children that which belongs to them; in short, sir, because -- "

"Because?"

"I was innocent!"

"That is what I was waiting for," said Judge Jarriquez.

And while his fingers tattooed a slightly more audible march, he made a sign with his head to Dacosta, which signified as clearly as possible, "Go on! Tell me your history. I know it, but I do not wish to interrupt you in telling it in your own way."

Joam Dacosta, who did not disregard the magistrate's far from encouraging attitude, could not but see this, and he told the history of his whole life. He spoke quietly without departing from the calm he had imposed upon himself, without omitting any circumstances which had preceded or succeeded his condemnation. In the same tone he insisted on the honored and honorable life he had led since his escape, on his duties as head of his family, as husband and father, which he had so worthily fulfilled. He laid stress only on one circumstance - that which had brought him to Manaos to urge on the revision of the proceedings against him, to procure his rehabilitation - and that he was compelled to do.

Judge Jarriquez, who was naturally prepossessed against all criminals, did not interrupt him. He contented himself with opening and shutting his eyes like a man who heard the story told for the hundredth time; and when Joam Dacosta laid on the table the memoir which he had drawn up, he made no movement to take it.

"You have finished?" he said.

"Yes, sir."

"And you persist in asserting that you only left Iquitos to procure the revision of the judgment against you."

"I had no other intention."

"What is there to prove that? Who can prove that, without the denunciation which had brought about your arrest, you would have given yourself up?"

"This memoir, in the first place."

"That memoir was in your possession, and there is nothing to show that had you not been arrested, you would have put it to the use you say you intended."

"At the least, sir, there was one thing that was not in

mypossession, and of the authenticity of which there can be no doubt."

"What?"

"The letter I wrote to your predecessor, Judge Ribeiro, the letter which gave him notice of my early arrival."

"Ah! you wrote?"

"Yes. And the letter which ought to have arrived at its destination should have been handed over to you."

"Really!" answered Judge Jarriquez, in a slightly incredulous tone. "You wrote to Judge Ribeiro."

"Before he was a judge in this province," answered Joam Dacosta, "he was an advocate at Villa Rica. He it was who defended me in the trial at Tijuco. He never doubted of the justice of my cause. He did all he could to save me. Twenty years later, when he had become chief justice at Manaos, I let him know who I was, where I was, and what I wished to attempt. His opinion about me had not changed, and it was at his advice I left the fazenda, and came in person to proceed with my rehabilitation. But death had unfortunately struck him, and maybe I shall be lost, sir, if in Judge Jarriquez I do not find another Judge Ribeiro."

The magistrate, appealed to so directly, was about to start up in defiance of all the traditions of the judicial bench, but he managed to restrain himself, and was contented with muttering:

"Very strong, indeed; very strong!"

Judge Jarriquez was evidently hard of heart, and proof against all surprise.

At this moment a guard entered the room, and handed a sealed packet to the magistrate.

He broke the seal and drew a letter from the envelope. He opened it and read it, not without a certain contraction of his eyebrows, and then said:

"I have no reason for hiding from you, Joam Dacosta, that this is the letter you have been speaking about, addressed by you to Judge Ribeiro and sent on to me. I have, therefore, no reason to doubt what you have said on the subject."

"Not only on that subject," answered Dacosta, "but on the subject of all the circumstances of my life which I have brought to your knowledge, and which are none of them open to question."

"Eh! Joam Dacosta," quickly replied Judge Jarriquez. "You protest your innocence; but all prisoners do as much! After all, you only offer moral presumptions. Have you any material proof?"

"Perhaps I have," answered Joam Dacosta.

At these words, Judge Jarriquez left his chair. This was too much for him, and he had to take two or three circuits of the room to recover himself.

CHAPTER V

MATERIAL PROOFS

.

WHEN THE MAGISTRATE had again taken his place, like a man who considered he was perfectly master of himself, he leaned back in his chair, and with his head raised and his eyes looking straight in front, as though not even noticing the accused, remarked, in a tone of the most perfect indifference:

"Go on."

Joam Dacosta reflected for a minute as if hesitating to resume the order of his thoughts, and then answered as follows:

"Up to the present, sir, I have only given you moral presumptions of my innocence grounded on the dignity, propriety, and honesty of the whole of my life. I should have thought that such proofs were those most worthy of being brought forward in matters of justice."

Judge Jarriquez could not restrain a movement of his shoulders, showing that such was not his opinion.

"Since they are not enough, I proceed with the material proofs which I shall perhaps be able to produce," continued Dacosta; "I say perhaps, for I do not yet know what credit to attach to them. And, sir, I have never spoken of these things to my wife or children, not wishing to raise a hope which might be destroyed."

"To the point," answered Jarriquez.

"I have every reason to believe, sir, that my arrest on the eve of the arrival of the raft at Manaos is due to information given to the chief of the police!"

"You are not mistaken, Joam Dacosta, but I ought to tell you that the information is anonymous."

"It matters little, for I know that it could only come from a scoundrel called Torres."

"And what right have you to speak in such a way of this - informer?"

"A scoundrel! Yes, sir!" replied Joam quickly. "This man, whom I received with hospitality, only came to me to propose that I should purchase his silence to offer me an odious bargain that I shall never regret having refused, whatever may be the consequences of his denunciation!"

"Always this method!" thought Judge Jarriquez; "accusing others to clear himself."

But he none the less listened with extreme attention to Joam's recital of his relations with the adventurer up to the moment when Torres let him know that he knew and could reveal the name of the true author of the crime of Tijuco.

"And what is the name of the guilty man?" asked

Jarriquez, shaken in his indifference.

"I do not know," answered Joam Dacosta. "Torres was too cautious to let it out."

"And the culprit is living?"

"He is dead."

The fingers of Judge Jarriquez tattooed more quickly, and he could not avoid exclaiming, "The man who can furnish the proof of a prisoner's innocence is always dead."

"If the real culprit is dead, sir," replied Dacosta, "Torres at least is living, and the proof, written throughout in the handwriting of the author of the crime, he has assured me is in his hands! He offered to sell it to me!"

"Eh! Joam Dacosta!" answered Judge Jarriquez, "that would not have been dear at the cost of the whole of your fortune!"

"If Torres had only asked my fortune, I would have given it to him and not one of my people would have demurred! Yes, you are right, sir; a man cannot pay too dearly for the redemption of his honor! But this scoundrel, knowing that I was at his mercy, required more than my fortune!"

"How so?"

"My daughter's hand was to be the cost of the bargain! I refused; he denounced me, and that is why I am now before you!"

"And if Torres had not informed against you," asked Judge Jarriquez - "if Torres had not met with you on your voyage, what would you have done on learning on your arrival of the death of Judge Ribeiro? Would you then have delivered yourself into the hands of justice?"

"Without the slightest hesitation," replied Joam, in a firm voice; "for, I repeat it, I had no other object in leaving Iquitos to come to Manaos."

This was said in such a tone of truthfulness that Judge Jarriquez experienced a kind of feeling making its way to that corner of the heart where convictions are formed, but he did not yet give in.

He could hardly help being astonished. A judge engaged merely in this examination, he knew nothing of what is known by those who have followed this history, and who cannot doubt but that Torres held in his hands the material proof of Joam Dacosta's innocence. They know that the document existed; that it contained this evidence; and perhaps they may be led to think that Judge Jarriquez was pitilessly incredulous. But they should remember that Judge Jarriquez was not in their position; that he was accustomed to the invariable protestations of the culprits who came before him. The document which Joam Dacosta appealed to was not produced; he did not really know if it actually existed; and to conclude, he had before him a man whose guilt had for him the certainty of a settled thing.

However, he wished, perhaps through curiosity, to drive Joam Dacosta behind his last entrenchments.

"And so," he said, "all your hope now rests on the declaration which has been made to you by Torres."

"Yes, sir, if my whole life does not plead for me."

"Where do you think Torres really is?"

"I think in Manaos."

"And you hope that he will speak - that he will consent to good-naturedly hand over to you the document for which you have declined to pay the price he asked?"

"I hope so, sir," replied Joam Dacosta; "the situation now is not the same for Torres; he has denounced me, and consequently he cannot retain any hope of resuming his bargaining under the previous conditions. But this document might still be worth a fortune if, supposing I am acquitted or executed, it should ever escape him. Hence his interest is to sell me the document, which can thus not injure him in any way, and I think he will act according to his interest."

The reasoning of Joam Dacosta was unanswerable, and Judge Jarriquez felt it to be so. He made the only possible objection.

"The interest of Torres is doubtless to sell you the document - if the document exists."

"If it does not exist," answered Joam Dacosta, in a penetrating voice, "in trusting to the justice of men, I must put my trust only in God!"

At these words Judge Jarriquez rose, and, in not quite such an indifferent tone, said, "Joam Dacosta, in examining you here, in allowing you to relate the particulars of your past life and to protest your innocence, I have gone further than my instructions allow me. An information has already been laid in this affair, and you have appeared before the jury at Villa Rica, whose verdict was given unanimously, and without even the addition of extenuating circumstances. You have been found guilty of the instigation of, and complicity in, the murder of the soldiers and the robbery of the diamonds at Tijuco, the capital sentence was pronounced on you, and it was only by flight that you escaped execution. But that you came here to deliver yourself over, or not, to the hands of justice twenty-three years afterward, you would never have been retaken. For the last time, you admit that you are Joam Dacosta, the condemned man of the diamond arrayal?"

"I am Joam Dacosta."

"You are ready to sign this declaration?"

"I am ready."

And with a hand without a tremble Joam Dacosta put his name to the foot of the declaration and the report which Judge Jarriquez had made his clerk draw up.

"The report, addressed to the minister of justice, is to be sent off to Rio Janeiro," said the magistrate. "Many days will elapse before we receive orders to carry out your sentence. If then, as you say, Torres possesses the proof of your innocence, do all you can yourself - do all you can through your friends - do everything, so that that proof can be produced in time. Once the order arrives no delay will be possible, and justice must take its course."

Joam Dacosta bowed slightly.

"Shall I be allowed in the meantime to see my wife and children?" he asked.

"After to-day, if you wish," answered Judge Jarriquez; "you are no longer in close confinement, and they can be brought to you as soon as they apply."

The magistrate then rang the bell. The guards entered the room, and took away Joam Dacosta.

Judge Jarriquez watched him as he went out, and shook his head and muttered:

"Well, well! This is a much stranger affair than I ever thought it would be!"

CHAPTER VI

THE LAST BLOW

WHILE JOAM DACOSTA was undergoing this examination, Yaquita, from an inquiry made by Manoel, ascertained that she and her children would be permitted to see the prisoner that very day about four o'clock in the afternoon.

Yaquita had not left her room since the evening before. Minha and Lina kept near her, waiting for the time when she would be admitted to see her husband.

Yaquita Garral or Yaquita Dacosta, he would still find her the devoted wife and brave companion he had ever known her to be.

About eleven o'clock in the morning Benito joined Manoel and Fragoso, who were talking in the bow of the jangada.

"Manoel," said he, "I have a favor to ask you."

"What is it?"

"And you too, Fragoso."

"I am at your service, Mr. Benito," answered

the barber.

"What is the matter?" asked Manoel, looking at his friend, whose expression was that of a man who had come to some unalterable resolution.

"You never doubt my father's innocence? Is that so?" said Benito.

"Ah!" exclaimed Fragoso. "Rather I think it was I who committed the crime."

"Well, we must now commence on the project I thought of yesterday."

"To find out Torres?" asked Manoel.

"Yes, and know from him how he found out my father's retreat. There is something inexplicable about it. Did he know it before? I cannot understand it, for my father never left Iquitos for more than twenty years, and this scoundrel is hardly thirty! But the day will not close before I know it; or, woe to Torres!"

Benito's resolution admitted of no discussion; and besides, neither Manoel nor Fragoso had the slightest thought of dissuading him.

"I will ask, then," continued Benito, "for both of you to accompany me. We shall start in a minute or two. It will not do to wait till Torres has left Manaos. He has no longer got his silence to sell, and the idea might occur to him. Let us be off!"

And so all three of them landed on the bank of the Rio Negro and started for the town.

Manaos was not so considerable that it could not be searched in a few hours. They had made up their minds to go from house to house, if necessary, to look for Torres, but their better plan seemed to be to apply in the first instance to the keepers of the taverns and lojas where the adventurer was most likely to put up. There could hardly be a doubt that the ex-captain of the woods would not have given his name; he might have personal reasons for avoiding all communication with the police. Nevertheless, unless he had left Manaos, it was almost impossible for him to escape the young fellows' search. In any case, there would be no use in applying to the police, for it was very probable - in fact, we know that it actually was so - that the information given to them had been anonymous.

For an hour Benito, Manoel, and Fragoso walked along the principal streets of the town, inquiring of the tradesmen in their shops, the tavern-keepers in their cabarets, and even the bystanders, without any one being able to recognize the individual whose description they so accurately gave.

Had Torres left Manaos? Would they have to give up all hope of coming across him?

In vain Manoel tried to calm Benito, whose head seemed on fire. Cost what it might, he must get at Torres!

Chance at last favored them, and it was Fragoso who put them on the right track.

In a tavern in Holy Ghost Street, from the description which the people received of the adventurer, they replied that the individual in question had put up at the loja the evening before.

"Did he sleep here?" asked Fragoso.

"Yes," answered the tavern-keeper.

"Is he here now?"

"No. He has gone out."

"But has he settled his bill, as a man would who has gone for good?"

"By no means; he left his room about an hour ago, and he will doubtless come back to supper."

"Do you know what road he took when he went out?"

"We saw him turning toward the Amazon, going through the lower town, and you will probably meet him on that side."

Fragoso did not want any more. A few seconds afterward he rejoined the young fellows, and said:

"I am on the track."

"He is there!" exclaimed Benito.

"No; he has just gone out, and they have seen him walking across to the bank of the Amazon."

"Come on!" replied Benito.

They had to go back toward the river, and the shortest way was for them to take the left bank of the Rio

Negro, down to its mouth.

Benito and his companions soon left the last houses of the town behind, and followed the bank, making a slight detour so as not to be observed from the jangada.

The plain was at this time deserted. Far away the view extended across the flat, where cultivated fields had replaced the former forests.

Benito did not speak; he could not utter a word. Manoel and Fragoso respected his silence. And so the three of them went along and looked about on all sides as they traversed the space between the bank of the Rio Negro and that of the Amazon. Three-quarters of an hour after leaving Manaos, and still they had seen nothing!

Once or twice Indians working in the fields were met with. Manoel questioned them, and one of them at length told him that a man, such as he described, had just passed in the direction of the angle formed by the two rivers at their confluence.

Without waiting for more, Benito, by an irresistible movement, strode to the front, and his two companions had to hurry on to avoid being left behind.

The left bank of the Amazon was then about a quarter of a mile off. A sort of cliff appeared ahead, hiding a part of the horizon, and bounding the view a few hundred paces in advance.

Benito, hurrying on, soon disappeared behind one of the sandy knolls.

"Quicker! quicker!" said Manoel to Fragoso. "We must not leave him alone for an instant."

And they were dashing along when a shout struck on their ears.

Had Benito caught sight of Torres? What had he seen? Had Benito and Torres already met?

Manoel and Fragoso, fifty paces further on, after swiftly running round one of the spurs of the bank, saw two men standing face to face to each other.

They were Torres and Benito.

In an instant Manoel and Fragoso had hurried up to them. It might have been supposed that in Benito's state of excitement he would be unable to restrain himself when he found himself once again in the presence of the adventurer. It was not so.

As soon as the young man saw himself face to face with Torres, and was certain that he could not escape, a complete change took place in his manner, his coolness returned, and he became once more master of himself.

The two men looked at one another for a few moments without a word.

Torres first broke silence, and, in the impudent tone habitual to him, remarked:

"Ah! How goes it, Mr. Benito Garral?"

"No, Benito Dacosta!" answered the young man.

"Quite so," continued Torres. "Mr. Benito Dacosta, accompanied by Mr. Manoel Valdez and my friend Fragoso!"

At the irritating qualification thus accorded him by the adventurer, Fragoso, who was by no means loath to do him some damage, was about to rush to the attack, when Benito, quite unmoved, held him back.

"What is the matter with you, my lad?" exclaimed Torres, retreating for a few steps. "I think I had better put myself on guard."

And as he spoke he drew from beneath his poncho his manchetta, the weapon, adapted at will for offense or defense, which a Brazilian is never without. And then, slightly stooping, and planted firmly on his feet, he waited for what was to follow.

"I have come to look for you, Torres," said Benito, who had not stirred in the least at this threatening attitude.

"To look for me?" answered the adventurer. "It is not very difficult to find me. And why have you come to look for me?"

"To know from your own lips what you appear to know of the past life of my father."

"Really?"

"Yes. I want to know how you recognized him, why you were prowling about our fazenda in the forest of Iquitos, and why you were waiting for us at Tabatinga."

"Well! it seems to me nothing could be clearer!" answered Torres, with a grin. "I was waiting to get a passage on the jangada, and I went on board with the intention of making him a very simple proposition - which possibly he was wrong in rejecting."

At these words Manoel could stand it no longer. With pale face and eye of fire he strode up to Torres.

Benito, wishing to exhaust every means of conciliation, thrust himself between them.

"Calm yourself, Manoel!" he said. "I am calm - even I."

And then continuing:

"Quite so, Torres; I know the reason of your coming on board the raft. Possessed of a secret which was doubtless given to you, you wanted to make it a means of extortion. But that is not what I want to know at present."

"What is it, then?"

"I want to know how you recognized Joam Dacosta in the fazenda of Iquitos?"

"How I recognized him?" replied Torres. "That is my business, and I see no reason why I should tell you. The important fact is, that I was not mistaken when I denounced in him the real author of the crime of Tijuco!"

"You say that to me?" exclaimed Benito, who began to lose his self-possession.

"I will tell you nothing," returned Torres; "Joam Dacosta declined my propositions! He refused to admit me into his family! Well! now that his secret is known, now that he is a prisoner, it is I who refuse to enter his family, the family of a thief, of a murderer, of a condemned felon, for whom the gallows now waits!"

"Scoundrel!" exclaimed Benito, who drew his manchetta from his belt and put himself in position.

Manoel and Fragoso, by a similar movement, quickly drew their weapons.

"Three against one!" said Torres.

"No! one against one!" answered Benito.

"Really! I should have thought an assassination would have better suited an assassin's son!"

"Torres!" exclaimed Benito, "defend yourself, or I will kill you like a mad dog!"

"Mad! so be it!" answered Torres. "But I bite, Benito Dacosta, and beware of the wounds!"

And then again grasping his manchetta, he put himself on guard and ready to attack his enemy.

Benito had stepped back a few paces.

"Torres," he said, regaining all his coolness, which for a moment he had lost; "you were the guest of my father, you threatened him, you betrayed him, you denounced him, you accused an innocent man, and with God's help I am going to kill you!"

Torres replied with the most insolent smile imaginable. Perhaps at the moment the scoundrel had an idea of stopping any struggle between Benito and him, and he could have done so. In fact he had seen that Joam Dacosta had said nothing about the document which formed the material proof of his innocence.

Had he revealed to Benito that he, Torres, possessed this proof, Benito would have been that instant disarmed. But his desire to wait till the very last moment, so as to get the very best price for the document he possessed, the recollection of the young man's insulting words, and the hate which he bore to all that belonged to him, made him forget his own interest.

In addition to being thoroughly accustomed to the manchetta, which he often had had occasion to use, the adventurer was strong, active, and artful, so that against an adversary who was scarcely twenty, who could have neither his strength nor his dexterity, the chances were greatly in his favor.

Manoel by a last effort wished to insist on fighting him instead of Benito.

"No, Manoel," was the cool reply, "it is for me alone to avenge my father, and as everything here ought to be in order, you shall be my second."

"Benito!"

"As for you, Fragoso, you will not refuse if I ask you to act as second for that man?"

"So be it," answered Fragoso, "though it is not an

office of honor. Without the least ceremony," he added, "I would have killed him like a wild beast."

The place where the duel was about to take place was a level bank about fifty paces long, on the top of a cliff rising perpendicularly some fifty feet above the Amazon. The river slowly flowed at the foot, and bathed the clumps of reeds which bristled round its base.

There was, therefore, none too much room, and the combatant who was the first to give way would quickly be driven over into the abyss.

The signal was given by Manoel, and Torres and Benito stepped forward.

Benito had complete command over himself. The defender of a sacred cause, his coolness was unruffled, much more so than that of Torres, whose conscience insensible and hardened as it was, was bound at the moment to trouble him.

The two met, and the first blow came from Benito. Torres parried it. They then jumped back, but almost at the same instant they rushed together, and with their left hands seized each other by the shoulder - never to leave go again.

Torres, who was the strongest, struck a side blow with his manchetta which Benito could not quite parry. His left side was touched, and his poncho was reddened with his blood. But he quickly replied, and slightly wounded Torres in the hand.

Several blows were then interchanged, but nothing

decisive was done. The ever silent gaze of Benito pierced the eyes of Torres like a sword blade thrust to his very heart. Visibly the scoundrel began to quail. He recoiled little by little, pressed back by his implacable foe, who was more determined on taking the life of his father's denouncer than in defending his own. To strike was all that Benito longed for; to parry was all that the other now attempted to do.

Soon Torres saw himself thrust to the very edge of the bank, at a spot where, slightly scooped away, it overhung the river. He perceived the danger; he tried to retake the offensive and regain the lost ground. His agitation increased, his looks grew livid. At length he was obliged to stoop beneath the arm which threatened him.

"Die, then!" exclaimed Benito.

The blow was struck full on its chest, but the point of the manchetta was stopped by a hard substance hidden beneath the poncho of the adventurer.

Benito renewed his attack, and Torres, whose return thrust did not touch his adversary, felt himself lost. He was again obliged to retreat. Then he would have shouted - shouted that the life of Joam Dacosta depended on his own! He had not time!

A second thrust of the manchetta pierced his heart. He fell backward, and the ground suddenly failing him, he was precipitated down the cliff. As a last effort his hands convulsively clutched at a clump of reeds, but they could not stop him, and he disappeared beneath the waters of the river.

Benito was supported on Manoel's shoulder; Fragoso grasped his hands. He would not even give his companions time to dress his wound, which was very slight.

"To the jangada!" he said, "to the jangada!"

Manoel and Fragoso with deep emotion followed him without speaking a word.

A quarter of an hour afterward the three reached the bank to which the raft was moored. Benito and Manoel rushed into the room where were Yaquita and Minha, and told them all that had passed.

"My son!" "My brother!"

The words were uttered at the same moment.

"To the prison!" said Benito.

"Yes! Come! come!" replied Yaquita.

Benito, followed by Manoel, hurried along his mother, and half an hour later they arrived before the prison.

Owing to the order previously given by Judge Jarriquez they were immediately admitted, and conducted to the chamber occupied by the prisoner.

The door opened. Joam Dacosta saw his wife, his son, and Manoel enter the room.

"Ah! Joam, my Joam!" exclaimed Yaquita.

"Yaquita! my wife! my children!" replied the prisoner,

who opened his arms and pressed them to his heart.

"My Joam, innocent!"

"Innocent and avenged!" said Benito.

"Avenged? What do you mean?"

"Torres is dead, father; killed by my hand!"

"Dead! - Torres! - Dead!" gasped Joam Dacosta. "My son! You have ruined me!"

CHAPTER VII

RESOLUTIONS

A FEW HOURS later the whole family had returned to the raft, and were assembled in the large room. All were there, except the prisoner, on whom the last blow had just fallen. Benito was quite overwhelmed, and accused himself of having destroyed his father, and had it not been for the entreaties of Yaquita, of his sister, of Padre Passanha, and of Manoel, the distracted youth would in the first moments of despair have probably made away with himself. But he was never allowed to get out of sight; he was never left alone. And besides, how could he have acted otherwise? Ah! why had not Joam Dacosta told him all before he left the jangada? Why had he refrained from speaking, except before a judge, of this material proof of his innocence? Why, in his interview with Manoel after the expulsion of Torres, had he been silent about the document which the adventurer pretended to hold in his hands? But, after all, what faith ought he to place in what Torres had said? Could he be certain that such a document was in the rascal's possession?

Whatever might be the reason, the family now knew everything, and that from the lips of Joam Dacosta himself. They knew that Torres had declared that the proof of the innocence of the convict of Tijuco actually existed; that the document had been written by the very hand of the author of the attack; that the criminal, seized by remorse at the moment of his death, had intrusted it to his companion, Torres; and that he, instead of fulfilling the wishes of the dying man, had made the handing over of the document an excuse for extortion. But they knew also that Torres had just been killed, and that his body was engulfed in the waters of the Amazon, and that he died without even mentioning the name of the guilty man.

Unless he was saved by a miracle, Joam Dacosta might now be considered as irrevocably lost. The death of Judge Ribeiro on the one hand, the death of Torres on the other, were blows from which he could not recover! It should here be said that public opinion at Manaos, unreasoning as it always is, was all against he prisoner. The unexpected arrest of Joam Dacosta had revived the memory of the terrible crime of Tijuco, which had lain forgotten for twenty-three years. The trial of the young clerk at the mines of the diamond arrayal, his capital sentence, his escape a few hours before his intended execution - all were remembered, analyzed, and commented on. An article which had just appeared in the *O Diario d'o Grand Para,* the most widely circulated journal in these parts, after giving a history of the circumstances of the crime, showed itself decidedly hostile to the prisoner. Why should these people believe in Joam Dacosta's innocence, when they were ignorant of all that his friends knew - of what they alone knew?

And so the people of Manaos became excited. A mob of Indians and negroes hurried, in their blind folly, to surround the prison and roar forth tumultuous shouts of death. In this part of the two Americas, where executions under Lynch law are of frequent occurrence, the mob soon surrenders itself to its cruel instincts, and it was feared that on this occasion it would do justice with its own hands.

What a night it was for the passengers from the fazenda! Masters and servants had been affected by the blow! Were not the servants of the fazenda members of one family? Every one of them would watch over the safety of Yaquita and her people! On the bank of the Rio Negro there was a constant coming and going of the natives, evidently excited by the arrest of Joam Dacosta, and who could say to what excesses these half-barbarous men might be led?

The time, however, passed without any demonstration against the jangada.

On the morrow, the 26th of August, as soon as the sun rose, Manoel and Fragoso, who had never left Benito for an instant during this terrible night, attempted to distract his attention from his despair. After taking him aside they made him understand that there was no time to be lost - that they must make up their minds to act.

"Benito," said Manoel, "pull yourself together! Be a man again! Be a son again!"

"My father!" exclaimed Benito. "I have killed him!"

"No!" replied Manoel. "With heaven's help it is possible that all may not be lost!"

"Listen to us, Mr. Benito," said Fragoso.

The young man, passing his hand over his eyes, made

a violent effort to collect himself.

"Benito," continued Manoel, "Torres never gave a hint to put us on the track of his past life. We therefore cannot tell who was the author of the crime of Tijuco, or under what conditions it was committed. To try in that direction is to lose our time."

"And time presses!" added Fragoso.

"Besides," said Manoel, "suppose we do find out who this companion of Torres was, he is dead, and he could not testify in any way to the innocence of Joam Dacosta. But it is none the less certain that the proof of this innocence exists, and there is not room to doubt the existence of a document which Torres was anxious to make the subject of a bargain. He told us so himself. The document is a complete avowal written in the handwriting of the culprit, which relates the attack in its smallest details, and which clears our father! Yes! A hundred times, yes! The document exists!"

"But Torres does not exist!" groaned Benito, "and the document has perished with him!"

"Wait, and don't despair yet!" answered Manoel. "You remember under what circumstances we made the acquaintance of Torres? It was in the depths of the forest of Iquitos. He was in pursuit of a monkey which had stolen a metal case, which it so strangely kept, and the chase had lasted a couple of hours when the monkey fell to our guns. Now, do you think that it was for the few pieces of gold contained in the case that Torres was in such a fury to recover it? and do you not remember the extraordinary satisfaction which he displayed when we gave him back the case which we had taken out of the monkey's paw?"

"Yes! yes!" answered Benito. "This case which I held - which I gave back to him! Perhaps it contained -- "

"It is more than probable! It is certain!" replied Manoel.

"And I beg to add," said Fragoso, "for now the fact recurs to my memory, that during the time you were at Ega I remained on board, at Lina's advice, to keep an eye on Torres, and I saw him - yes, I saw him - reading, and again reading, an old faded paper, and muttering words which I could not understand."

"That was the document!" exclaimed Benito, who snatched at the hope - the only one that was left. "But this document; had he not put it in some place of security?"

"No," answered Manoel - "no; it was too precious for Torres to dream of parting with it. He was bound to carry it always about with him, and doubtless in that very case."

"Wait! wait, Manoel!" exclaimed Benito; "I remember - yes, I remember. During the struggle, at the first blow I struck Torres in his chest, my manchetta was stopped by some hard substance under his poncho, like a plate of metal -- "

"That was the case!" said Fragoso.

"Yes," replied Manoel; "doubt is impossible! That was the case; it was in his breast-pocket."

"But the corpse of Torres?"

"We will recover it!"

"But the paper! The water will have stained it, perhaps destroyed it, or rendered it undecipherable!"

"Why," answered Manoel, "if the metal case which held it was water-tight?"

"Manoel," replied Benito, who seized on the last hope, "you are right! The corpse of Torres must be recovered! We will ransack the whole of this part of the river, if necessary, but we will recover it!"

The pilot Araujo was then summoned and informed of what they were going to do.

"Good!" replied he; "I know all the eddies and currents where the Rio Negro and the Amazon join, and we shall succeed in recovering the body. Let us take two pirogues, two ubas, a dozen of our Indians, and make a start."

Padre Passanha was then coming out of Yaquita's room.

Benito went to him, and in a few words told him what they were going to do to get possession of the document. "Say nothing to my mother or my sister," he added; "if this last hope fails it will kill them!"

"Go, my lad, go," replied Passanha, "and may God help you in your search."

Five minutes afterward the four boats started from the

raft. After descending the Rio Negro they arrived near the bank of the Amazon, at the very place where Torres, mortally wounded, had disappeared beneath the waters of the stream.

CHAPTER VIII

THE FIRST SEARCH

THE SEARCH had to commence at once, and that for two weighty reasons.

The first of these was - and this was a question of life or death - that this proof of Joam Dacosta's innocence must be produced before the arrival of the order from Rio Janeiro. Once the identity of the prisoner was established, it was impossible that such an order could be other than the order for his execution.

The second was that the body of Torres should be got out of the water as quickly as possible so as to regain undamaged the metal case and the paper it ought to contain.

At this juncture Araujo displayed not only zeal and intelligence, but also a perfect knowledge of the state of the river at its confluence with the Rio Negro.

"If Torres," he said to the young men, "had been from the first carried away by the current, we should have to drag the river throughout a large area, for we shall have a good many days to wait for his body to reappear on the surface through the effects of decomposition."

"We cannot do that," replied Manoel. "This very day we ought to succeed."

"If, on the contrary," continued the pilot, "the corpse has got stuck among the reeds and vegetation at the foot of the bank, we shall not be an hour before we find it."

"To work, then!" answered Benito.

There was but one way of working. The boats approached the bank, and the Indians, furnished with long poles, began to sound every part of the river at the base of the bluff which had served for the scene of combat.

The place had been easily recognized. A track of blood stained the declivity in its chalky part, and ran perpendicularly down it into the water; and there many a clot scattered on the reeds indicated the very spot where the corpse had disappeared.

About fifty feet down stream a point jutted out from the riverside and kept back the waters in a kind of eddy, as in a large basin. There was no current whatever near the shore, and the reeds shot up out of the river unbent. Every hope then existed that Torres' body had not been carried away by the main stream. Where the bed of the river showed sufficient slope, it was perhaps possible for the corpse to have rolled several feet along the ridge, and even there no effect of the current could be traced.

The ubas and the pirogues, dividing the work among them, limited the field of their researches to the extreme edge of the eddy, and from the circumference to the center the crews' long poles left not a single point unexplored. But no amount of sounding discovered the body of the adventurer, neither among the clumps of reeds nor on the bottom of the river, whose slope was then carefully examined.

Two hours after the work had begun they had been led to think that the body, having probably struck against the declivity, had fallen off obliquely and rolled beyond the limits of this eddy, where the action of the current commenced to be felt.

"But that is no reason why we should despair," said Manoel, "still less why we should give up our search."

"Will it be necessary," exclaimed Benito, "to search the river throughout its breadth and its length?"

"Throughout its breadth, perhaps," answered Araujo, "throughout its length, no - fortunately."

"And why?" asked Manoel.

"Because the Amazon, about a mile away from its junction with the Rio Negro, makes a sudden bend, and at the same time its bed rises, so that there is a kind of natural barrier, well known to sailors as the Bar of Frias, which things floating near the surface are alone able to clear. In short, the currents are ponded back, and they cannot possibly have any effect over this depression."

This was fortunate, it must be admitted. But was Araujo mistaken? The old pilot of the Amazon could be relied on. For the thirty years that he had followed his profession the crossing of the Bar of Frias, where the current was increased in force by its decrease in depth, had often given him trouble. The narrowness of the channel and the elevation of the bed made the passage exceedingly difficult, and many a raft had there come to grief.

And so Araujo was right in declaring that if the corpse of Torres was still retained by its weight on the sandy bed of the river, it could not have been dragged over the bar. It is true that later on, when, on account of the expansion of the gases, it would again rise to the surface, the current would bear it away, and it would then be irrevocably lost down the stream, a long way beyond the obstruction. But this purely physical effect would not take place for several days.

They could not have applied to a man who was more skillful or more conversant with the locality than Araujo, and when he affirmed that the body could not have been borne out of the narrow channel for more than a mile or so, they were sure to recover it if they thoroughly sounded that portion of the river.

Not an island, not an islet, checked the course of the Amazon in these parts. Hence, when the foot of the two banks had been visited up to the bar, it was in the bed itself, about five hundred feet in width, that more careful investigations had to be commenced.

The way the work was conducted was this. The boats taking the right and left of the Amazon lay alongside the banks. The reeds and vegetation were tried with the poles. Of the smallest ledges in the banks in which a body could rest, not one escaped the scrutiny of Araujo and his Indians.

But all this labor produced no result, and half the day had elapsed without the body being brought to the surface of the stream.

An hour's rest was given to the Indians. During this time they partook of some refreshment, and then they returned to their task.

Four of the boats, in charge of the pilot, Benito, Fragoso, and Manoel, divided the river between the Rio Negro and the Bar of Frias into four portions. They set to work to explore its very bed. In certain places the poles proved insufficient to thoroughly search among the deeps, and hence a few dredges - or rather harrows, made of stones and old iron, bound round with a solid bar - were taken on board, and when the boats had pushed off these rakes were thrown in and the river bottom stirred up in every direction.

It was in this difficult task that Benito and his companions were employed till the evening. The ubas and pirogues, worked by the oars, traversed the whole surface of the river up to the bar of Frias.

There had been moments of excitement during this spell of work, when the harrows, catching in something at the bottom, offered some slight resistance. They were then hauled up, but in place of the body so eagerly searched for, there would appear only heavy stones or tufts of herbage which they had dragged from their sandy bed. No one, however, had an idea of giving up the enterprise. They none of them thought of themselves in this work of salvation. Benito, Manoel, Araujo had not even to stir up the Indians or to encourage them. The gallant fellows knew that they were working for the fazender of

Iquitos - for the man whom they loved, for the chief of the excellent family who treated their servants so well.

Yes; and so they would have passed the night in dragging the river. Of every minute lost all knew the value.

A little before the sun disappeared, Araujo, finding it useless to continue his operations in the gloom, gave the signal for the boats to join company and return together to the confluence of the Rio Negro and regain the jangada.

The work so carefully and intelligently conducted was not, however, at an end.

Manoel and Fragoso, as they came back, dared not mention their ill success before Benito. They feared that the disappointment would only force him to some act of despair.

But neither courage nor coolness deserted the young fellow; he was determined to follow to the end this supreme effort to save the honor and the life of his father, and he it was who addressed his companions, and said: "To-morrow we will try again, and under better conditions if possible."

"Yes," answered Manoel; "you are right, Benito. We can do better. We cannot pretend to have entirely explored the river along the whole of the banks and over the whole of its bed."

"No; we cannot have done that," replied Araujo; "and I maintain what I said - that the body of Torres is there, and that it is there because it has not been carried away, because it could not be drawn over the Bar of Frias, and because it will take many days before it rises to the surface and floats down the stream. Yes, it is there, and not a demijohn of tafia will pass my lips until I find it!"

This affirmation from the pilot was worth a good deal, and was of a hope-inspiring nature.

However, Benito, who did not care so much for words as he did for things, thought proper to reply, "Yes, Araujo; the body of Torres is in the river, and we shall find it if -- "

"If?" said the pilot.

"If it has not become the prey of the alligators!"

Manoel and Fragoso waited anxiously for Araujo's reply.

The pilot was silent for a few moments; they felt that he was reflecting before he spoke. "Mr. Benito," he said at length, "I am not in the habit of speaking lightly. I had the same idea as you; but listen. During the ten hours we have been at work have you seen a single cayman in the river?"

"Not one," said Fragoso.

"If you have not seen one," continued the pilot, "it was because there were none to see, for these animals have nothing to keep them in the white waters when, a quarter of a mile off, there are large stretches of the black waters, which they so greatly prefer. When the raft was attacked by some of these creatures it was in a part where there was no place for them to flee to. Here it is quite different. Go to the Rio Negro, and there you will see caymans by the score. Had Torres' body fallen into that tributary there might be no chance of recovering it. But it was in the Amazon that it was lost, and in the Amazon it will be found."

Benito, relieved from his fears, took the pilot's hand and shook it, and contented himself with the reply, "To-morrow, my friends!"

Ten minutes later they were all on board the jangada. During the day Yaquit had passed some hours with her husband. But before she started, and when she saw neither the pilot, nor Manoel, nor Benito, nor the boats, she had guessed the search on which they had gone, but she said nothing to Joam Dacosta, as she hoped that in the morning she would be able to inform him of their success.

But when Benito set foot on the raft she perceived that their search had been fruitless. However, she advanced toward him. "Nothing?" she asked.

"Nothing," replied Benito. "But the morrow is left to us."

The members of the family retired to their rooms, and nothing more was said as to what had passed.

Manoel tried to make Benito lie down, so as to take a few hours' rest.

"What is the good of that?" asked Benito. "Do you think I could sleep?"

CHAPTER IX

THE SECOND ATTEMPT

ON THE MORROW, the 27th of August, Benito took Manoel apart, before the sun had risen, and said to him: "Our yesterday's search was vain. If we begin again under the same conditions we may be just as unlucky."

"We must do so, however," replied Manoel.

"Yes," continued Benito; "but suppose we do not find the body, can you tell me how long it will be before it rises to the surface?"

"If Torres," answered Manoel, "had fallen into the water living, and not mortally wounded, it would take five or six days; but as he only disappeared after being so wounded, perhaps two or three days would be enough to bring him up again."

This answer of Manoel, which was quite correct, requires some explanation. Every human body which falls into the water will float if equilibrium is established between its density and that of its liquid bed. This is well known to be the fact, even when a person does not know how to swim. Under such circumstances, if you are entirely submerged, and only keep your mouth and nose away from the water, you are sure to float. But this is not generally done. The first movement of a drowning man is to try and hold as much as he can of himself above the water; he holds up his head and lifts up his arms, and these parts of his body, being no longer supported by the liquid, do not lose that amount of weight which they would do if completely immersed. Hence an excess of weight, and eventually entire submersion, for the water makes its way to the lungs through the mouth, takes the place of the air which fills them, and the body sinks to the bottom.

On the other hand, when the man who falls into the water is already dead the conditions are different, and more favorable for his floating, for then the movements of which we have spoken are checked, and the liquid does not make its way to the lungs so copiously, as there is no attempt to respire, and he is consequently more likely to promptly reappear. Manoel then was right in drawing the distinction between the man who falls into the water living and the man who falls into it dead. In the one case the return to the surface takes much longer than in the other.

The reappearance of the body after an immersion more or less prolonged is always determined by the decomposition, which causes the gases to form. These bring about the expansion of the cellular tissues, the volume augments and the weight decreases, and then, weighing less than the water it displaces, the body attains the proper conditions for floating.

"And thus," continued Manoel, "supposing the conditions continue favorable, and Torres did not live after he fell into the water, if the decomposition is not modified by circumstances which we cannot foresee, he will not reappear before three days."

"We have not got three days," answered Benito. "We cannot wait, you know; we must try again, and in some new way."

"What can you do?" answered Manoel.

"Plunge down myself beneath the waters," replied Benito, "and search with my eyes - with my hands."

"Plunge in a hundred times - a thousand times!" exclaimed Manoel. "So be it. I think, like you, that we ought to go straight at what we want, and not struggle on with poles and drags like a blind man who only works by touch. I also think that we cannot wait three days. But to jump in, come up again, and go down again will give only a short period for the exploration. No; it will never do, and we shall only risk a second failure."

"Have you no other plan to propose, Manoel?" asked Benito, looking earnestly at his friend.

"Well, listen. There is what would seem to be a Providential circumstance that may be of use to us."

"What is that?"

"Yesterday, as we hurried through Manaos, I noticed that they were repairing one of the quays on the bank of the Rio Negro. The submarine works were being carried on with the aid of a diving-dress. Let us borrow, or hire, or buy, at any price, this apparatus, and then we may resume our researches under more favorable conditions."

"Tell Araujo, Fragoso, and our men, and let us be off," was the instant reply of Benito.

The pilot and the barber were informed of the decision with regard to Manoel's project. Both were ordered to go with the four boats and the Indians to the basin of Frias, and there to wait for the two young men.

Manoel and Benito started off without losing a moment, and reached the quay at Manaos. There they offered the contractor such a price that he put the apparatus at their service for the whole day.

"Will you not have one of my men," he asked, "to help you?"

"Give us your foreman and one of his mates to work the air-pump," replied Manoel.

"But who is going to wear the diving-dress?"

"I am," answered Benito.

"You!" exclaimed Manoel.

"I intend to do so."

It was useless to resist.

An hour afterward the raft and all the instruments necessary for the enterprise had drifted down to the bank where the boats were waiting.

The diving-dress is well known. By its means men can descend beneath the waters and remain there a certain time without the action of the lungs being in any way injured. The diver is clothed in a waterproof suit of India rubber, and his feet are attached to leaden shoes, which allow him to retain his upright position beneath the surface. At the collar of the dress, and about the height of the neck, there is fitted a collar of copper, on which is screwed a metal globe with a glass front. In this globe the diver places his head, which he can move about at his ease. To the globe are attached two pipes; one used for carrying off the air ejected from the lungs, and which is unfit for respiration, and the other in communication with a pump worked on the raft, and bringing in the fresh air. When the diver is at work the raft remains immovable above him; when the diver moves about on the bottom of the river the raft follows his movements, or he follows those of the raft, according to his convenience.

These diving-dresses are now much improved, and are less dangerous than formerly. The man beneath the liquid mass can easily bear the additional pressure, and if anything was to be feared below the waters it was rather some cayman who might there be met with. But, as had been observed by Araujo, not one of these amphibians had been seen, and they are well known to prefer the black waters of the tributaries of the Amazon. Besides, in case of danger, the diver has always his check-string fastened to the raft, and at the least warning can be quickly hauled to the surface.

Benito, invariably very cool once his resolution was taken, commenced to put his idea into execution, and got into the diving dress. His head disappeared in the metal globe, his hand grasped a sort of iron spear with which to stir up the vegetation and detritus accumulated in the river bed, and on his giving the signal he was lowered into the stream.

The men on the raft immediately commenced to work the air-pump, while four Indians from the jangada, under the orders of Araujo, gently propelled it with their long poles in the desired direction.

The two pirogues, commanded one by Fragoso, the other by Manoel, escorted the raft, and held themselves ready to start in any direction, should Benito find the corpse of Torres and again bring it to the surface of the Amazon.

CHAPTER X

A CANNON SHOT

BENITO THEN HAD disappeared beneath the vast sheet which still covered the corpse of the adventurer. Ah! If he had had the power to divert the waters of the river, to turn them into vapor, or to drain them off - if he could have made the Frias basin dry down stream, from the bar up to the influx of the Rio Negro, the case hidden in Torres' clothes would already have been in his hand! His father's innocence would have been recognized! Joam Dacosta, restored to liberty, would have again started on the descent of the river, and what terrible trials would have been avoided!

Benito had reached the bottom. His heavy shoes made the gravel on the bed crunch beneath him. He was in some ten or fifteen feet of water, at the base of the cliff, which was here very steep, and at the very spot where Torres had disappeared.

Near him was a tangled mass of reeds and twigs and aquatic plants, all laced together, which assuredly during the researches of the previous day no pole could have penetrated. It was consequently possible that the body was entangled among the submarine shrubs, and still in the place where it had originally fallen.

Hereabouts, thanks to the eddy produced by the prolongation of one of the spurs running out into the stream, the current was absolutely *nil*. Benito guided his movements by those of the raft, which the long poles of the Indians kept just over his head.

The light penetrated deep through the clear waters, and the magnificent sun, shining in a cloudless sky, shot its rays down into them unchecked. Under ordinary conditions, at a depth of some twenty feet in water, the view becomes exceedingly blurred, but here the waters seemed to be impregnated with a luminous fluid, and Benito was able to descend still lower without the darkness concealing the river bed.

The young man slowly made his way along the bank. With his iron-shod spear he probed the plants and rubbish accumulated along its foot. Flocks of fish, if we can use such an expression, escaped on all sides from the dense thickets like flocks of birds. It seemed as though the thousand pieces of a broken mirror glimmered through the waters. At the same time scores of crustaceans scampered over the sand, like huge ants hurrying from their hills.

Notwithstanding that Benito did not leave a single point of the river unexplored, he never caught sight of the object of his search. He noticed, however, that the slope of the river bed was very abrupt, and he concluded that Torres had rolled beyond the eddy toward the center of the stream. If so, he would probably still recover the body, for the current could hardly touch it at the depth, which was already great, and seemed sensibly to increase. Benito then resolved to pursue his investigations on the side where he had begun to probe the vegetation. This was why he continued to advance in that direction, and the raft had to follow him during a quarter of an hour, as had been previously arranged.

The quarter of an hour had elapsed, and Benito had found nothing. He felt the need of ascending to the surface, so as to once more experience those physiological conditions in which he could recoup his strength. In certain spots, where the depth of the river necessitated it, he had had to descend about thirty feet. He had thus to support a pressure almost equal to an atmosphere, with the result of the physical fatigue and mental agitation which attack those who are not used to this kind of work. Benito then pulled the communication cord, and the men on the raft commenced to haul him in, but they worked slowly, taking a minute to draw him up two or three feet so as not to produce in his internal organs the dreadful effects of decompression.

As soon as the young man had set foot on the raft the metallic sphere of the diving-dress was raised, and he took a long breath and sat down to rest.

The pirogues immediately rowed alongside. Manoel, Fragoso, and Araujo came close to him, waiting for him to speak.

"Well?" asked Manoel.

"Still nothing! Nothing!"

"Have you not seen a trace?"

"Not one!"

"Shall I go down now?"

"No, Manoel," answered Benito; "I have begun; I know where to go. Let me do it!"

Benito then explained to the pilot that his intention was to visit the lower part of the bank up to the Bar of Frias, for there the slope had perhaps stopped the corpse, if, floating between the two streams, it had in the least degree been affected by the current. But first he wanted to skirt the bank and carefully explore a sort of hole formed in the slope of the bed, to the bottom of which the poles had evidently not been able to penetrate. Araujo approved of this plan, and made the necessary preparations.

Manoel gave Benito a little advice. "As you want to pursue your search on that side," he said, "the raft will have to go over there obliquely; but mind what you are doing, Benito. That is much deeper than where you have been yet; it may be fifty or sixty feet, and you will have to support a pressure of quite two atmospheres. Only venture with extreme caution, or you may lose your presence of mind, or no longer know where you are or what to do. If your head feels as if in a vice, and your ears tingle, do not hesitate to give us the signal, and we will at once haul you up. You can then begin again if you like, as you will have got accustomed to move about in the deeper parts of the river."

Benito promised to attend to these hints, of which he recognized the importance. He was particularly struck with the fact that his presence of mind might abandon him at the very moment he wanted it most.

Benito shook hands with Manoel; the sphere of the diving-dress was again screwed to his neck, the pump began to work, and the diver once more disappeared beneath the stream.

The raft was then taken about forty feet along the left bank, but as it moved toward the center of the river the current increased in strength, the ubas were moored, and the rowers kept it from drifting, so as only to allow it to advance with extreme slowness.

Benito descended very gently, and again found himself on the firm sand. When his heels touched the ground it could be seen, by the length of the haulage cord, that he was at a depth of some sixty-five or seventy feet. He was therefore in a considerable hole, excavated far below the ordinary level.

The liquid medium was more obscure, but the limpidity of these transparent waters still allowed the light to penetrate sufficiently for Benito to distinguish the objects scattered on the bed of the river, and to approach them with some safety. Besides, the sand, sprinkled with mica flakes, seemed to form a sort of reflector, and the very grains could be counted glittering like luminous dust.

Benito moved on, examining and sounding the smallest cavities with his spear. He continued to advance very slowly; the communication cord was paid out, and as the pipes which served for the inlet and outlet of the air were never tightened, the pump was worked under the proper conditions.

Benito turned off so as to reach the middle of the bed of the Amazon, where there was the greatest depression. Sometimes profound obscurity thickened around him, and then he could see nothing, so feeble was the light; but this was a purely passing phenomenon, and due to the raft, which, floating above his head, intercepted the solar rays and made the night replace the day. An instant afterward the huge shadow would be dissipated, and the reflection of the sands appear again in full force.

All the time Benito was going deeper. He felt the increase of the pressure with which his body was wrapped by the liquid mass. His respiration became less easy; the retractibility of his organs no longer worked with as much ease as in the midst of an atmosphere more conveniently adapted for them. And so he found himself under the action of physiological effects to which he was unaccustomed. The rumbling grew louder in his ears, but as his thought was always lucid, as he felt that the action of his brain was quite clear - even a little more so than usual - he delayed giving the signal for return, and continued to go down deeper still.

Suddenly, in the subdued light which surrounded him, his attention was attracted by a confused mass. It seemed to take the form of a corpse, entangled beneath a clump of aquatic plants. Intense excitement seized him. He stepped toward the mass; with his spear he felt it. It was the carcass of a huge cayman, already reduced to a skeleton, and which the current of the Rio Negro had swept into the bed of the Amazon. Benito recoiled, and, in spite of the assertions of the pilot, the thought recurred to him that some living cayman might even then be met with in the deeps near the Bar of Frias!

But he repelled the idea, and continued his progress, so as to reach the bottom of the depression.

And now he had arrived at a depth of from eighty to a hundred feet, and consequently was experiencing a pressure of three atmospheres. If, then, this cavity was also drawn blank, he would have to suspend his researches.

Experience has shown that the extreme limit for such submarine explorations lies between a hundred and twenty and a hundred and thirty feet, and that below this there is great danger, the human organism not only being hindered from performing his functions under such a pressure, but the apparatus failing to keep up a sufficient supply of air with the desirable regularity.

But Benito was resolved to go as far as his mental powers and physical energies would let him. By some strange presentiment he was drawn toward this abyss; it seemed to him as though the corpse was very likely to have rolled to the bottom of the hole, and that Torres, if he had any heavy things about him, such as a belt containing either money or arms, would have sunk to the very lowest point. Of a sudden, in a deep hollow, he saw a body through the gloom! Yes! A corpse, still clothed, stretched out like a man asleep, with his arms folded under his head!

Was that Torres? In the obscurity, then very dense, he found it difficult to see; but it was a human body that lay there, less than ten paces off, and perfectly motionless!

A sharp pang shot through Benito. His heart, for an instant, ceased to beat. He thought he was going to lose consciousness. By a supreme effort he recovered himself. He stepped toward the corpse.

Suddenly a shock as violent as unexpected made his whole frame vibrate! A long whip seemed to twine round his body, and in spite of the thick diving-dress he felt himself lashed again and again.

"A gymnotus!" he said.

It was the only word that passed his lips.

In fact, it was a *"puraque,"* the name given by the Brazilians to the gymnotus, or electric snake, which had just attacked him.

It is well known that the gymnotus is a kind of eel, with a blackish, slimy skin, furnished along the back and tail with an apparatus composed of plates joined by vertical lamellæ, and acted on by nerves of considerable power. This apparatus is endowed with singular electrical properties, and is apt to produce very formidable results. Some of these gymnotuses are about the length of a common snake, others are about ten feet long, while others, which, however, are rare, even reach fifteen or twenty feet, and are from eight to ten inches in diameter.

Gymnotuses are plentiful enough both in the Amazon and its tributaries; and it was one of these living coils, about ten feet long, which, after uncurving itself like a bow, again attacked the diver.

Benito knew what he had to fear from this formidable animal. His clothes were powerless to protect him. The discharges of the gymnotus, at first somewhat weak, become more and more violent, and there would come a time when, exhausted by the shocks, he would be rendered powerless.

Benito, unable to resist the blows, half-dropped upon the sand. His limbs were becoming paralyzed little by little under the electric influences of the gymnotus, which lightly touched his body as it wrapped him in its folds. His arms even he could not lift, and soon his spear escaped him, and his hand had not strength enough left to pull the cord and give the signal.

Benito felt that he was lost. Neither Manoel nor his companions could suspect the horrible combat which was going on beneath them between the formidable puraque and the unhappy diver, who only fought to suffer, without any power of defending himself.

And that at the moment when a body - the body of Torres without a doubt! - had just met his view.

By a supreme instinct of self-preservation Benito uttered a cry. His voice was lost in the metallic sphere from which not a sound could escape!

And now the puraque redoubled its attacks; it gave forth shock after shock, which made Benito writhe on the sand like the sections of a divided worm, and his muscles were wrenched again and again beneath the living lash.

Benito thought that all was over; his eyes grew dim, his limbs began to stiffen.

But before he quite lost his power of sight and reason he became the witness of a phenomenon, unexpected, inexplicable, and marvelous in the extreme.

A deadened roar resounded through the liquid depths. It was like a thunder-clap, the reverberations of which rolled along the river bed, then violently agitated by the electrical discharges of the gymnotus. Benito felt himself bathed as it were in the dreadful booming which found an echo in the very deepest of the river depths.

And then a last cry escaped him, for fearful was the vision which appeared before his eyes!

The corpse of the drowned man which had been stretched on the sand arose! The undulations of the water lifted up the arms, and they swayed about as if with some peculiar animation. Convulsive throbs made the movement of the corpse still more alarming.

It was indeed the body of Torres. One of the suns rays shot down to it through the liquid mass, and Benito recognized the bloated, ashy features of the scoundrel who fell by his own hand, and whose last breath had left him beneath the waters.

And while Benito could not make a single movement with his paralyzed limbs, while his heavy shoes kept him down as if he had been nailed to the sand, the corpse straightened itself up, the head swayed to and fro, and disentangling itself from the hole in which it had been kept by a mass of aquatic weeds, it slowly ascended to the surface of the Amazon.

CHAPTER XI

THE CONTENTS OF THE CASE

WHAT WAS it that had happened? A purely physical phenomenon, of which the following is the explanation.

The gunboat Santa Ana, bound for Manaos, had come up the river and passed the bar at Frias. Just before she reached the *embouchure* of the Rio Negro she hoisted her colors and saluted the Brazilian flag. At the report vibrations were produced along the surface of the stream, and these vibrations making their way down to the bottom of the river, had been sufficient to raise the corpse of Torres, already lightened by the commencement of its decomposition and the distension of its cellular system. The body of the drowned man had in the ordinary course risen to the surface of the water.

This well-known phenomenon explains the reappearance of the corpse, but it must be admitted that the arrival of the Santa Ana was a fortunate coincidence.

By a shout from Manoel, repeated by all his companions, one of the pirogues was immediately steered for the body, while the diver was at the same time hauled up to the raft.

Great was Manoel's emotion when Benito, drawn on to the platform, was laid there in a state of complete inertia, not a single exterior movement betraying that he still lived.

Was not this a second corpse which the waters of the Amazon had given up?

As quickly as possible the diving-dress was taken off him.

Benito had entirely lost consciousness beneath the violent shocks of the gymnotus.

Manoel, distracted, called to him, breathed into him, and endeavored to recover the heart's pulsation.

"It beats! It beats!" he exclaimed.

Yes! Benito's heart did still beat, and in a few minutes Manoel's efforts restored him to life.

"The body! the Body!"

Such were the first words, the only ones which escaped from Benito's lips.

"There it is!" answered Fragoso, pointing to a pirogue then coming up to the raft with the corpse.

"But what has been the matter, Benito?" asked Manoel. "Has it been the want of air?"

"No!" said Benito; "a puraque attacked me! But the noise? The detonation?"

"A cannon shot!" replied Manoel. "It was the cannon shot which brought the corpse to the surface."

At this moment the pirogue came up to the raft with the body of Torres, which had been taken on board by the Indians. His sojourn in the water had not disfigured him very much. He was easily recognizable, and there was no doubt as to his identity.

Fragoso, kneeling down in the pirogue, had already begun to undo the clothes of the drowned man, which came away in fragments.

At the moment Torres' right arm, which was now left bare, attracted his attention. On it there appeared the distinct scar of an old wound produced by a blow from a knife.

"That scar!" exclaimed Fragoso. "But - that is good! I remember now -- "

"What?" demanded Manoel.

"A quarrel! Yes! a quarrel I witnessed in the province of Madeira three years ago. How could I have forgotten it! This Torres was then a captain of the woods. Ah! I know now where I had seen him, the scoundrel!"

"That does not matter to us now!" cried Benito. "The case! the case! Has he still got that?" and Benito was about to tear away the last coverings of the corpse to get at it.

Manoel stopped him.

"One moment, Benito," he said; and then, turning to the men on the raft who did not belong to the jangada, and whose evidence could not be suspected at any future time:

"Just take note, my friends," he said, "of what we are doing here, so that you can relate before the magistrate what has passed."

The men came up to the pirogue.

Fragoso undid the belt which encircled the body of Torres underneath the torn poncho, and feeling his breast-pocket, exclaimed:

"The case!"

A cry of joy escaped from Benito. He stretched forward to seize the case, to make sure than it contained --

"No!" again interrupted Manoel, whose coolness did not forsake him. "It is necessary that not the slightest possible doubt should exist in the mind of the magistrate! It is better that disinterested witnesses should affirm that this case was really found on the corpse of Torres!"

"You are right," replied Benito.

"My friend," said Manoel to the foreman of the raft, "just feel in the pocket of the waistcoat."

The foreman obeyed. He drew forth a metal case, with the cover screwed on, and which seemed to have suffered in no way from its sojourn in the water.

"The paper! Is the paper still inside?" exclaimed Benito, who could not contain himself.

"It is for the magistrate to open this case!" answered Manoel. "To him alone belongs the duty of verifying that the document was found within it."

"Yes, yes. Again you are right, Manoel," said Benito. "To Manaos, my friends - to Manaos!"

Benito, Manoel, Fragoso, and the foreman who held the case, immediately jumped into one of the pirogues, and were starting off, when Fragoso said:

"And the corpse?"

The pirogue stopped.

In fact, the Indians had already thrown back the body into the water, and it was drifting away down the river.

"Torres was only a scoundrel," said Benito. "If I had to fight him, it was God that struck him, and his body ought not to go unburied!"

And so orders were given to the second pirogue to recover the corpse, and take it to the bank to await its burial.

But at the same moment a flock of birds of prey, which skimmed along the surface of the stream, pounced on the floating body. They were urubus, a kind of small vulture, with naked necks and long claws, and black as crows. In South America they are known as gallinazos, and their voracity is unparalleled. The body, torn open by their beaks, gave forth the gases which inflated it, its density increased, it sank down little by little, and for the last time what remained of Torres disappeared beneath the waters of the Amazon.

Ten minutes afterward the pirogue arrived at Manaos. Benito and his companions jumped ashore, and hurried through the streets of the town. In a few minutes they had reached the dwelling of Judge Jarriuez, and informed him, through one of his servants, that they wished to see him immediately.

The judge ordered them to be shown into his study.

There Manoel recounted all that had passed, from the moment when Torres had been killed until the moment when the case had been found on his corpse, and taken from his breast-pocket by the foreman.

Although this recital was of a nature to corroborate all that Joam Dacosta had said on the subject of Torres, and of the bargain which he had endeavored to make, Judge Jarriquez could not restrain a smile of incredulity.

"There is the case, sir," said Manoel. "For not a single instant has it been in our hands, and the man who gives it to you is he who took it from the body of Torres."

The magistrate took the case and examined it with care, turning it over and over as though it were made of some precious material. Then he shook it, and a few coins inside sounded with a metallic ring. Did not, then, the case contain the document which had been so much sought after - the document written in the very hand of the true author of the crime of Tijuco, and which Torres had wished to sell at such an ignoble price to Joam Dacosta? Was this material proof of the convict's innocence irrevocably lost?

We can easily imagine the violent agitation which had seized upon the spectators of this scene. Benito could scarcely utter a word, he felt his heart ready to burst. "Open it, sir! open the case!" he at last exclaimed, in a broken voice.

Judge Jarriquez began to unscrew the lid; then, when the cover was removed, he turned up the case, and from it a few pieces of gold dropped out and rolled on the table.

"But the paper! the paper!" again gasped Benito, who clutched hold of the table to save himself from falling.

The magistrate put his fingers into the case and drew out, not without difficulty, a faded paper, folded with care, and which the water did not seem to have even touched.

"The document! that is the document!" shouted Fragoso; "that is the very paper I saw in the hands of Torres!"

Judge Jarriquez unfolded the paper and cast his eyes over it, and then he turned it over so as to examine it on the back and the front, which were both covered with writing. "A document it really is!" said he; "there is no doubt of that. It is indeed a document!"

"Yes," replied Benito; "and that is the document which proves my father's innocence!"

"I do not know that," replied Judge Jarriquez; "and I

am much afraid it will be very difficult to know it."

"Why?" exclaimed Benito, who became pale as death.

"Because this document is a cryptogram, and -"

"Well?"

"We have not got the key!"

CHAPTER XII

THE DOCUMENT

THIS WAS a contingency which neither Joam Dacosta nor his people could have anticipated. In fact, as those who have not forgotten the first scene in this story are aware, the document was written in a disguised form in one of the numerous systems used in cryptography.

But in which of them?

To discover this would require all the ingenuity of which the human brain was capable.

Before dismissing Benito and his companions, Judge Jarriquez had an exact copy made of the document, and, keeping the original, handed it over to them after due comparison, so that they could communicate with the prisoner.

Then, making an appointment for the morrow, they retired, and not wishing to lose an instant in seeing Joam Dacosta, they hastened on to the prison, and there, in a short interview, informed him of all that had passed.

Joam Dacosta took the document and carefully examined it. Shaking his head, he handed it back to his son. "Perhaps," he said, "there is therein written the proof I shall never be able to produce. But if that proof escapes me, if the whole tenor of my life does not plead for me, I have nothing more to expect from the justice of men, and my fate is in the hands of God!"

And all felt it to be so. If the document remained indecipherable, the position of the convict was a desperate one.

"We shall find it, father!" exclaimed Benito. "There never was a document of this sort yet which could stand examination. Have confidence - yes, confidence! Heaven has, so to speak, miraculously given us the paper which vindicates you, and, after guiding our hands to recover it, it will not refuse to direct our brains to unravel it."

Joam Dacosta shook hands with Benito and Manoel, and then the three young men, much agitated, retired to the jangada, where Yaquita was awaiting them.

Yaquita was soon informed of what had happened since the evening - the reappearance of the body of Torres, the discovery of the document, and the strange form under which the real culprit, the companion of the adventurer, had thought proper to write his confession - doubtless, so that it should not compromise him if it fell into strange hands.

Naturally, Lina was informed of this unexpected complication, and of the discovery made by Fragoso that Torres was an old captain of the woods belonging to the gang who were employed about the mouths of the Madeira.

"But under what circumstances did you meet him?" asked the young mulatto.

"It was during one of my runs across the province of Amazones," replied Fragoso, "when I was going from village to village, working at my trade."

"And the scar?"

"What happened was this: One day I arrived at the mission of Aranas at the moment that Torres, whom I had never before seen, had picked a quarrel with one of his comrades - and a bad lot they are! - and this quarrel ended with a stab from a knife, which entered the arm of the captain of the woods. There was no doctor there, and so I took charge of the wound, and that is how I made his acquaintance."

"What does it matter after all," replied the young girl, "that we know what Torres had been? He was not the author of the crime, and it does not help us in the least."

"No, it does not," answered Fragoso; "for we shall end by reading the document, and then the innocence of Joam Dacosta will be palpable to the eyes of all."

This was likewise the hope of Yaquita, of Benito, of Manoel, and of Minha, and, shut up in the house, they passed long hours in endeavoring to decipher the writing.

But if it was their hope - and there is no need to insist on that point - it was none the less that of Judge Jarriquez.

After having drawn up his report at the end of his examination establishing the identity of Joam Dacosta, the magistrate had sent it off to headquarters, and therewith he thought he had finished with the affair so far as he was concerned. It could not well be otherwise.

On the discovery of the document, Jarriquez suddenly found himself face to face with the study of which he was a master. He, the seeker after numerical combinations, the solver of amusing problems, the answerer of charades, rebuses, logogryphs, and such things, was at last in his true element.

At the thought that the document might perhaps contain the justification of Joam Dacosta, he felt all the instinct of the analyst aroused. Here, before his very eyes, was a cryptogram! And so from that moment he thought of nothing but how to discover its meaning, and it is scarcely necessary to say that he made up his mind to work at it continuously, even if he forgot to eat or to drink.

After the departure of the young people, Judge Jarriquez installed himself in his study. His door, barred against every one, assured him of several hours of perfect solitude. His spectacles were on his nose, his snuff-box on the table. He took a good pinch so as to develop the finesse and sagacity of his mind. He picked up the document and became absorbed in meditation, which soon became materialized in the shape of a monologue. The worthy justice was one of those unreserved men who think more easily aloud than to himself. "Let us proceed with method," he said. "No method, no logic; no logic, no success."

Then, taking the document, he ran through it from beginning to end, without understanding it in the least.

The document contained a hundred lines, which were divided into half a dozen paragraphs.

"Hum!" said the judge, after a little reflection; "to try every paragraph, one after the other, would be to lose precious time, and be of no use. I had better select one of these paragraphs, and take the one which is likely to prove the most interesting. Which of them would do this better than the last, where the recital of the whole affair is probably summed up? Proper names might put me on the track, among others that of Joam Dacosta; and if he had anything to do with this document, his name will evidently not be absent from its concluding paragraph."

The magistrate's reasoning was logical, and he was decidedly right in bringing all his resources to bear in the first place on the gist of the cryptogram as contained in its last paragraph.

Here is the paragraph, for it is necessary to again bring it before the eyes of the reader so as to show how an analyst set to work to discover its meaning.

"P h y j s l y d d q f d z x g a s g z z q q e h x g k f n d r x u j u g l o c y t d x v k s b x h h u y p o h d v y r y m h u h p u y d k j o x p h e t o z l s l e t n p m v f f o v p d p a j x h y y n o j y g g a y m e q y n f u q l n m v l y f g s u z m q I z t l b q q y u g s q e u b v n r c r e d g r u z b l r m x y u h q h p z d r r g c r o h e p q x u f I v v r p l p h o n t h v d d q f h q s n t z h h h n f e p m q k y u u e x k t o g z g k y u u m f v I j d q d p z j q s y k r p l x h x q r y m v k l o h h h o t o z v d k s p p s u v j h d."

At the outset, Judge Jarrizuez noticed that the lines of the document were not divided either into words or phrases, and that there was a complete absence of punctuation. This fact could but render the reading of the document more difficult.

"Let us see, however," he said, "if there is not some assemblage of letters which appears to form a word - I mean a pronounceable word, whose number of consonants is in proportion to its vowels. And at the beginning I see the word *phy*; further on the word *gas*. Halloo! *ujugi*. Does that mean the African town on the banks of Tanganyika? What has that got to do with all this? Further on here is the word *ypo*. Is it Greek, then? Close by here is *rym* and *puy*, and *jox*, and *phetoz*, and *jyggay*, and *mv*, and *qruz*. And before that we have got *red* and *let*. That is good! those are two English words. Then *ohe - syk;* then *rym* once more, and then the word *oto.*"

Judge Jarriquez let the paper drop, and thought for a few minutes.

"All the words I see in this thing seem queer!" he said. "In fact, there is nothing to give a clue to their origin. Some look like Greek, some like Dutch; some have an English twist, and some look like nothing at all! To say nothing of these series of consonants which are not wanted in any human pronunciation. Most assuredly it will not be very easy to find the key to this cryptogram."

The magistrate's fingers commenced to beat a tattoo on his desk - a kind of reveille to arouse his dormant faculties.

"Let us see," he said, "how many letters there are in the paragraph."

He counted them, pen in hand.

"Two hundred and seventy-six!" he said. "Well, now let us try what proportion these different letters bear to each other."

This occupied him for some time. The judge took up the document, and, with his pen in his hand, he noted each letter in alphabetical order.

In a quarter of an hour he had obtained the following table:

a = 3 times
b = 4 -
c = 3 -
d = 16 -
e = 9 -
f = 10 -
g = 13 -
h = 23 -
i = 4 -
j = 8 -
k = 9 -
l = 9 -
m = 9 -
n = 9 -
o = 12 -
p = 16 -
q = 16 -
r = 12 -
s = 10 -
t = 8 -

Jules Verne

$u = 17$ -
$v = 13$ -
$x = 12$ -
$y = 19$ -
$z = 12$ -
- - - - - - - -
Total . . . 276 times.

"Ah, ah!" he exclaimed. "One thing strikes me at once, and that is that in this paragraph all the letters of the alphabet are not used. That is very strange. If we take up a book and open it by chance it will be very seldom that we shall hit upon two hundred and seventy-six letters without all the signs of the alphabet figuring among them. After all, it may be chance," and then he passed to a different train of thought. "One important point is to see if the vowels and consonants are in their normal proportion."

And so he seized his pen, counted up the vowels, and obtained the following result:

$a = 3$ times
$e = 9$ -
$i = 4$ -
$o = 12$ -
$u = 17$ -
$y = 19$ -
- - - - - - - -
Total . . . 276 times.

"And thus there are in this paragraph, after we have done our subtraction, sixty-four vowels and two hundred and twelve consonants. Good! that is the normal proportion. That is about a fifth, as in the alphabet, where there are six vowels among twenty-six letters. It is possible, therefore, that the document is written in the language of our country, and that only the signification of each letter is changed. If it has been modified in regular order, and a *b* is always represented by an *l,* and *o* by a *v* a *g* by a *k*, an *u* by an *r,* etc., I will give up my judgeship if I do not read it. What can I do better than follow the method of that great analytical genius, Edgar Allan Poe?"

Judge Jarriquez herein alluded to a story by the great American romancer, which is a masterpiece. Who has not read the "Gold Bug?" In this novel a cryptogram, composed of ciphers, letters, algebraic signs, asterisks, full-stops, and commas, is submitted to a truly mathematical analysis, and is deciphered under extraordinary conditions, which the admirers of that strange genius can never forget. On the reading of the American document depended only a treasure, while on that of this one depended a man's life. Its solution was consequently all the more interesting.

The magistrate, who had often read and re-read his "Gold Bug," was perfectly acquainted with the steps in the analysis so minutely described by Edgar Poe, and he resolved to proceed in the same way on this occasion. In doing so he was certain, as he had said, that if the value or signification of each letter remained constant, he would, sooner or later, arrive at the solution of the document.

"What did Edgar Poe do?" he repeated. "First of all he began by finding out the sign - here there are only letters, let us say the letter - which was reproduced the oftenest. I see that that is *h,* for it is met with twenty-three times. This enormous proportion shows, to begin with, that *h* does not stand for *h*, but, on the contrary, that it represents the letter which recurs most frequently in our language, for I suppose the document is written in Portuguese. In English or French it would certainly be *e,* in Italian it would be *i* or *a,* in Portuguese it will be *a* or *o.* Now let us say that it signifies *a* or *o.* "

After this was done, the judge found out the letter which recurred most frequently after *h,* and so on, and he formed the following table:

h = 23 times
y = 19 -
u = 17 -
$d\,p\,q$ = 16 -
$g\,v$ = 13 -
$o\,r\,x\,z$ = 12 -
$f\,s$ = 10 -
$e\,k\,l\,m\,n$ = 9 -
$j\,t$ = 8 -
$b\,i$ = 8 -
$a\,c$ = 8 -

"Now the letter *a* only occurs thrice!" exclaimed the judge, "and it ought to occur the oftenest. Ah! that clearly proves that the meaning had been changed. And now, after *a* or *o,* what are the letters which figure oftenest in our language? Let us see," and Judge Jarriquez, with truly remarkable sagacity, which denoted a very observant mind, started on this new quest. In this he was only imitating the American romancer, who, great analyst as he was, had, by simple induction, been able to construct an alphabet corresponding to the signs of the cryptogram and by means of it to eventually read the pirate's parchment note with ease.

The magistrate set to work in the same way, and we may affirm that he was no whit inferior to his illustrious master. Thanks to his previous work at logogryphs and squares, rectangular arrangements and other enigmas, which depend only on an arbitrary disposition of the letters, he was already pretty strong in such mental pastimes. On this occasion he sought to establish the order in which the letters were reproduced - vowels first, consonants afterward.

Three hours had elapsed since he began. He had before his eyes an alphabet which, if his procedure were right, would give him the right meaning of the letters in the document. He had only to successively apply the letters of his alphabet to those of his paragraph. But before making this application some slight emotion seized upon the judge. He fully experienced the intellectual gratification - much greater than, perhaps, would be thought - of the man who, after hours of obstinate endeavor, saw the impatiently sought-for sense of the logogryph coming into view.

"Now let us try," he said; "and I shall be very much surprised if I have not got the solution of the enigma!"

Judge Jarriquez took off his spectacles and wiped the glasses; then he put them back again and bent over the table. His special alphabet was in one hand, the cryptogram in the other. He commenced to write under the first line of the paragraph the true letters, which, according to him, ought to correspond exactly with each of the cryptographic letters. As with the first line so did he with the second, and the third, and the fourth, until he reached the end of the paragraph.

Oddity as he was, he did not stop to see as he wrote if

the assemblage of letters made intelligible words. No; during the first stage his mind refused all verification of that sort. What he desired was to give himself the ecstasy of reading it all straight off at once.

And now he had done.

"Let us read!" he exclaimed.

And he read. Good heavens! what cacophony! The lines he had formed with the letters of his alphabet had no more sense in them that those of the document! It was another series of letters, and that was all. They formed no word; they had no value. In short, they were just as hieroglyphic.

"Confound the thing!" exclaimed Judge Jarriquez.

CHAPTER XIII

IS IT A MATTER OF FIGURES?

IT WAS SEVEN o'clock in the evening. Judge Jarriquez had all the time been absorbed in working at the puzzle - and was no further advanced - and had forgotten the time of repast and the time of repose, when there came a knock at his study door.

It was time. An hour later, and all the cerebral substance of the vexed magistrate would certainly have evaporated under the intense heat into which he had worked his head.

At the order to enter - which was given in an impatient tone - the door opened and Manoel presented himself.

The young doctor had left his friends on board the jangada at work on the indecipherable document, and had come to see Judge Jarriquez. He was anxious to know if he had been fortunate in his researches. He had come to ask if he had at length discovered the system on which the cryptogram had been written.

The magistrate was not sorry to see Manoel come in. He was in that state of excitement that solitude was exasperating to him. He wanted some one to speak to, some one as anxious to penetrate the mystery as he was. Manoel was just the man.

"Sir," said Manoel as he entered, "one question! Have you succeeded better than we have?"

"Sit down first," exclaimed Judge Jarriquez, who got up and began to pace the room. "Sit down. If we are both of us standing, you will walk one way and I shall walk the other, and the room will be too narrow to hold us."

Manoel sat down and repeated his question.

"No! I have not had any success!" replied the magistrate; "I do not think I am any better off. I have got nothing to tell you; but I have found out a certainty."

"What is that, sir?"

"That the document is not based on conventional signs, but on what is known in cryptology as a cipher, that is to say, on a number."

"Well, sir," answered Manoel, "cannot a document of that kind always be read?"

"Yes," said Jarriquez, "if a letter is invariably represented by the same letter; if an *a*, for example, is always a *p*, and a *p* is always an *x*; if not, it cannot."

"And in this document?"

"In this document the value of the letter changes with the arbitrarily selected cipher which necessitates it. So a *b* will in one place be represented by a *k* will later on become a *z*, later on an *u* or an *n* or an *f*, or any other letter."

"And then?"

"And then, I am sorry to say, the cryptogram is indecipherable."

"Indecipherable!" exclaimed Manoel. "No, sir; we shall end by finding the key of the document on which the man's life depends."

Manoel had risen, a prey to the excitement he could not control; the reply he had received was too hopeless, and he refused to accept it for good.

At a gesture from the judge, however, he sat down again, and in a calmer voice asked:

"And in the first place, sir, what makes you think that the basis of this document is a number, or, as you call it, a cipher?"

"Listen to me, young man," replied the judge, "and you will be forced to give in to the evidence."

The magistrate took the document and put it before the eyes of Manoel and showed him what he had done.

"I began," he said, "by treating this document in the proper way, that is to say, logically, leaving nothing to chance. I applied to it an alphabet based on the proportion the letters bear to one another which is usual in our language, and I sought to obtain the meaning by following the precepts of our immortal analyst, Edgar Poe. Well, what succeeded with him collapsed with me."

"Collapsed!" exclaimed Manoel.

"Yes, my dear young man, and I at once saw that success sought in that fashion was impossible. In truth, a stronger man than I might have been deceived."

"But I should like to understand," said Manoel, "and I do not -- "

"Take the document," continued Judge Jarriquez; "first look at the disposition of the letters, and read it through."

Manoel obeyed.

"Do you not see that the combination of several of the letters is very strange?" asked the magistrate.

"I do not see anything," said Manoel, after having for perhaps the hundredth time read through the document.

"Well! study the last paragraph! There you understand the sense of the whole is bound to be summed up. Do you see anything abnormal?"

"Nothing."

"There is, however, one thing which absolutely proves that the language is subject to the laws of number."

"And that is?"

"That is that you see three *h's* coming together in two different places."

What Jarriquez said was correct, and it was of a nature to attract attention. The two hundred and fourth, two hundred and fifth, and two hundred and sixth letters of the paragraph, and the two hundred and fifty-eight, two hundred and fifty-ninth, and two hundred and sixtieth letters of the paragraph were consecutive *h's*. At first this peculiarity had not struck the magistrate.

"And that proves?" asked Manoel, without divining the deduction that could be drawn from the combination.

"That simply proves that the basis of the document is a number. It shows *à priori* that each letter is modified in virtue of the ciphers of the number and according to the place which it occupies."

"And why?"

"Because in no language will you find words with three consecutive repetitions of the letter *h.*"

Manoel was struck with the argument; he thought about it, and, in short, had no reply to make.

"And had I made the observation sooner," continued the magistrate, "I might have spared myself a good deal of trouble and a headache which extends from my occiput to my sinciput."

"But, sir," asked Manoel, who felt the little hope vanishing on which he had hitherto rested, "what do you mean by a cipher?"

"Tell me a number."

"Any number you like."

"Give me an example and you will understand the explanation better."

Judge Jarriquez sat down at the table, took up a sheet of paper and a pencil, and said:

"Now, Mr. Manoel, let us choose a sentence by chance, the first that comes; for instance:

Judge Jarriquez has an ingenious mind.

I write this phrase so as to space the letters different and I get:

Judgejarriquezhasaningeniousmind.

"That done," said the magistrate, to whom the phrase seemed to contain a proposition beyond dispute, looking Manoel straight in the face, "suppose I take a number by chance, so as to give a cryptographic form to this natural succession of words; suppose now this word is composed of three ciphers, and let these ciphers be 2, 3, and 4. Now on the line below I put the number 234, and repeat it as many times as are necessary to get to the end of the phrase, and so that every cipher comes underneath a letter. This is what we get:

J u d g e j a r r I q u e z h a s a n I n g e n I o u s m I n
d 2 3 4 2 3 4 2 3 4 2 3 4 2 3 4 2 3 4 2 3 4 2 3 4 2 3 4 2 3 4 2
3 4 2 3 4 And now, Mr. Manoel, replacing each letter by the letter in advance of it in alphabetical order according to the value of the cipher, we get:

$$j + 2 = l$$
$$u + 3 = x$$

$$d + 4 = h$$
$$g + 2 = i$$
$$e + 3 = h$$
$$j + 4 = n$$
$$a + 2 = c$$
$$r + 3 = u$$
$$r + 4 = v$$
$$i + 2 = k$$
$$q + 3 = t$$
$$u + 4 = y$$
$$e + 2 = g$$
$$a + 3 = c$$
$$h + 4 = t$$
$$a + 2 = c$$
$$s + 3 = v$$
$$a + 4 = e$$
$$n + 2 = p$$
$$i + 3 = l$$
$$n + 4 = r$$
$$g + 2 = i$$
$$e + 3 = h$$
$$n + 4 = r$$
$$i + 2 = k$$
$$o + 3 = r$$
$$u + 4 = y$$
$$s + 2 = u$$

and so on.

"If, on account of the value of the ciphers which compose the number I come to the end of the alphabet without having enough complementary letters to deduct, I begin again at the beginning. That is what happens at the end of my name when the z is replaced by the 3. As after z the alphabet has no more letters, I commence to count from a, and so get the c. That done, when I get to the end of this cryptographic system, made up of the 234 - which was arbitrarily selected, do not forget! - the phrase which you recognize above is replaced by

lxhihncuvktygclveplrihrkryupmpg.

"And now, young man, just look at it, and do you not think it is very much like what is in the document? Well, what is the consequence? Why, that the signification of the letters depends on a cipher which chance puts beneath them, and the cryptographic letter which answers to a true one is not always the same. So in this phrase the first *j* is represented by an *l* the second by an *n;* the first *e* by an *h,* the second b a *g,* the third by an *h*; the first *d* is represented by an *h* the last by a *g;* the first *u* by an *x,* the last by a *y;* the first and second *a's* by a *c,* the last by an *e;* and in my own name one *r* is represented by a *u,* the other by a *v.* and so on. Now do you see that if you do not know the cipher 234 you will never be able to read the lines, and consequently if we do not know the number of the document it remains undecipherable."

On hearing the magistrate reason with such careful logic, Manoel was at first overwhelmed, but, raising his head, he exclaimed:

"No, sir, I will not renounce the hope of finding the number!"

"We might have done so," answered Judge Jarriquez, "if the lines of the document had been divided into words."

"And why?"

"For this reason, young man. I think we can assume that in the last paragraph all that is written in these earlier paragraphs is summed up. Now I am convinced that in it will be found the name of Joam Dacosta. Well, if the lines had been divided into words, in trying the words one after the other - I mean the words composed of seven letters, as the name of Dacosta is - it would not have been impossible to evolve the number which is the key of the document."

"Will you explain to me how you ought to proceed to do that, sir?" asked Manoel, who probably caught a glimpse of one more hope.

"Nothing can be more simple," answered the judge. "Let us take, for example, one of the words in the sentence we have just written - my name, if you like. It is represented in the cryptogram by this queer succession of letters, *ncuvktygc*. Well, arranging these letters in a column, one under the other, and then placing against them the letters of my name and deducting one from the other the numbers of their places in alphabetical order, I see the following result:

$$\text{Between } n \text{ and } j \text{ we have 4 letters}$$
$$- c - a - 2 -$$
$$- u - r - 3 -$$
$$- v - r - 4 -$$
$$- k - i - 2 -$$
$$- t - q - 3 -$$
$$- y - u - 4 -$$
$$- g - e - 2 -$$
$$- c - z - 3 -$$

"Now what is the column of ciphers made up of that we have got by this simple operation? Look here! 423

423 423, that is to say, of repetitions of the numbers 423, or 234, or 342."

"Yes, that is it!" answered Manoel.

"You understand, then, by this means, that in calculating the true letter from the false, instead of the false from the true, I have been able to discover the number with ease; and the number I was in search of is really the 234 which I took as the key of my cryptogram."

"Well, sir!" exclaimed Manoel, "if that is so, the name of Dacosta is in the last paragraph; and taking successively each letter of those lines for the first of the seven letters which compose his name, we ought to get -- "

"That would be impossible," interrupted the judge, "except on one condition."

"What is that?"

"That the first cipher of the number should happen to be the first letter of the word Dacosta, and I think you will agree with me that that is not probable."

"Quite so!" sighed Manoel, who, with this improbability, saw the last chance vanish.

"And so we must trust to chance alone," continued Jarriquez, who shook his head, "and chance does not often do much in things of this sort."

"But still," said Manoel, "chance might give us this number."

"This number," exclaimed the magistrate - "this number? But how many ciphers is it composed of? Of two, or three, or four, or nine, or ten? Is it made of different ciphers only or of ciphers in different order many times repeated? Do you not know, young man, that with the ordinary ten ciphers, using all at a time, but without any repetition, you can make three million two hundred and sixty-eight thousand and eight hundred different numbers, and that if you use the same cipher more than once in the number, these millions of combinations will be enormously increased! And do you not know that if we employ every one of the five hundred and twenty-five thousand and six hundred minutes of which the year is composed to try at each of these numbers, it would take you six years, and that you would want three centuries if each operation took you an hour? No! You ask the impossible!"

"Impossible, sir?" answered Manoel. "An innocent man has been branded as guilty, and Joam Dacosta is to lose his life and his honor while you hold in your hands the material proof of his innocence! That is what is impossible!"

"Ah! young man!" exclaimed Jarriquez, "who told you, after all, that Torres did not tell a lie? Who told you that he really did have in his hands a document written by the author of the crime? that this paper was the document, and that this document refers to Joam Dacosta?"

"Who told me so?" repeated Manoel, and his face was hidden in his hands.

In fact, nothing could prove for certain that the

document had anything to do with the affair in the diamond province. There was, in fact, nothing to show that it was not utterly devoid of meaning, and that it had been imagined by Torres himself, who was as capable of selling a false thing as a true one!

"It does not matter, Manoel," continued the judge, rising; "it does not matter! Whatever it may be to which the document refers, I have not yet given up discovering the cipher. After all, it is worth more than a logogryph or a rebus!"

At these words Manoel rose, shook hands with the magistrate, and returned to the jangada, feeling more hopeless when he went back than when he set out.

CHAPTER XIV

CHANCE!

A COMPLETE change took place in public opinion on the subject of Joam Dacosta. To anger succeeded pity. The population no longer thronged to the prison of Manaos to roar out cries of death to the prisoner. On the contrary, the most forward of them in accusing him of being the principal author of the crime of Tijuco now averred that he was not guilty, and demanded his immediate restoration to liberty. Thus it always is with the mob - from one extreme they run to the other. But the change was intelligible.

The events which had happened during the last few days - the struggle between Benito and Torres; the search for the corpse, which had reappeared under such extraordinary circumstances; the finding of the "indecipherable" document, if we can so call it; the information it concealed, the assurance that it contained, or rather the wish that it contained, the material proof of the guiltlessness of Joam Dacosta; and the hope that it was written by the real culprit - all these things had contributed to work the change in public opinion. What the people had desired and impatiently demanded forty-eight hours before, they now feared, and that was the arrival of the instructions due from Rio de Janeiro.

These, however, were not likely to be delayed.

Joam Dacosta had been arrested on the 24th of August, and examined next day. The judge's report was sent off on the 26th. It was now the 28th. In three or four days more the minister would have come to a decision regarding the convict, and it was only too certain that justice would take its course.

There was no doubt that such would be the case. On the other hand, that the assurance of Dacosta's innocence would appear from the document, was not doubted by anybody, neither by his family nor by the fickle population of Manaos, who excitedly followed the phases of this dramatic affair.

But, on the other hand, in the eyes of disinterested or indifferent persons who were not affected by the event, what value could be assigned to this document? and how could they even declare that it referred to the crime in the diamond arrayal? It existed, that was undeniable; it had been found on the corpse of Torres, nothing could be more certain. It could even be seen, by comparing it with the letter in which Torres gave the information about Joam Dacosta, that the document was not in the handwriting of the adventurer. But, as had been suggested by Judge Jarriquez, why should not the scoundrel have invented it for the sake of his bargain? And this was less unlikely to be the case, considering that Torres had declined to part with it until after his marriage with Dacosta's daughter - that is to say, when it would have been impossible to undo an accomplished fact.

All these views were held by some people in some form, and we can quite understand what interest the affair created. In any case, the situation of Joam Dacosta was most hazardous. If the document were not deciphered, it would be just the same as if it did not exist; and if the secret of the cryptogram were not miraculously divined or revealed before the end of the three days, the supreme sentence would inevitably be suffered by the doomed man of Tijuco. And this miracle a man attempted to perform! The man was Jarriquez, and he now really set to work more in the interest of Joam Dacosta than for the satisfaction of his analytical faculties. A complete change had also taken place in his opinion. Was not this man, who had voluntarily abandoned his retreat at Iquitos, who had come at the risk of his life to demand his rehabilitation at the hands of Brazilian justice, a moral enigma worth all the others put together? And so the judge had resolved never to leave the document until he had discovered the cipher. He set to work at it in a fury. He ate no more; he slept no more! All his time was passed in inventing combinations of numbers, in forging a key to force this lock!

This idea had taken possession of Judge Jarriquez's brain at the end of the first day. Suppressed frenzy consumed him, and kept him in a perpetual heat. His whole house trembled; his servants, black or white, dared not come near him. Fortunately he was a bachelor; had there been a Madame Jarriquez she would have had a very uncomfortable time of it. Never had a problem so taken possession of this oddity, and he had thoroughly made up his mind to get at the solution, even if his head exploded like an overheated boiler under the tension of its vapor.

It was perfectly clear to the mind of the worthy magistrate that the key to the document was a number, composed of two or more ciphers, but what this number was all investigation seemed powerless to discover.

This was the enterprise on which Jarriquez, in quite a fury, was engaged, and during this 28th of August he brought all his faculties to bear on it, and worked away almost superhumanly.

To arrive at the number by chance, he said, was to lose himself in millions of combinations, which would absorb the life of a first-rate calculator. But if he could in no respect reckon on chance, was it impossible to proceed by reasoning? Decidedly not! And so it was "to reason till he became unreasoning" that Judge Jarriquez gave himself up after vainly seeking repose in a few hours of sleep. He who ventured in upon him at this moment, after braving the formal defenses which protected his solitude, would have found him, as on the day before, in his study, before his desk, with the document under his eyes, the thousands of letters of which seemed all jumbled together and flying about his head.

"Ah!" he explained, "why did not the scoundrel who wrote this separate the words in this paragraph? We might - we will try - but no! However, if there is anything here about the murder and the robbery, two or three words there must be in it - 'arrayal,' 'diamond,' 'Tijuco,' 'Dacosta,' and others; and in putting down their cryptological equivalents the number could be arrived at. But there is nothing - not a single break! - not one word by itself! One word of two hundred and seventy-six letters! I hope the wretch may be blessed two hundred and seventy-six times for complicating his system in this way! He ought to be hanged two hundred and seventy-six times!"

And a violent thump with his fist on the document emphasized this charitable wish.

"But," continued the magistrate, "if I cannot find one of the words in the body of the document, I might at least try my hand at the beginning and end of each paragraph. There may be a chance there that I ought not to miss."

And impressed with this idea Judge Jarriquez successively tried if the letters which commenced or . finished the different paragraphs could be made to correspond with those which formed the most important word, which was sure to be found somewhre, that of *Dacosta*.

He could do nothing of the kind.

In fact, to take only the last paragraph with which he began, the formula was:

$$P = D$$
$$h = a$$
$$y = c$$
$$f = o$$
$$s = s$$
$$l = t$$
$$y = a$$

Now, at the very first letter Jarriquez was stopped in his calculations, for the difference in alphabetical position between the *d* and the *p* gave him not one cipher, but two, namely, 12, and in this kind of cryptograph only one letter can take the place of another.

It was the same for the seven last letters of the paragraph, *p s u v j h d,* of which the series also commences with a *p,* and which in no case could stand for the *d* in *Dacosta,* because these letters were in like manner twelve spaces apart.

So it was not his name that figured here.

The same observation applies to the words *arrayal* and *Tijuco,* which were successively tried, but whose construction did not correspond with the cryptographic series.

After he had got so far, Judge Jarriquez, with his head nearly splitting, arose and paced his office, went for fresh air to the window, and gave utterance to a growl, at the noise of which a flock of hummingbirds, murmuring among the foliage of a mimosa tree, betook themselves to flight. Then he returned to the document.

He picked it up and turned it over and over.

"The humbug! the rascal!" he hissed; "it will end by driving me mad! But steady! Be calm! Don't let our spirits go down! This is not the time!"

And then, having refreshed himself by giving his head a thorough sluicing with cold water:

"Let us try another way," he said, "and as I cannot hit upon the number from the arrangement of the letters, let us see what number the author of the document would have chosen in confessing that he was the author of the crime at Tijuco."

This was another method for the magistrate to enter upon, and maybe he was right, for there was a certain amount of logic about it.

"And first let us try a date! Why should not the culprit have taken the date of the year in which Dacosta, the innocent man he allowed to be sentenced in his own place, was born? Was he likely to forget a number which was so important to him? Then Joam Dacosta was born in 1804. Let us see what 1804 will give us as a cryptographical number."

And Judge Jarriquez wrote the first letters of the paragraph, and putting over them the number 1804 repeated thrice, he obtained

1804 1804 1804
phyj slyd dqfd

Then in counting up the spaces in alphabetical order, he obtained

s.yf rdy. cif.

And this was meaningless! And he wanted three letters which he had to replace by points, because the ciphers, 8, 4, and 4, which command the three letters, *h, d,* and *d,* do not give corresponding letters in ascending the series.

"That is not it again!" exclaimed Jarriquez. "Let us try another number."

And he asked himself, if instead of this first date the author of the document had not rather selected the date of the year in which the crime was committed.

This was in 1826.

And so proceeding as above, he obtained.

1826 1826 1826
phyj slyd dqfd

and that gave

o.vd rdv. cid.

the same meaningless series, the same absence of
sense, as many letters wanting as in the former
instance, and for the same reason.

"Bother the number!" exclaimed the magistrate. "We
must give it up again. Let us have another one! Perhaps
the rascal chose the number of contos representing the
amount of the booty!"

Now the value of the stolen diamonds was estimated at
eight hundred and thirty-four contos, or about
2,500,000 francs, and so the formula became

834 834 834 834
phy jsl ydd qfd

and this gave a result as little gratifying as the others --

het bph pa. ic.

"Confound the document and him who imagined it!"
shouted Jarriquez, throwing down the paper, which
was wafted to the other side of the room. "It would try
the patience of a saint!"

But the short burst of anger passed away, and the magistrate, who had no idea of being beaten, picked up the paper. What he had done with the first letters of the different paragraphs he did with the last - and to no purpose. Then he tried everything his excited imagination could suggest.

He tried in succession the numbers which represented Dacosta's age, which would have been known to the author of the crime, the date of his arrest, the date of the sentence at the Villa Rica assizes, the date fixed for the execution, etc., etc., even the number of victims at the affray at Tijuco!

Nothing! All the time nothing!

Judge Jarriquez had worked himself into such a state of exasperation that there really was some fear that his mental faculties would lose their balance. He jumped about, and twisted about, and wrestled about as if he really had got hold of his enemy's body. Then suddenly he cried, "Now for chance! Heaven help me now, logic is powerless!"

His hand seized a bell-pull hanging near his table. The bell rang furiously, and the magistrate strode up to the door, which he opened. "Bobo!" he shouted.

A moment or two elapsed.

Bobo was a freed negro, who was the privileged servant of Jarriquez. He did not appear; it was evident that Bobo was afraid to come into his master's room.

Another ring at the bell; another call to Bobo, who, for his own safety, pretended to be deaf on this occasion.

Jules Verne

And now a third ring at the bell, which unhitched the crank and broke the cord.

This time Bobo came up. "What is it, sir?" asked Bobo, prudently waiting on the threshold.

"Advance, without uttering a single word!" replied the judge, whose flaming eyes made the negro quake again.

Bobo advanced.

"Bobo," said Jarriquez, "attend to what I say, and answer immediately; do not even take time to think, or I -- "

Bobo, with fixed eyes and open mouth, brought his feet together like a soldier and stood at attention.

"Are you ready?" asked his master.

"I am."

"Now, then, tell me, without a moment's thought - you understand - the first number than comes into your head."

"76223," answered Bobo, all in a breath. Bobo thought he would please his master by giving him a pretty large one!

Judge Jarriquez had run to the table, and, pencil in hand, had made out a formula with the number given by Bobo, and which Bobo had in this way only given him at a venture.

It is obvious that it was most unlikely that a number such as 76223 was the key of the document, and it produced no other result than to bring to the lips of Jarriquez such a vigorous ejaculation that Bobo disappeared like a shot!

CHAPTER XV

THE LAST EFFORTS

THE MAGISTRATE, however, was not the only one who passed his time unprofitably. Benito, Manoel, and Minha tried all they could together to extract the secret from the document on which depended their father's life and honor. On his part, Fragoso, aided by Lina, could not remain quiet, but all their ingenuity had failed, and the number still escaped them.

"Why don't you find it, Fragoso?" asked the young mulatto.

"I will find it," answered Fragoso.

And he did not find it!

Here we should say that Fragoso had an idea of a project of which he had not even spoken to Lina, but which had taken full possession of his mind. This was to go in search of the gang to which the ex-captain of the woods had belonged, and to find out who was the probable author of this cipher document, which was supposed to be the confession of the culprit of Tijuco. The part of the Amazon where these people were employed, the very place where Fragoso had met Torres a few years before, was not very far from

Manaos. He would only have to descend the river for about fifty miles, to the mouth of the Madeira, a tributary coming in on the right, and there he was almost sure to meet the head of these *"capitaes do mato,"* to which Torres belonged. In two days, or three days at the outside, Fragoso could get into communication with the old comrades of the adventurer.

"Yes! I could do that," he repeated to himself; "but what would be the good of it, supposing I succeeded? If we are sure that one of Torres' companions has recently died, would that prove him to be the author of this crime? Would that show that he gave Torres a document in which he announced himself the author of this crime, and exonerated Joam Dacosta? Would that give us the key of the document? No! Two men only knew the cipher - the culprit and Torres! And these two men are no more!"

So reasoned Fragoso. It was evident that his enterprise would do no good. But the thought of it was too much for him. An irresistible influence impelled him to set out, although he was not even sure of finding the band on the Madeira. In fact, it might be engaged in some other part of the province, and to come up with it might require more time than Fragoso had at his disposal! And what would be the result?

It is none the less true, however, that on the 29th of August, before sunrise, Fragoso, without saying anything to anybody, secretly left the jangada, arrived at Manaos, and embarked in one of the egariteas which daily descend the Amazon.

And great was the astonishment when he was not seen on board, and did not appear during the day. No one, not even Lina, could explain the absence of so devoted a servant at such a crisis.

Some of them even asked, and not without reason, if the poor fellow, rendered desperate at having, when he met him on the frontier, personally contributed to bringing Torres on board the raft, had not made away with himself.

But if Fragoso could so reproach himself, how about Benito? In the first place at Iquitos he had invited Torres to visit the fazenda; in the second place he had brought him on board the jangada, to become a passenger on it; and in the third place, in killing him, he had annihilated the only witness whose evidence could save the condemned man.

And so Benito considered himself responsible for everything - the arrest of his father, and the terrible events of which it had been the consequence.

In fact, had Torres been alive, Benito could not tell but that, in some way or another, from pity or for reward, he would have finished by handing over the document. Would not Torres, whom nothing could compromise, have been persuaded to speak, had money been brought to bear upon him? Would not the long-sought-for proof have been furnished to the judge? Yes, undoubtedly! And the only man who could have furnished this evidence had been killed through Benito!

Such was what the wretched man continually repeated to his mother, to Manoel, and to himself. Such were the cruel responsibilities which his conscience laid to his charge.

Between her husband, with whom she passed all the time that was allowed her, and her son, a prey to despair which made her tremble for his reason, the brave Yaquita lost none of her moral energy. In her they found the valiant daughter of Magalhaës, the worthy wife of the fazender of Iquitos.

The attitude of Joam Dacosta was well adapted to sustain her in this ordeal. That gallant man, that rigid Puritan, that austere worker, whose whole life had been a battle, had not yet shown a moment of weakness.

The most terrible blow which had struck him without prostrating him had been the death of Judge Ribeiro, in whose mind his innocence did not admit of a doubt. Was it not with the help of his old defender that he had hoped to strive for his rehabilitation? The intervention of Torres he had regarded throughout as being quite secondary for him. And of this document he had no knowledge when he left Iquitos to hand himself over to the justice of his country. He only took with him moral proofs. When a material proof was unexpectedly produced in the course of the affair, before or after his arrest, he was certainly not the man to despise it. But if, on account of regrettable circumstances, the proof disappeared, he would find himself once more in the same position as when he passed the Brazilian frontier - the position of a man who came to say, "Here is my past life; here is my present; here is an entirely honest existence of work and devotion which I bring you. You passed on me at first an erroneous judgment. After twenty-three years of exile I have come to give myself up! Here I am; judge me again!"

The death of Torres, the impossibility of reading the

document found on him, had thus not produced on Joam Dacosta the impression which it had on his children, his friends, his household, and all who were interested in him.

"I have faith in my innocence," he repeated to Yaquita, "as I have faith in God. If my life is still useful to my people, and a miracle is necessary to save me, that miracle will be performed; if not, I shall die! God alone is my judge!"

The excitement increased in Manaos as the time ran on; the affair was discussed with unexampled acerbity. In the midst of this enthrallment of public opinion, which evoked so much of the mysterious, the document was the principal object of conversation.

At the end of this fourth day not a single person doubted but that it contained the vindication of the doomed man. Every one had been given an opportunity of deciphering its incomprehensible contents, for the "Diario d'o Grand Para" had reproduced it in facsimile. Autograph copies were spread about in great numbers at the suggestion of Manoel, who neglect nothing that might lead to the penetration of the mystery - not even chance, that "nickname of Providence," as some one has called it.

In addition, a reward of one hundred contos (or three hundred thousand francs) was promised to any one who could discover the cipher so fruitlessly sought after - and read the document. This was quite a fortune, and so people of all classes forgot to eat, drink, or sleep to attack this unintelligible cryptogram.

Up to the present, however, all had been useless, and

probably the most ingenious analysts in the world would have spent their time in vain. It had been advertised that any solution should be sent, without delay, to Judge Jarriquez, to his house in God-the-Son Street; but the evening of the 29th of August came and none had arrived, nor was any likely to arrive.

Of all those who took up the study of the puzzle, Judge Jarriquez was one of the most to be pitied. By a natural association of ideas, he also joined in the general opinion that the document referred to the affair at Tijuco, and that it had been written by the hand of the guilty man, and exonerated Joam Dacosta. And so he put even more ardor into his search for the key. It was not only the art for art's sake which guided him, it was a sentiment of justice, of pity toward a man suffering under an unjust condemnation. If it is the fact that a certain quantity of phosphorus is expended in the work of the brain, it would be difficult to say how many milligrammes the judge had parted with to excite the network of his "sensorium," and after all, to find out nothing, absolutely nothing.

But Jarriquez had no idea of abandoning the inquiry. If he could only now trust to chance, he would work on for that chance. He tried to evoke it by all means possible and impossible. He had given himself over to fury and anger, and, what was worse, to impotent anger!

During the latter part of this day he had been trying different numbers - numbers selected arbitrarily - and how many of them can scarcely be imagined. Had he had the time, he would not have shrunk from plunging into the millions of combinations of which the ten symbols of numeration are capable. He would have given his whole life to it at the risk of going mad before the year was out. Mad! was he not that already? He had had the idea that the document might be read through the paper, and so he turned it round and exposed it to the light, and tried it in that way.

Nothing! The numbers already thought of, and which he tried in this new way, gave no result. Perhaps the document read backward, and the last letter was really the first, for the author would have done this had he wished to make the reading more difficult.

Nothing! The new combination only furnished a series of letters just as enigmatic.

At eight o'clock in the evening Jarriquez, with his face in his hands, knocked up, worn out mentally and physically, had neither strength to move, to speak, to think, or to associate one idea with another.

Suddenly a noise was heard outside. Almost immediately, notwithstanding his formal orders, the door of his study was thrown open. Benito and Manoel were before him, Benito looking dreadfully pale, and Manoel supporting him, for the unfortunate young man had hardly strength to support himself.

The magistrate quickly arose.

"What is it, gentlemen? What do you want?" he asked.

"The cipher! the cipher!" exclaimed Benito, mad with grief - "the cipher of the document."

"Do you know it, then?" shouted the judge.

"No, sir," said Manoel. "But you?"

"Nothing! nothing!"

"Nothing?" gasped Benito, and in a paroxysm of despair he took a knife from his belt and would have plunged it into his breast had not the judge and Manoel jumped forward and managed to disarm him.

"Benito," said Jarriquez, in a voice which he tried to keep calm, "if you father cannot escape the expiation of a crime which is not his, you could do something better than kill yourself."

"What?" said Benito.

"Try and save his life!"

"How?"

"That is for you to discover," answered the magistrate, "and not for me to say."

CHAPTER XVI

PREPARATIONS

ON THE FOLLOWING day, the 30th of August, Benito and Manoel talked matters over together. They had understood the thought to which the judge had not dared to give utterance in their presence, and were engaged in devising some means by which the condemned man could escape the penalty of the law.

Nothing else was left for them to do. It was only too certain that for the authorities at Rio Janeiro the undeciphered document would have no value whatever, that it would be a dead letter, that the first verdict which declared Joam Dacosta the perpetrator of the crime at Tijuco would not be set aside, and that, as in such cases no commutation of the sentence was possible, the order for his execution would inevitably be received.

Once more, then, Joam Dacosta would have to escape by flight from an unjust imprisonment.

It was at the outset agreed between the two young men that the secret should be carefully kept, and that neither Yaquita nor Minha should be informed of preparations, which would probably only give rise to hopes destined never to be realized. Who could tell if, owing to some unforeseen circumstance, the attempt at escape would not prove a miserable failure?

The presence of Fragoso on such an occasion would have been most valuable. Discreet and devoted, his services would have been most welcome to the two young fellows; but Fragoso had not reappeared. Lina, when asked, could only say that she knew not what had become of him, nor why he had left the raft without telling her anything about it.

And assuredly, had Fragoso foreseen that things would have turned out as they were doing, he would never have left the Dacosta family on an expedition which appeared to promise no serious result. Far better for him to have assisted in the escape of the doomed man than to have hurried off in search of the former comrades of Torres!

But Fragoso was away, and his assistance had to be dispensed with.

At daybreak Benito and Manoel left the raft and proceeded to Manaos. They soon reached the town, and passed through its narrow streets, which at that early hour were quite deserted. In a few minutes they arrived in front of the prison. The waste ground, amid which the old convent which served for a house of detention was built, was traversed by them in all directions, for they had come to study it with the utmost care.

Fifty-five feet from the ground, in an angle of the building, they recognized the window of the cell in which Joam Dacosta was confined. The window was secured with iron bars in a miserable state of repair, which it would be easy to tear down or cut through if they could only get near enough. The badly jointed stones in the wall, which were crumbled away every here and there, offered many a ledge for the feet to rest on, if only a rope could be fixed to climb up by. One of the bars had slipped out of its socket, and formed a hook over which it might be possible to throw a rope. That done, one or two of the bars could be removed, so as to permit a man to get through. Benito and Manoel would then have to make their way into the prisoner's room, and without much difficulty the escape could be managed by means of the rope fastened to the projecting iron. During the night, if the sky were very cloudy, none of these operations would be noticed before the day dawned. Joam Dacosta could get safely away.

Manoel and Benito spent an hour about the spot, taking care not to attract attention, but examining the locality with great exactness, particularly as regarded the position of the window, the arrangement of the iron bars, and the place from which it would be best to throw the line.

"That is agreed," said Manoel at length. "And now, ought Joam Dacosta to be told about this?"

"No, Manoel. Neither to him, any more than to my mother, ought we to impart the secret of an attempt in which there is such a risk of failure."

"We shall succeed, Benito!" continued Manoel. "However, we must prepare for everything; and in case the chief of the prison should discover us at the moment of escape -- "

"We shall have money enough to purchase his silence," answered Benito.

"Good!" replied Manoel. "But once your father is out of prison he cannot remain hidden in the town or on the jangada. Where is he to find refuge?"

This was the second question to solve: and a very difficult one it was.

A hundred paces away from the prison, however, the waste land was crossed by one of those canals which flow through the town into the Rio Negro. This canal afforded an easy way of gaining the river if a pirogue were in waiting for the fugitive. From the foot of the wall to the canal side was hardly a hundred yards.

Benito and Manoel decided that about eight o'clock in the evening one of the pirogues, with two strong rowers, under the command of the pilot Araujo, should start from the jangada. They could ascend the Rio Negro, enter the canal, and, crossing the waste land, remain concealed throughout the night under the tall vegetation on the banks.

But once on board, where was Joam Dacosta to seek refuge? To return to Iquitos was to follow a road full of difficulties and peril, and a long one in any case, should the fugitive either travel across the country or by the river. Neither by horse not pirogue could he be got out of danger quickly enough, and the fazenda was no longer a safe retreat. He would not return to it as the fazender, Joam Garral, but as the convict, Joam Dacosta, continually in fear of his extradition. He could never dream of resuming his former life.

To get away by the Rio Negro into the north of the province, or even beyond the Brazilian territory, would require more time than he could spare, and his first care must be to escape from immediate pursuit.

To start again down the Amazon? But stations, village, and towns abounded on both sides of the river. The description of the fugitive would be sent to all the police, and he would run the risk of being arrested long before he reached the Atlantic. And supposing he reached the coast, where and how was he to hide and wait for a passage to put the sea between himself and his pursuers?

On consideration of these various plans, Benito and Manoel agreed that neither of them was practicable. One, however, did offer some chance of safety, and that was to embark in the pirogue, follow the canal into the Rio Negro, descend this tributary under the guidance of the pilot, reach the confluence of the rivers, and run down the Amazon along its right bank for some sixty miles during the nights, resting during the daylight, and so gaining the *embouchure* of the Madeira.

This tributary, which, fed by a hundred affluents, descends from the watershed of the Cordilleras, is a regular waterway opening into the very heart of Bolivia. A pirogue could pass up it and leave no trace of its passage, and a refuge could be found in some town or village beyond the Brazilian frontier. There Joam Dacosta would be comparatively safe, and there for several months he could wait for an opportunity of reaching the Pacific coast and taking passage in some vessel leaving one of its ports; and if the ship were bound for one of the States of North America he would be free. Once there, he could sell the fazenda, leave his country forever, and seek beyond the sea, in the Old World, a final retreat in which to end an existence so cruelly and unjustly disturbed. Anywhere he might go, his family - not excepting Manoel, who was bound to him by so many ties - would assuredly follow without the slightest hesitation.

"Let us go," said Benito; "we must have all ready before night, and we have no time to lose."

The young men returned on board by way of the canal bank, which led along the Rio Negro. They satisfied themselves that the passage of the pirogue would be quite possible, and that no obstacles such as locks or boats under repair were there to stop it. They then descended the left bank of the tributary, avoiding the slowly-filling streets of the town, and reached the jangada.

Benito's first care was to see his mother. He felt sufficiently master of himself to dissemble the anxiety which consumed him. He wished to assure her that all hope was not lost, that the mystery of the document would be cleared up, that in any case public opinion was in favor of Joam, and that, in face of the agitation which was being made in his favor, justice would grant all the necessary time for the production of the material proof his innocence. "Yes, mother," he added, "before to-morrow we shall be free from anxiety."

"May heaven grant it so!" replied Yaquita, and she looked at him so keenly that Benito could hardly meet her glance.

On his part, and as if by pre-arrangement, Manoel had

tried to reassure Minha by telling her that Judge Jarriquez was convinced of the innocence of Joam, and would try to save him by every means in his power.

"I only wish he would, Manoel," answered she, endeavoring in vain to restrain her tears.

And Manoel left her, for the tears were also welling up in his eyes and witnessing against the words of hope to which he had just given utterance.

And now the time had arrived for them to make their daily visit to the prisoner, and Yaquita and her daughter set off to Manaos.

For an hour the young men were in consultation with Araujo. They acquainted him with their plan in all its details, and they discussed not only the projected escape, but the measures which were necessary for the safety of the fugitive.

Araujo approved of everything; he undertook during the approaching night to take the pirogue up the canal without attracting any notice, and he knew its course thoroughly as far as the spot where he was to await the arrival of Joam Dacosta. To get back to the mouth of the Rio Negro was easy enough, and the pirogue would be able to pass unnoticed among the numerous craft continually descending the river.

Araujo had no objection to offer to the idea of following the Amazon down to its confluence with the Madeira. The course of the Madeira was familiar to him for quite two hundred miles up, and in the midst of these thinly-peopled provinces, even if pursuit took place in their direction, all attempts at capture could be easily frustrated; they could reach the interior of Bolivia, and if Joam decided to leave his country he could procure a passage with less danger on the coast of the Pacific than on that of the Atlantic.

Araujo's approval was most welcome to the young fellows; they had great faith in the practical good sense of the pilot, and not without reason. His zeal was undoubted, and he would assuredly have risked both life and liberty to save the fazender of Iquitos.

With the utmost secrecy Araujo at once set about his preparations. A considerable sum in gold was handed over to him by Benito to meet all eventualities during the voyage on the Madeira. In getting the pirogue ready, he announced his intention of going in search of Fragoso, whose fate excited a good deal of anxiety among his companions. He stowed away in the boat provisions for many days, and did not forget the ropes and tools which would be required by the young men when they reached the canal at the appointed time and place.

These preparations evoked no curiosity on the part of the crew of the jangada, and even the two stalwart negroes were not let into the secret. They, however, could be absolutely depended on. Whenever they learned what the work of safety was in which they were engaged - when Joam Dacosta, once more free, was confided to their charge - Araujo knew well that they would dare anything, even to the risk of their own lives, to save the life of their master.

By the afternoon all was ready, and they had only the night to wait for. But before making a start Manoel wished to call on Judge Jarriquez for the last time. The magistrate might perhaps have found out something new about the document. Benito preferred to remain on the raft and wait for the return of his mother and sister.

Manoel then presented himself at the abode of Judge Jarriquez, and was immediately admitted.

The magistrate, in the study which he never quitted, was still the victim of the same excitement. The document crumpled by his impatient fingers, was still there before his eyes on the table.

"Sir," said Manoel, whose voice trembled as he asked the question, "have you received anything from Rio de Janeiro."

"No," answered the judge; "the order has not yet come to hand, but it may at any moment."

"And the document?"

"Nothing yet!" exclaimed he. "Everything my imagination can suggest I have tried, and no result."

"None?"

"Nevertheless, I distinctly see one word in the document - only one!"

"What is that - what is the word?"

"'Fly'!"

Manoel said nothing, but he pressed the hand which

Jarriquez held out to him, and returned to the jangada to wait for the moment of action.

CHAPTER XVII

THE LAST NIGHT

THE VISIT of Yaquita and her daughter had been like all such visits during the few hours which each day the husband and wife spent together. In the presence of the two beings whom Joam so dearly loved his heart nearly failed him. But the husband - the father – retained his self-command. It was he who comforted the two poor women and inspired them with a little of the hope of which so little now remained to him. They had come with the intention of cheering the prisoner. Alas! far more than he they themselves were in want of cheering! But when they found him still bearing himself unflinchingly in the midst of his terrible trial, they recovered a little of their hope.

Once more had Joam spoken encouraging words to them. His indomitable energy was due not only to the feeling of his innocence, but to his faith in that God, a portion of whose justice yet dwells in the hearts of men. No! Joam Dacosta would never lose his life for the crime of Tijuco!

Hardly ever did he mention the document. Whether it were apocryphal or no, whether it were in the hand-writing of Torres or in that of the real perpetrator of the crime, whether it contained or did not contain the longed-for vindication, it was on no such doubtful hypothesis that Joam Dacosta presumed to trust. No; he reckoned on a better argument in his favor, and it was to his long life of toil and honor that he relegated the task of pleading for him.

This evening, then, his wife and daughter, strengthened by the manly words, which thrilled them to the core of their hearts, had left him more confident than they had ever been since his arrest. For the last time the prisoner had embraced them, and with redoubled tenderness. It seemed as though the *dénouement* was nigh.

Joam Dacosta, after they had left, remained for some time perfectly motionless. His arms rested on a small table and supported his head. Of what was he thinking? Had he at last been convinced that human justice, after failing the first time, would at length pronounce his acquittal?

Yes, he still hoped. With the report of Judge Jarriquez establishing his identity, he knew that his memoir, which he had penned with so much sincerity, would have been sent to Rio de Janeiro, and was now in the hands of the chief justice. This memoir, as we know, was the history of his life from his entry into the offices of the diamond arrayal until the very moment when the jangada stopped before Manaos. Joam Dacosta was pondering over his whole career. He again lived his past life from the moment when, as an orphan, he had set foot in Tijuco. There his zeal had raised him high in the offices of the governor-general, into which he had been admitted when still very young. The future smiled on him; he would have filled some important position. Then this sudden catastrophe; the robbery of the diamond convoy, the massacre of the escort, the suspicion directed against him as the only official who could have divulged the secret of the expedition, his arrest, his appearance before the jury, his conviction in spite of all the efforts of his advocate, the last hours spent in the condemned cell at Villa Rica, his escape under conditions which betokened almost superhuman courage, his flight through the northern provinces, his arrival on the Peruvian frontier, and the reception which the starving fugitive had met with from the hospitable fazender Magalhaës.

The prisoner once more passed in review these events, which had so cruelly marred his life. And then, lost in his thoughts and recollections, he sat, regardless of a peculiar noise on the outer wall of the convent, of the jerkings of a rope hitched on to a bar of his window, and of grating steel as it cut through iron, which ought at once to have attracted the attention of a less absorbed man.

Joam Dacosta continued to live the years of his youth after his arrival in Peru. He again saw the fazender, the clerk, the partner of the old Portuguese, toiling hard for the prosperity of the establishment at Iquitos. Ah! why at the outset had he not told all to his benefactor? He would never have doubted him. It was the only error with which he could reproach himself. Why had he not confessed to him whence he had come, and who he was - above all, at the moment when Magalhaës had place in his hand the hand of the daughter who would never have believed that he was the author of so frightful a crime.

And now the noise outside became loud enough to attract the prisoner's attention. For an instant Joam raised his head; his eyes sought the window, but with a vacant look, as though he were unconscious, and the next instant his head again sank into his hands. Again he was in thought back at Iquitos.

There the old fazender was dying; before his end he longed for the future of his daughter to be assured, for his partner to be the sole master of the settlement which had grown so prosperous under his management. Should Dacosta have spoken then? Perhaps; but he dared not do it. He again lived the happy days he had spent with Yaquita, and again thought of the birth of his children, again felt the happiness which had its only trouble in the remembrances of Tijuco and the remorse that he had not confessed his terrible secret.

The chain of events was reproduced in Joam's mind with a clearness and completeness quite remarkable.

And now he was thinking of the day when his daughter's marriage with Manoel had been decided. Could he allow that union to take place under a false name without acquainting the lad with the mystery of his life? No! And so at the advice of Judge Ribeiro he resolved to come and claim the revision of his sentence, to demand the rehabilitation which was his due! He was starting with his people, and then came the intervention of Torres, the detestable bargain proposed by the scoundrel, the indignant refusal of the father to hand over his daughter to save his honor and his life, and then the denunciation and the arrest!

Suddenly the window flew open with a violent push from without.

Joam started up; the souvenire of the past vanished like a shadow.

Benito leaped into the room; he was in the presence of his father, and the next moment Manoel, tearing down the remaining bars, appeared before him.

Joam Dacosta would have uttered a cry of surprise. Benito left him no time to do so.

"Father," he said, "the window grating is down. A rope leads to the ground. A pirogue is waiting for you on the canal not a hundred yards off. Araujo is there ready to take you far away from Manaos, on the other bank of the Amazon where your track will never be discovered. Father, you must escape this very moment! It was the judge's own suggestion!"

"It must be done!" added Manoel.

"Fly! I! - Fly a second time! Escape again?"

And with crossed arms, and head erect, Joam Dacosta stepped forward.

"Never!" he said, in a voice so firm that Benito and Manoel stood bewildered.

The young men had never thought of a difficulty like this. They had never reckoned on the hindrances to escape coming from the prisoner himself.

Benito advanced to his father, and looking him straight in the face, and taking both his hands in his, not to force him, but to try and convince him, said:

"Never, did you say, father?"

"Never!"

"Father," said Manoel - "for I also have the right to call you father - listen to us! If we tell you that you ought to fly without losing an instant, it is because if you remain you will be guilty toward others, toward yourself!"

"To remain," continued Benito, "is to remain to die! The order for execution may come at any moment! If you imagine that the justice of men will nullify a wrong decision, if you think it will rehabilitate you whom it condemned twenty years since, you are mistaken! There is hope no longer! You must escape! Come!"

By an irresistible impulse Benito seized his father and drew him toward the window.

Joam Dacosta struggled from his son's grasp and recoiled a second time.

"To fly," he answered, in the tone of a man whose resolution was unalterable, "is to dishonor myself, and you with me! It would be a confession of my guilt! Of my own free will I surrendered myself to my country's judges, and I will await their decision, whatever that decision may be!"

"But the presumptions on which you trusted are insufficient," replied Manoel, "and the material proof of your innocence is still wanting! If we tell you that you ought to fly, it is because Judge Jarriquez himself told us so. You have now only this one chance left to escape from death!"

"I will die, then," said Joam, in a calm voice. "I will die protesting against the decision which condemned me! The first time, a few hours before the execution - I fled! Yes! I was then young. I had all my life before me in which to struggle against man's injustice! But to save myself now, to begin again the miserable existence of a felon hiding under a false name, whose every effort is required to avoid the pursuit of the police, again to live the life of anxiety which I have led for twenty-three years, and oblige you to share it with me; to wait each day for a denunciation which sooner or later must come, to wait for the claim for extradition which would follow me to a foreign country! Am I to live for that? No! Never!"

"Father," interrupted Benito, whose mind threatened to give way before such obstinacy, "you shall fly! I will have it so!" And he caught hold of Joam Dacosta, and tried by force to drag him toward the window.

"No! no!"

"You wish to drive me mad?"

"My son," exclaimed Joam Dacosta, "listen to me! Once already I escaped from the prison at Villa Rica, and people believed I fled from well-merited punishment. Yes, they had reason to think so. Well, for the honor of the name which you bear I shall not do so again."

Benito had fallen on his knees before his father. He held up his hands to him; he begged him:

"But this order, father," he repeated, "this order which is due to-day - even now - it will contain your sentence of death."

"The order may come, but my determination will not change. No, my son! Joam Dacosta, guilty, might fly! Joam Dacosta, innocent, will not fly!"

The scene which followed these words was heart-rending. Benito struggled with his father. Manoel, distracted, kept near the window ready to carry off the prisoner - when the door of the room opened.

On the threshold appeared the chief of the police, accompanied by the head warder of the prison and a few soldiers. The chief of the police understood at a glance that an attempt at escape was being made; but he also understood from the prisoner's attitude that he it was who had no wish to go! He said nothing. The sincerest pity was depicted on his face. Doubtless he also, like Judge Jarriquez, would have liked Dacosta to have escaped.

It was too late!

The chief of the police, who held a paper in his hand, advanced toward the prisoner.

"Before all of you," said Joam Dacosta, "let me tell you, sir, that it only rested with me to get away, and that I would not do so."

The chief of the police bowed his head, and then, in a voice which he vainly tried to control:

"Joam Dacosta," he said, "the order has this moment arrived from the chief justice at Rio Janeiro."

"Father!" exclaimed Manoel and Benito.

"This order," asked Joam Dacosta, who had crossed his arms, "this order requires the execution of my sentence?"

"Yes!"

"And that will take place?"

"To-morrow."

Benito threw himself on his father. Again would he have dragged him from his cell, but the soldiers came and drew away the prisoner from his grasp.

At a sign from the chief of the police Benito and Manoel were taken away. An end had to be put to this painful scene, which had already lasted too long.

"Sir," said the doomed man, "before to-morrow, before the hour of my execution, may I pass a few moments with Padre Passanha, whom I ask you to tell?"

"It will be forbidden."

"May I see my family, and embrace for a last time my wife and children?"

"You shall see them."

"Thank you, sir," answered Joam; "and now keep guard over that window; it will not do for them to take me out of here against my will."

And then the chief of the police, after a respectful bow, retired with the warder and the soldiers.

The doomed man, who had now but a few hours to live, was left alone.

CHAPTER XVIII

FRAGOSO

AND SO the order had come, and, as Judge Jarriquez had foreseen, it was an order requiring the immediate execution of the sentence pronounced on Joam Dacosta. No proof had been produced; justice must take its course.

It was the very day - the 31st of August, at nine o'clock in the morning of which the condemned man was to perish on the gallows.

The death penalty in Brazil is generally commuted except in the case of negroes, but this time it was to be suffered by a white man.

Such are the penal arrangements relative to crimes in the diamond arrayal, for which, in the public interest, the law allows no appear to mercy.

Nothing could now save Joam Dacosta. It was not only life, but honor that he was about to lose.

But on the 31st of August a man was approaching Manaos with all the speed his horse was capable of, and such had been the pace at which he had come that half a mile from the town the gallant creature fell, incapable of carrying him any further.

The rider did not even stop to raise his steed. Evidently he had asked and obtained from it all that was possible, and, despite the state of exhaustion in which he found himself, he rushed off in the direction of the city.

The man came from the eastern provinces, and had followed the left bank of the river. All his means had gone in the purchase of this horse, which, swifter far than any pirogue on the Amazon, had brought him to Manaos.

It was Fragoso!

Had, then, the brave fellow succeeded in the enterprise of which he had spoken to nobody? Had he found the party to which Torres belonged? Had he discovered some secret which would yet save Joam Dacosta?

He hardly knew. But in any case he was in great haste to acquaint Judge Jarriquez with what he had ascertained during his short excursion.

And this is what had happened.

Fragoso had made no mistake when he recognized Torres as one of the captains of the party which was employed in the river provinces of the Madeira.

He set out, and on reaching the mouth of that tributary he learned that the chief of these *capitaes da mato* was then in the neighborhood.

Without losing a minute, Fragoso started on the search, and, not without difficulty, succeeded in meeting him.

To Fragoso's questions the chief of the party had no hesitation in replying; he had no interest in keeping silence with regard to the few simple matters on which he was interrogated. In fact, three questions only of importance were asked him by Fragoso, and these were:

"Did not a captain of the woods named Torres belong to your party a few months ago?"

"Yes."

"At that time had he not one intimate friend among his companions who has recently died?"

"Just so!"

"And the name of that friend was?"

"Ortega."

This was all that Fragoso had learned. Was this information of a kind to modify Dacosta's position? It was hardly likely.

Fragoso saw this, and pressed the chief of the band to tell him what he knew of this Ortega, of the place where he came from, and of his antecedents generally. Such information would have been of great importance if Ortega, as Torres had declared, was the true author of the crime of Tijuco. But unfortunately the chief could give him no information whatever in the matter.

What was certain was that Ortega had been a member of the band for many years, that an intimate friendship existed between him and Torres, that they were always seen together, and that Torres had watched at his bedside when he died.

This was all the chief of the band knew, and he could tell no more. Fragoso, then, had to be contented with these insignificant details, and departed immediately.

But if the devoted fellow had not brought back the proof that Ortega was the author of the crime of Tijuco, he had gained one thing, and that was the knowledge that Torres had told the truth when he affirmed that one of his comrades in the band had died, and that he had been present during his last moments.

The hypothesis that Ortega had given him the document in question had now become admissible. Nothing was more probable than that this document had reference to the crime of which Ortega was really the author, and that it contained the confession of the culprit, accompanied by circumstances which permitted of no doubt as to its truth.

And so, if the document could be read, if the key had been found, if the cipher on which the system hung were known, no doubt of its truth could be entertained.

But this cipher Fragoso did not know. A few more presumptions, a half-certainty that the adventurer had invented nothing, certain circumstances tending to prove that the secret of the matter was contained in the document - and that was all that the gallant fellow brought back from his visit to the chief of the gang of which Torres had been a member.

Nevertheless, little as it was, he was in all haste to relate it to Judge Jarriquez. He knew that he had not an hour to lose, and that was why on this very morning, at about eight o'clock, he arrived, exhausted with fatigue, within half a mile of Manaos. The distance between there and the town he traversed in a few minutes. A kind of irresistible presentiment urged him on, and he had almost come to believe that Joam Dacosta's safety rested in his hands.

Suddenly Fragoso stopped as if his feet had become rooted in the ground. He had reached the entrance to a small square, on which opened one of the town gates.

There, in the midst of a dense crowd, arose the gallows, towering up some twenty feet, and from it there hung the rope!

Fragoso felt his consciousness abandon him. He fell; his eyes involuntarily closed. He did not wish to look, and these words escaped his lips: "Too late! too late!" But by a superhuman effort he raised himself up. No; it was *not* too late, the corpse of Joam Dacosta was *not* hanging at the end of the rope!

"Judge Jarriquez! Judge Jarriquez!" shouted Fragoso, and panting and bewildered he rushed toward the city gate, dashed up the principal street of Manaos, and fell half-dead on the threshold of the judge's house. The door was shut. Fragoso had still strength enough left to knock at it.

One of the magistrate's servants came to open it; his master would see no one.

In spite of this denial, Fragoso pushed back the man who guarded the entrance, and with a bound threw himself into the judge's study.

"I come from the province where Torres pursued his calling as captain of the woods!" he gasped. "Mr. Judge, Torres told the truth. Stop - stop the execution?"

"You found the gang?"

"Yes."

"And you have brought me the cipher of the document?"

Fragoso did not reply.

"Come, leave me alone! leave me alone!" shouted Jarriquez, and, a prey to an outburst of rage, he grasped the document to tear it to atoms.

Fragoso seized his hands and stopped him. "The truth is there!" he said.

"I know," answered Jarriquez; "but it is a truth which will never see the light!"

"It will appear - it must! it must!"

"Once more, have you the cipher?"

"No," replied Fragoso; "but, I repeat, Torres has not lied. One of his companions, with whom he was very intimate, died a few months ago, and there can be no doubt but that this man gave him the document he came to sell to Joam Dacosta."

"No," answered Jarriquez - "no, there is no doubt about it - as far as we are concerned; but that is not enough for those who dispose of the doomed man's life. Leave me!"

Fragoso, repulsed, would not quit the spot. Again he threw himself at the judge's feet. "Joam Dacosta is innocent!" he cried; "you will not leave him to die? It was not he who committed the crime of Tijuco; it was the comrade of Torres, the author of that document! It was Ortega!"

As he uttered the name the judge bounded backward. A kind of calm swiftly succeeded to the tempest which raged within him. He dropped the document from his clenched hand, smoothed it out on the table, sat down, and, passing his hand over his eyes - "That name?" he said - "Ortega? Let us see," and then he proceeded with the new name brought back by Fragoso as he had done with the other names so vainly tried by himself.

After placing it above the first six letters of the paragraph he obtained the following formula:

O r t e g a
P h y j s l

"Nothing!" he said. "That give us - nothing!"

And in fact the *h* placed under the *r* could not be expressed by a cipher, for, in alphabetical order, this letter occupies an earlier position to that of the *r*.

The *p,* the *y,* the *j,* arranged beneath the letters *o, t, e,* disclosed the cipher 1, 4, 5, but as for the *s* and the *l* at the end of the word, the interval which separated them from the *g* and the *a* was a dozen letters, and hence impossible to express by a single cipher, so that they corresponded to neither *g* nor *a*.

And here appalling shouts arose in the streets; they were the cries of despair.

Fragoso jumped to one of the windows, and opened it before the judge could hinder him.

The people filled the road. The hour had come at which the doomed man was to start from the prison, and the crowd was flowing back to the spot where the gallows had been erected.

Judge Jarriquez, quite frightful to look upon, devoured the lines of the document with a fixed stare.

"The last letters!" he muttered. "Let us try once more the last letters!"

It was the last hope.

And then, with a hand whose agitation nearly prevented him from writing at all, he placed the name of Ortega over the six last letters of the paragraph, as he had done over the first.

An exclamation immediately escaped him. He saw, at first glance, that the six last letters were inferior in alphabetical order to those which composed Ortega's name, and that consequently they might yield the number.

And when he reduced the formula, reckoning each later letter from the earlier letter of the word, he obtained.

Ortega
4 3 2 5 1 3
S u v j h d

The number thus disclosed was 432513.

But was this number that which had been used in the document? Was it not as erroneous as those he had previously tried?

At this moment the shouts below redoubled - shouts of pity which betrayed the sympathy of the excited crowd. A few minutes more were all that the doomed man had to live!

Fragoso, maddened with grief, darted from the room! He wished to see, for the last time, his benefactor who was on the road to death! He longed to throw himself before the mournful procession and stop it, shouting, "Do not kill this just man! do not kill him!"

But already Judge Jarriquez had placed the given number above the first letters of the paragraph, repeating them as often as was necessary, as follows:

4 3 2 5 1 3 4 3 2 5 1 3 4 3 2 5 1 3 4 3 2 5 1 3
P h y j s l y d d q f d z x g a s g z z q q e h

And then, reckoning the true letters according to their alphabetical order, he read:

"Le véritable auteur du vol de -- "

A yell of delight escaped him! This number, 432513, was the number sought for so long! The name of Ortega had enabled him to discover it! At length he held the key of the document, which would incontestably prove the innocence of Joam Dacosta, and without reading any more he flew from his study into the street, shouting:

"Halt! Halt!"

To cleave the crowd, which opened as he ran, to dash to the prison, whence the convict was coming at the last moment, with his wife and children clinging to him with the violence of despair, was but the work of a minute for Judge Jarriquez.

Stopping before Joam Dacosta, he could not speak for a second, and then these words escaped his lips:

"Innocent! Innocent!"

CHAPTER XIX

THE CRIME OF TIJUCO

ON THE ARRIVAL of the judge the mournful procession halted. A roaring echo had repeated after him and again repeated the cry which escaped from every mouth:

"Innocent! Innocent!"

Then complete silence fell on all. The people did not want to lose one syllable of what was about to be proclaimed.

Judge Jarriquez sat down on a stone seat, and then, while Minha, Benito, Manoel, and Fragoso stood round him, while Joam Dacosta clasped Yaquita to his heart, he first unraveled the last paragraph of the document by means of the number, and as the words appeared by the institution of the true letters for the cryptological ones, he divided and punctuated them, and then read it out in a loud voice. And this is what he read in the midst of profound silence:

Le véritable auteur du vol des diamants et de
43 251343251 343251 34 325 134 32513432 51 34
Ph yjslyddf dzxgas gz zqq ehx gkfndrxu ju gi

l'assassinat des soldats qui escortaient le convoi,
32513432513 432 5134325 134 32513432513 43
251343 *ocytdxvksbx bhu ypohdvy rym huhpuydkjox ph etozsl*

commis dans la nuit du vingt-deux janvier mil 251343
2513 43 2513 43 251343251 3432513 432 *etnpmv ffov pd pajx hy ynojyggay meqynfu q1n*

huit-cent vingt-six, n'est donc pas Joam Dacosta,
5134 3251 3425 134 3251 3432 513 4325 1343251
mvly fgsu zmqiz tlb qgyu gsqe uvb nrcc edgruzb

injustement condamné à mort, c'est moi, les misérable
34325134325 13432513 4 3251 3432 513 43
251343251 *l4msyuhqpz drrgcroh e pqxu fivv rpl ph onthvddqf*

employé de l'administration du district diamantin,
3432513 43 251343251343251 34 32513432
513432513 *hqsntzh hh nfepmqkyuuexkto gz gkyuumfv ijdqdpzjq*

out, moi seul, qui signe de mon vrai nom, Ortega.
432 513 4325 134 32513 43 251 3432 513 432513
syk rpl xhxq rym vkloh hh oto zvdk spp suvjhd.

"The real author of the robbery of the diamonds and of the murder of the soldiers who escorted the convoy, committed during the night of the twenty-second of January, one thousand eight hundred and twenty-six, was thus not Joam Dacosta, unjustly condemned to death; it was I, the wretched servant of the Administration of the diamond district; yes, I alone, who sign this with my true name, Ortega."

The reading of this had hardly finished when the air was rent with prolonged hurrahs.

What could be more conclusive than this last paragraph, which summarized the whole of the document, and proclaimed so absolutely the innocence of the fazender of Iquitos, and which snatched from the gallows this victim of a frightful judicial mistake!

Joam Dacosta, surrounded by his wife, his children, and his friends, was unable to shake the hands which were held out to him. Such was the strength of his character that a reaction occurred, tears of joy escaped from his eyes, and at the same instant his heart was lifted up to that Providence which had come to save him so miraculously at the moment he was about to offer the last expiation to that God who would not permit the accomplishment of that greatest of crimes, the death of an innocent man!

Yes! There could be no doubt as to the vindication of Joam Dacosta. The true author of the crime of Tijuco confessed of his own free will, and described the circumstances under which it had been perpetrated!

By means of the number Judge Jarriquez interpreted the whole of the cryptogram.

And this was what Ortega confessed.

He had been the colleague of Joam Dacosta, employed, like him, at Tijuco, in the offices of the governor of the diamond arrayal. He had been the official appointed to accompany the convoy to Rio de Janeiro, and, far from recoiling at the horrible idea of enriching himself by means of murder and robbery, he had informed the smugglers of the very day the convoy was to leave Tijuco.

During the attack of the scoundrels, who awaited the convoy just beyond Villa Rica, he pretended to defend himself with the soldiers of the escort, and then, falling among the dead, he was carried away by his accomplices. Hence it was that the solitary soldier who survived the massacre had reported that Ortega had perished in the struggle.

But the robbery did not profit the guilty man in the long run, for, a little time afterward, he was robbed by those whom he had helped to commit the crime.

Penniless, and unable to enter Tijuco again, Ortega fled away to the provinces in the north of Brazil, to those districts of the Upper Amazon where the *capitaes da mato* are to be found. He had to live somehow, and so he joined this not very honorable company; they neither asked him who he was nor whence he came, and so Ortega became a captain of the woods, and for many years he followed the trade of a chaser of men.

During this time Torres, the adventurer, himself in absolute want, became his companion. Ortega and he became most intimate. But, as he had told Torres, remorse began gradually to trouble the scoundrel's life. The remembrance of his crime became horrible to him. He knew that another had been condemned in his place! He knew subsequently that the innocent man had escaped from the last penalty, but that he would never be free from the shadow of the capital sentence! And then, during an expedition of his party for several months beyond the Peruvian frontier, chance caused

Ortega to visit the neighborhood of Iquitos, and there in Joam Garral, who did not recognize him, he recognized Joam Dacosta.

Henceforth he resolved to make all the reparation he could for the injustice of which his old comrade had been the victim. He committed to the document all the facts relative to the crime of Tijuco, writing it first in French, which had been his mother's native tongue, and then putting it into the mysterious form we know, his intention being to transmit it to the fazender of Iquitos, with the cipher by which it could be read.

Death prevented his completing his work of reparation. Mortally wounded in a scuffle with some negroes on the Madeira, Ortega felt he was doomed. His comrade Torres was then with him. He thought he could intrust to his friend the secret which had so grievously darkened his life. He gave him the document, and made him swear to convey it to Joam Dacosta, whose name and address he gave him, and with his last breath he whispered the number 432513, without which the document would remain undecipherable.

Ortega dead, we know how the unworthy Torres acquitted himself of his mission, how he resolved to turn to his own profit the secret of which he was the possessor, and how he tried to make it the subject of an odious bargain.

Torres died without accomplishing his work, and carried his secret with him. But the name of Ortega, brought back by Fragoso, and which was the signature of the document, had afforded the means of unraveling the cryptogram, thanks to the sagacity of Judge Jarriquez. Yes, the material proof sought after for so long was the incontestable witness of the innocence of Joam Dacosta, returned to life, restored to honor.

The cheers redoubled when the worthy magistrate, in a loud voice, and for the edification of all, read from the document this terrible history.

And from that moment Judge Jarriquez, who possessed this indubitable proof, arranged with the chief of the police, and declined to allow Joam Dacosta, while waiting new instructions from Rio Janeiro, to stay in any prison but his own house.

There could be no difficulty about this, and in the center of the crowd of the entire population of Manaos, Joam Dacosta, accompanied by all his family, beheld himself conducted like a conquerer to the magistrate's residence.

And in that minute the honest fazender of Iquitos was well repaid for all that he had suffered during the long years of exile, and if he was happy for his family's sake more than for his own, he was none the less proud for his country's sake that this supreme injustice had not been consummated!

And in all this what had become of Fragoso?

Well, the good-hearted fellow was covered with caresses! Benito, Manoel, and Minha had over-whelmed him, and Lina had by no means spared him. He did not know what to do, he defended himself as best he could. He did not deserve anything like it. Chance alone had done it. Were any thanks due to him for having recognized Torres as a captain of the woods? No, certainly not. As to his idea of hurrying off in search of the band to which Torres had belonged, he did not think it had been worth much, and as to the name of Ortega, he did not even know its value.

Gallant Fragoso! Whether he wished it or no, he had none the less saved Joam Dacosta!

And herein what a strange succession of different events all tending to the same end. The deliverance of Fragoso at the time when he was dying of exhaustion in the forest of Iquitos; the hospitable reception he had met with at the fazenda, the meeting with Torres on the Brazilian frontier, his embarkation on the jangada; and lastly, the fact that Fragoso had seen him somewhere before.

"Well, yes!" Fragoso ended by exclaiming; "but it is not to me that all this happiness is due, it is due to Lina!"

"To me?" replied the young mulatto.

"No doubt of it. Without the liana, without the idea of the liana, could I ever have been the cause of so much happiness?"

So that Fragoso and Lina were praised and petted by all the family, and by all the new friends whom so many trials had procured them at Manaos, need hardly be insisted on.

But had not Judge Jarriquez also had his share in this rehabilitation of an innocent man? If, in spite of all the shrewdness of his analytical talents, he had not been able to read the document, which was absolutely undecipherable to any one who had not got the key, had he not at any rate discovered the system on which the cryptogram was composed? Without him what could have been done with only the name of Ortega to reconstitute the number which the author of the crime and Torres, both of whom were dead, alone knew?

And so he also received abundant thanks.

Needless to say that the same day there was sent to Rio de Janeiro a detailed report of the whole affair, and with it the original document and the cipher to enable it to be read. New instructions from the minister of justice had to be waited for, though there could be no doubt that they would order the immediate discharge of the prisoner. A few days would thus have to be passed at Manaos, and then Joam Dacosta and his people, free from all constraint, and released from all apprehension, would take leave of their host to go on board once more and continue their descent of the Amazon to Para, where the voyage was intended to terminate with the double marriage of Minha and Manoel and Lina and Fragoso.

Four days afterward, on the fourth of September, the order of discharge arrived. The document had been recognized as authentic. The handwriting was really that of Ortega, who had been formerly employed in the diamond district, and there could be no doubt that the confession of his crime, with the minutest details that were given, had been entirely written with his own hand.

The innocence of the convict of Villa Rica was at length admitted. The rehabilitation of Joam Dacosta was at last officially proclaimed.

That very day Judge Jarriquez dined with the family on board the giant raft, and when evening came he shook hands with them all. Touching were the adieus, but an engagement was made for them to see him again on their return at Manaos, and later on the fazenda of Iquitos.

On the morning of the morrow, the fifth of September, the signal for departure was given. Joam Dacosta and Yaquita, with their daughter and sons, were on the deck of the enormous raft. The jangada had its moorings slackened off and began to move with the current, and when it disappeared round the bend of the Rio Negro, the hurrahs of the whole population of Manaos, who were assembled on the bank, again and again re-echoed across the stream.

CHAPTER XX

THE LOWER AMAZON

LITTLE REMAINS to tell of the second part of the voyage down the mighty river. It was but a series of days of joy. Joam Dacosta returned to a new life, which shed its happiness on all who belonged to him.

The giant raft glided along with greater rapidity on the waters now swollen by the floods. On the left they passed the small village of Don Jose de Maturi, and on the right the mouth of that Madeira which owes its name to the floating masses of vegetable remains and trunks denuded of their foliage which it bears from the depths of Bolivia. They passed the archipelago of Caniny, whose islets are veritable boxes of palms, and before the village of Serpa, which, successively transported from one back to the other, has definitely settled on the left of the river, with its little houses, whose thresholds stand on the yellow carpet of the beach.

The village of Silves, built on the left of the Amazon, and the town of Villa Bella, which is the principal guarana market in the whole province, were soon left behind by the giant raft. And so was the village of Faro and its celebrated river of the Nhamundas, on which, in 1539, Orellana asserted he was attacked by female warriors, who have never been seen again since, and thus gave us the legend which justifies the immortal name of the river of the Amazons.

Here it is that the province of Rio Negro terminates. The jurisdiction of Para then commences; and on the 22d of September the family, marveling much at a valley which has no equal in the world, entered that portion of the Brazilian empire which has no boundary to the east except the Atlantic.

"How magnificent!" remarked Minha, over and over again.

"How long!" murmured Manoel.

"How beautiful!" repeated Lina.

"When shall we get there?" murmured Fragoso.

And this was what might have been expected of these folks from the different points of view, though time passed pleasantly enough with them all the same. Benito, who was neither patient nor impatient, had recovered all his former good humor.

Soon the jangada glided between interminable plantations of cocoa-trees with their somber green flanked by the yellow thatch or ruddy tiles of the roofs of the huts of the settlers on both banks from Obidos up to the town of Monto Alegre.

Then there opened out the mouth of the Rio Trombetas, bathing with its black waters the houses of Obidos, situated at about one hundred and eighty miles from Belem, quite a small town, and even a *"citade"* with large streets bordered with handsome habitations, and a great center for cocoa produce. Then they saw another tributary, the Tapajos, with its greenish-gray waters descending from the south-west; and then Santarem, a wealthy town of not less than five thousand inhabitants, Indians for the most part, whose nearest houses were built on the vast beach of white sand.

After its departure from Manaos the jangada did not stop anywhere as it passed down the much less encumbered course of the Amazon. Day and night it moved along under the vigilant care of its trusty pilot; no more stoppages either for the gratification of the passengers or for business purposes. Unceasingly it progressed, and the end rapidly grew nearer.

On leaving Alemquer, situated on the left bank, a new horizon appeared in view. In place of the curtain of forests which had shut them in up to then, our friends beheld a foreground of hills, whose undulations could be easily descried, and beyond them the faint summits of veritable mountains vandyked across the distant depth of sky. Neither Yaquita, nor her daughter, nor Lina, nor old Cybele, had ever seen anything like this.

But in this jurisdiction of Para, Manoel was at home, and he could tell them the names of the double chain which gradually narrowed the valley of the huge river.

"To the right," said he, "that is the Sierra de Paracuarta, which curves in a half-circle to the south! To the left, that is the Sierra de Curuva, of which we have already passed the first outposts."

"Then they close in?" asked Fragoso.

"They close in!" replied Manoel.

And the two young men seemed to understand each other, for the same slight but significant nodding of the head accompanied the question and reply.

At last, notwithstanding the tide, which since leaving Obidos had begun to be felt, and which somewhat checked the progress of the raft, the town of Monto Alegre was passed, then that of Pravnha de Onteiro, then the mouth of the Xingu, frequented by Yurumas Indians, whose principal industry consists in preparing their enemies' heads for natural history cabinets.

To what a superb size the Amazon had now developed as already this monarch of rivers gave signs of opening out like a sea! Plants from eight to ten feet high clustered along the beach, and bordered it with a forest of reeds. Porto de Mos, Boa Vista, and Gurupa, whose prosperity is on the decline, were soon among the places left in the rear.

Then the river divided into two important branches, which flowed off toward the Atlantic, one going away northeastward, the other eastward, and between them appeared the beginning of the large island of Marajo. This island is quite a province in itself. It measures no less than a hundred and eighty leagues in circumference. Cut up by marshes and rivers, all savannah to the east, all forest to the west, it offers most excellent advantages for the raising of cattle, which can here be seen in their thousands. This immense barricade of Marajo is the natural obstacle which has compelled the Amazon to divide before precipitating its torrents of water into the sea. Following the upper branch, the jangada, after passing the islands of Caviana and Mexiana, would have found an *embouchure* of some fifty leagues across, but it would also have met with the bar of the prororoca, that terrible eddy which, for the three days preceding the new or full moon, takes but two minutes instead of six hours to raise the river from twelve to fifteen feet above ordinary high-water mark.

This is by far the most formidable of tide-races. Most fortunately the lower branch, known as the Canal of Breves, which is the natural area of the Para, is not subject to the visitations of this terrible phenomenon, and its tides are of a more regular description. Araujo, the pilot, was quite aware of this. He steered, therefore, into the midst of magnificent forests, here and there gliding past island covered with muritis palms; and the weather was so favorable that they did not experience any of the storms which so frequently rage along this Breves Canal.

A few days afterward the jangada passed the village of the same name, which, although built on the ground flooded for many months in the year, has become, since 1845, an important town of a hundred houses. Throughout these districts, which are frequented by Tapuyas, the Indians of the Lower Amazon become more and more commingled with the white population, and promise to be completely absorbed by them.

And still the jangada continued its journey down the river. Here, at the risk of entanglement, it grazed the branches of the mangliers, whose roots stretched down into the waters like the claws of gigantic crustaceans; then the smooth trunks of the paletuviers, with their pale-green foliage, served as the resting-places for the long poles of the crew as they kept the raft in the strength of the current.

Then came the Tocantins, whose waters, due to the different rivers of the province of Goyaz, mingle with those of the Amazon by an *embouchure* of great size, then the Moju, then the town of Santa Ana.

Majestically the panorama of both banks moved along without a pause, as though some ingenious mechanism necessitated its unrolling in the opposite direction to that of the stream.

Already numerous vessels descending the river, ubas, egariteas, vigilandas, pirogues of all builds, and small coasters from the lower districts of the Amazon and the Atlantic seaboard, formed a procession with the giant raft, and seemed like sloops beside some might man-of-war.

At length there appeared on the left Santa Maria de Belem do Para - the "town" as they call it in that country - with its picturesque lines of white houses at many different levels, its convents nestled among the palm-trees, the steeples of its cathedral and of Nostra Senora de Merced, and the flotilla of its brigantines, brigs, and barks, which form its commercial communications with the old world.

The hearts of the passengers of the giant raft beat high. At length they were coming to the end of the voyage which they had thought they would never reach. While the arrest of Joam detained them at Manaos, halfway on their journey, could they ever have hoped to see the capital of the province of Para?

It was in the course of this day, the 15th of October -

four months and a half after leaving the fazenda of Iquitos - that, as they rounded a sharp bend in the river, Belem came into sight.

The arrival of the jangada had been signaled for some days. The whole town knew the story of Joam Dacosta. They came forth to welcome him, and to him and his people accorded a most sympathetic reception.

Hundreds of craft of all sorts conveyed them to the fazender, and soon the jangada was invaded by all those who wished to welcome the return of their compatriot after his long exile. Thousands of sight-seers - or more correctly speaking, thousands of friends crowded on to the floating village as soon as it came to its moorings, and it was vast and solid enough to support the entire population. Among those who hurried on board one of the first pirogues had brought Madame Valdez. Manoel's mother was at last able to clasp to her arms the daughter whom her son had chosen. If the good lady had not been able to come to Iquitos, was it not as though a portion of the fazenda, with her new family, had come down the Amazon to her?

Before evening the pilot Araujo had securely moored the raft at the entrance of a creek behind the arsenal. That was to be its last resting-place, its last halt, after its voyage of eight hundred leagues on the great Brazilian artery. There the huts of the Indians, the cottage of the negroes, the store-rooms which held the valuable cargo, would be gradually demolished; there the principal dwelling, nestled beneath its verdant tapestry of flowers and foliage, and the little chapel whose humble bell was then replying to the sounding clangor from the steeples of Belem, would each in its turn disappear.

But, ere this was done, a ceremony had to take place on the jangada - the marriage of Manoel and Minha, the marriage of Lina and Fragoso. To Father Passanha fell the duty of celebrating the double union which promised so happily. In that little chapel the two couples were to receive the nuptial benediction from his hands.

If it happened to be so small as to be only capable of holding the members of Dacosta's family, was not the giant raft large enough to receive all those who wished to assist at the ceremony? and if not, and the crowd became so great, did not the ledges of the river banks afford sufficient room for as many others of the sympathizing crowd as were desirous of welcoming him whom so signal a reparation had made the hero of the day?

It was on the morrow, the 16th of October, that with great pomp the marriages were celebrated.

It was a magnificent day, and from about ten o'clock in the morning the raft began to receive its crowd of guests. On the bank could be seen almost the entire population of Belem in holiday costume. On the river, vessels of all sorts crammed with visitors gathered round the enormous mass of timber, and the waters of the Amazon literally disappeared even up to the left bank beneath the vast flotilla.

When the chapel bell rang out its opening note it seemed like a signal of joy to ear and eye. In an instant the churches of Belem replied to the bell of the jangada. The vessels in the port decked themselves with flags up to their mastheads, and the Brazilian colors were saluted by the many other national flags. Discharges of musketry reverberated on all sides, and it was only with difficulty that their joyous detonations could cope with the loud hurrahs from the assembled thousands.

The Dacosta family came forth from their house and moved through the crowd toward the little chapel. Joam was received with absolutely frantic applause. He gave his arm to Madame Valdez; Yaquita was escorted by the governor of Belem, who, accompanied by the friends of the young army surgeon, had expressed a wish to honor the ceremony with his presence. Manoel walked by the side of Minha, who looked most fascinating in her bride's costume, and then came Fragoso, holding the hand of Lina, who seemed quite radiant with joy. Then followed Benito, then old Cybele and the servants of the worthy family between the double ranks of the crew of the jangada.

Padre Passanha awaited the two couples at the entrance of the chapel. The ceremony was very simple, and the same bands which had formerly blessed Joam and Yaquita were again stretched forth to give the nuptial benediction to their child.

So much happiness was not likely to be interrupted by the sorrow of long separation. In fact, Manoel Valdez almost immediately sent in his resignation, so as to join the family at Iquitos, where he is still following the profession of a country doctor.

Naturally the Fragosos did not hesitate to go back with those who were to them friends rather than masters.

Madame Valdez had no desire to separate so happy a group, but she insisted on one thing, and that was that they should often come and see her at Belem. Nothing could be easier. Was not the mighty river a bond of communication between Belem and Iquitos? In a few days the first mail steamer was to begin a regular and rapid service, and it would then only take a week to ascend the Amazon, on which it had taken the giant raft so many months to drift. The important commercial negotiations, ably managed by Benito, were carried through under the best of conditions, and soon of what had formed this jangada - that is to say, the huge raft of timber constructed from an entire forest at Iquitos - there remained not a trace.

A month afterward the fazender, his wife, his son, Manoel and Minha Valdez, Lina and Fragoso, departed by one of the Amazon steamers for the immense establishment at Iquitos of which Benito was to take the management.

Joam Dacosta re-entered his home with his head erect, and it was indeed a family of happy hearts which he brought back with him from beyond the Brazilian frontier. As for Fragoso, twenty times a day was he heard to repeat, "What! without the liana?" and he wound up by bestowing the name on the young mulatto who, by her affection for the gallant fellow, fully justified its appropriateness. "If it were not for the one letter," he said, "would not Lina and Liana be the same?"

Choose from Thousands of 1stWorldLibrary Classics By

A. M. Barnard
Ada Leverson
Adolphus William Ward
Aesop
Agatha Christie
Alexander Aaronsohn
Alexander Kielland
Alexandre Dumas
Alfred Gatty
Alfred Ollivant
Alice Duer Miller
Alice Turner Curtis
Alice Dunbar
Ambrose Bierce
Amelia E. Barr
Amory H. Bradford
Andrew Lang
Andrew McFarland Davis
Andy Adams
Anna Sewell
Annie Besant
Annie Hamilton Donnell
Annie Payson Call
Annonaymous
Anton Chekhov
Arnold Bennett
Arthur Conan Doyle
Arthur M. Winfield
Arthur Ransome
Atticus
B.H. Baden-Powell
B. M. Bower
Baroness Emmuska Orczy
Baroness Orczy
Basil King
Bayard Taylor
Ben Macomber
Bertha Muzzy Bower
Bjornstjerne Bjornson
Booth Tarkington
Boyd Cable
Bram Stoker
C. Collodi
C. E. Orr
C. M. Ingleby
Carolyn Wells
Catherine Parr Traill
Charles A. Eastman
Charles Dickens

Charles Dudley Warner
Charles Farrar Browne
Charles Ives
Charles Kingsley
Charles Klein
Charles Amory Beach
Charles Hanson Towne
Charles Lathrop Pack
Charles Whibley
Charles Willing Beale
Charlotte M. Braeme
Charlotte M. Yonge
Charlotte Perkins Stetson
Clair W. Hayes
Clarence Day Jr.
Clarence E. Mulford
Clemence Housman
Confucius
Cornelis DeWitt Wilcox
Cyril Burleigh
D. H. Lawrence
Daniel Defoe
David Garnett
Dinah Craik
Don Carlos Janes
Donald Keyhoe
Dorothy Kilner
Dougan Clark
Douglas Fairbanks
E. Nesbit
E.P.Roe
E. Phillips Oppenheim
Earl Barnes
Edgar Rice Burroughs
Edith Van Dyne
Edith Wharton
Edward J. O'Biren
Edward S. Ellis
Edwin L. Arnold
Eleanor Atkins
Eliot Gregory
Elizabeth Gaskell
Elizabeth McCracken
Elizabeth Von Arnim
Ellem Key
Emerson Hough
Emilie F. Carlen
Emily Dickinson
Enid Bagnold

Enilor Macartney Lane
Erasmus W. Jones
Ernie Howard Pie
Ethel Turner
Ethel Watts Mumford
Eugenie Foa
Eugene Wood
Eustace Hale Ball
Evelyn Everett-green
Everard Cotes
F. H. Cheley
F. J. Cross
Federick Austin Ogg
Ferdinand Ossendowski
Francis Bacon
Francis Darwin
Frances Hodgson Burnett
Frances Parkinson Keyes
Frank Gee Patchin
Frank Harris
Frank Jewett Mather
Frank L. Packard
Frank V. Webster
Frederic Stewart Isham
Frederick Trevor Hill
Frederick Winslow Taylor
Friedrich Kerst
Friedrich Nietzsche
Fyodor Dostoyevsky
G.A. Henty
G.K. Chesterton
Gabrielle E. Jackson
Garrett P. Serviss
Gaston Leroux
George A. Warren
George Ade
Geroge Bernard Shaw
George Durston
George Ebers
George Eliot
George Gissing
George MacDonald
George Meredith
George Orwell
George Sylvester Viereck
George Tucker
George W. Cable
George Wharton James
Gertrude Atherton

Grace E. King
Grace Gallatin
Grant Allen
Guillermo A. Sherwell
Gulielma Zollinger
Gustav Flaubert
H. A. Cody
H. B. Irving
H.C. Bailey
H. G. Wells
H. H. Munro
H. Irving Hancock
H. Rider Haggard
H. W. C. Davis
Hamilton Wright Mabie
Hans Christian Andersen
Harold Avery
Harold McGrath
Harriet Beecher Stowe
Harry Houidini
Helent Hunt Jackson
Helen Nicolay
Hendrik Conscience
Hendy David Thoreau
Henri Barbusse
Henrik Ibsen
Henry Adams
Henry Ford
Henry Frost
Henry James
Henry Jones Ford
Henry Seton Merriman
Henry W Longfellow
Herbert A. Giles
Herbert N. Casson
Herman Hesse
Homer
Honore De Balzac
Horace Walpole
Horatio Alger Jr.
Howard Pyle
Howard R. Garis
Hugh Lofting
Hugh Walpole
Humphry Ward
Ian Maclaren
Inez Haynes Gillmore
Irving Bacheller
Israel Abrahams
Ivan Turgenev
J.G.Austin

J. Henri Fabre
J. M. Barrie
J. Macdonald Oxley
J. S. Fletcher
J. S. Knowles
J. Storer Clouston
Jack London
Jacob Abbott
James Allen
James Andrews
James Baldwin
James DeMille
James Joyce
James Lane Allen
James Lane Allen
James Oliver Curwood
James Oppenheim
James Otis
James R. Driscoll
Jane Austen
Janet Aldridge
Jens Peter Jacobsen
Jerome K. Jerome
John Burroughs
John Cournos
John F. Kennedy
John Gay
John Glasworthy
John Habberton
John Joy Bell
John Kendrick Bangs
John Milton
John Philip Sousa
Jonas Lauritz Idemil Lie
Jonathan Swift
Joseph A. Altsheler
Joseph Carey
Joseph Conrad
Joseph E. Badger Jr
Joseph Hergesheimer
Joseph Jacobs
Jules Vernes
Julian Hawthrone
Julie A Lippmann
Justin Huntly McCarthy
Kakuzo Okakura
Kenneth Grahame
Kenneth McGaffey
Kate Langley Bosher
Kate Langley Bosher
Katherine Cecil Thurston

Katherine Stokes
L. A. Abbot
L. T. Meade
L. Frank Baum
Latta Griswold
Laura Lee Hope
Laurence Housman
Lawrence Beasley
Leo Tolstoy
Leonid Andreyev
Lewis Carroll
Lewis Sperry Chafer
Lilian Bell
Lloyd Osbourne
Louis Hughes
Louis Tracy
Louisa May Alcott
Lucy Fitch Perkins
Lucy Maud Montgomery
Lydia Miller Middleton
Lyndon Orr
M. Corvus
M. H. Adams
Margaret E. Sangster
Margaret Vandercook
Margret Penrose
Maria Edgeworth
Maria Thompson Daviess
Mariano Azuela
Marion Polk Angellotti
Mark Overton
Mark Twain
Mary Austin
Mary Catherine Crowley
Mary Cole
Mary Hastings Bradley
Mary Roberts Rinehart
Mary Rowlandson
M. Wollstonecraft Shelley
Maud Lindsay
Max Beerbohm
Myra Kelly
Nathaniel Hawthrone
Nicolo Machiavelli
O. F. Walton
Oscar Wilde
Owen Johnson
P.G. Wodehouse
Paul and Mabel Thorne
Paul G. Tomlinson
Paul Severing

Percy Brebner
Peter B. Kyne
Plato
R. Derby Holmes
R. L. Stevenson
R. S. Ball
Rabindranath Tagore
Rahul Alvares
Ralph Bonehill
Ralph Henry Barbour
Ralph Victor
Ralph Waldo Emmerson
Rene Descartes
Rex Beach
Rex E. Beach
Richard Harding Davis
Richard Jefferies
Richard Le Gallienne
Robert Barr
Robert Frost
Robert Gordon Anderson
Robert L. Drake
Robert Lansing
Robert Lynd
Robert Michael Ballantyne
Robert W. Chambers
Rosa Nouchette Carey
Rudyard Kipling
Samuel B. Allison

Samuel Hopkins Adams
Sarah Bernhardt
Sarah C. Hallowell
Selma Lagerlof
Sherwood Anderson
Sigmund Freud
Standish O'Grady
Stanley Weyman
Stella Benson
Stephen Crane
Stewart Edward White
Stijn Streuvels
Swami Abhedananda
Swami Parmananda
T. S. Ackland
T. S. Arthur
The Princess Der Ling
Thomas A. Janvier
Thomas A Kempis
Thomas Anderton
Thomas Bailey Aldrich
Thomas Bulfinch
Thomas De Quincey
Thomas H. Huxley
Thomas Hardy
Thomas More
Thornton W. Burgess
U. S. Grant
Valentine Williams

Various Authors
Vaughan Kester
Victor Appleton
Virginia Woolf
Walter Camp
Walter Scott
Washington Irving
Wilbur Lawton
Wilkie Collins
Willa Cather
Willard F. Baker
William Dean Howells
William le Queux
W. Makepeace Thackeray
William W. Walter
Winston Churchill
Yei Theodora Ozaki
Yogi Ramacharaka
Young E. Allison
Zane Grey